FINDING DAD

For Mum

PAUL BESSELL

FINDING DAD

MIRROR BOOKS

MIRROR BOOKS

All of the events in this story are true, but some names and details have been changed to protect the identities of some individuals where appropriate.

1

Published in Great Britain and Ireland in 2026 by
Mirror Books, a Reach PLC business.

www.mirrorbooks.co.uk
@TheMirrorBooks

Print ISBN 9781917439572
eBook ISBN 9781917439589

Editing and Production: Christine Costello, Nick Webster
Cover Design: Chris Collins

Photographic Acknowledgements: Paul Bessell Personal Collection, MirrorPix, Alamy

Printed and bound in Great Britain by
CPI Group (UK) Ltd, Croydon, CR0 4YY

FSC www.fsc.org
MIX
Paper | Supporting responsible forestry
FSC® C013604

CONTENTS

AUTHOR'S NOTE

MUCH OF THE dialogue in this book is accurate almost to the word, particularly during events at which I was present. Some is taken from my father Peter Bessell's privately printed memoir, *Cover-Up*, while other reported speech draws on the memoir notes of his second wife, my mother, Pauline Bessell, in which she describes conversations, but does not necessarily transcribe actual dialogue. In this case I have written dialogue based on my knowledge of the events, the memoir notes and subsequent conversations with Pauline.

PROLOGUE

Oceanside, California, October 1984

MY FATHER WAS waiting outside the house. His previously lithe frame appeared shrunken; his formerly always impeccably tailored clothes were replaced by a woollen polo neck, a jumper and slacks. Peter Bessell, the once glamorous, always controversial MP, trans-atlantic jet-setter and confidant to the rich and powerful was gone. In his place, stood a frail figure, racked by emphysema and unable to take more than a few steps at a time without the aid of an oxygen cylinder, which he pushed around on a trolley.

My father was dying.

In the decade since he mysteriously vanished, at the height of his notoriety, I had barely spoken to him. His abrupt disappearance ruptured my family and shattered my faith in him.

It was Sunday, 13 January 1974, when, at the age of 21, I woke to find my father had disappeared. This was the man I loved and looked up to my whole life. Whilst I wished I could have spent more time with him, I understood he was important and often needed elsewhere, but he had always made sure that his family wanted for nothing.

Yet now he was gone, leaving only a brief note letting us know that his business had collapsed, and he may have acted fraudulently. To avoid arrest and public humiliation, he was running away to somewhere from where he couldn't be extradited. Mercifully, it appeared he hadn't committed suicide, though we feared he might have done. He had simply gone, leaving his family with nothing more than a few pounds and our clothes.

Some months later, he reappeared in California. In the subsequent 10 years, I saw him just four times, and on two of those occasions he'd been visiting the UK in the full glare of the media coverage of the so-called 'Trial of the Century', of the former leader of the Liberal Party, Jeremy Thorpe, for conspiracy to murder – hardly ideal circumstances in which to attempt to rebuild a relationship. Now, though, in 1984, time was running out.

It was a glorious California day. Palm trees gently swayed, and the roaring Pacific waves were packed with surfers. My father's house was right on the beach. It should have been an idyllic setting for a reunion and reconciliation, but it was not to be. One of the curses of the Bessells is that we seem incapable of facing issues head on, and, throughout our three weeks together, I avoided any discussion of the deep fractures in our family. I had so many questions, but I genuinely feared the answers.

When the time came to say goodbye, we hugged, but there were no tears. We both remained trapped in our English reserve. As I reversed out of the driveway, I looked back at my father. He was waving slowly, holding his precious dog. I knew this would be the last time I saw him. Yet nothing had been resolved. I felt devastated; the look on his face told me he felt the same way.

My father died a year later, in 1985. I never did ask him the questions, which, for a decade, had come between us. He never did explain the many mysteries of his life. Instead, he left me his personal papers, hoping, I think, that after his death, I might find the courage to delve into them to find the answers. I did not.

Instead, I was left simply with the accusations of others who variously described him as a mass-murderer and Chief of Stalin's NKVD; an MI6 agent; a CIA agent; an FBI agent; a secret adviser to the US Government; a South African Bureau of State Security spy; an MI5 F Division agent; a fraud; a bankrupt; a charlatan; a lounge lizard; a murderer; a compulsive liar; a fantasist; a 'grass' and a 'man who operated in a shadowy world of politicians, bankers, fixers, con men and criminals'. His personal life was epitomised in a *Daily Mirror* headline which read, 'Bessell and His Birds'. These accusations were not made as tittle-tattle at private dinner parties; they were made publicly in respectable publications. The 'liar' accusation was made by a judge; and the 'charlatan' by Henry Kissinger, the former US Secretary of State, Machiavellian diplomat, and controversial Nobel Peace Prize winner.

But are any of these claims true? Perhaps all of them are?

Recently, during a barbecue under the stars in my village, my hostess suddenly blurted out, 'I didn't know we had the son of a famous person living in the village.'

'Or infamous,' said her husband.

It was exactly the kind of put-down I'd had to live with for almost 50 years. I'd reached the point where I could either retreat from the world and become a recluse, or finally face the truth, whatever that might be.

What happened to my father, Peter Bessell? Why did he disappear, devastating his wife's life as well as his own? His actions had a profound impact on many people in a very public way.

Was he a patriotic British, Liberal Party MP, offered a Cabinet post in Harold Wilson's Labour Government, or was he a shadowy British or American intelligence asset? Was he an internationally successful businessman or a shameless fraudster? Was he a Christian pacifist or a pro-war, right-wing hawk? Was he the witness to a murder plot, who honourably testified against his closest friend, Jeremy Thorpe, or a traitorous Judas who turned on his friend to benefit himself? Was he a dedicated family man or a serial womaniser? At points, he was *all* of these things.

I grew up cocooned by my father's wealth and reputation. We lived in a large family home in Cornwall, waited on by servants. My mother looked and lived like a film star. From the age of nine, my sister and I were educated at expensive private schools. I was showered with gifts as a child, also as an adult – a flash American car and a speed-boat. I had a flat in Chelsea and an apartment in Midtown Manhattan. At a time when travel between the US and the UK was confined to the jet set, I flitted between London and New York practically weekly. People were interested in me simply because I was Peter Bessell's son. Unsurprisingly, throughout my childhood and early adult years, I idolised my father.

All that was torn away.

My father's disappearance was infinitely worse for my mother. She was middle-aged, did not have a job and lost her home. Above all, though, the love of her life vanished into thin air, with no explanation. It was a brutal betrayal from which she never fully recovered. Forty years later, the memories of her husband's disappearance would survive even the dementia, which took everything else from her .

When my father resurfaced, thrust back into the limelight, Jeremy Thorpe, a leading light in UK politics, had been charged with conspiracy to kill his gay lover, Norman Scott. This was an international sensation. Never before had a British MP faced a murder charge, and my father, as Thorpe's closest friend and confidant, had witnessed first-hand Thorpe's insistence that Scott be murdered. My father was under enormous pressure to give evidence as, without his testimony, the prosecution would stand little chance of success. It was a difficult decision to make: agreeing to testify could lead to the revelation of any number of bizarre events in his own life.

Both my mother and my father left substantial quantities of papers. My father's included a copy of his privately printed memoir, *Cover-Up*. For more than 30 years, I put off looking at these papers, fearful of what they might reveal.

When, finally, I plucked up the courage to examine them, I discovered hundreds of personal letters, statements and affidavits detailing my father's extraordinarily colourful life, warts and all. I found I had made a fundamental mistake. My father hadn't had 'a life'; he'd had several, running at the same time, and all largely secret.

Uncovering the real Peter Bessell was a long and, at times, painful journey. It challenged everything I thought I knew, and revealed much that I could never have imagined.

This book is an account of my belated journey into my father's many lives. There have been times when I've wished that I hadn't started the journey. I discovered aspects of my father's character and incidents in his long and colourful career which made me question whether I had ever really known him. The true story of his life is indeed stranger than fiction.

CHAPTER ONE

SOMEONE TO GET RID OF

IN THE SUMMER of 2002, I had lunch with my then 77-year-old mother, in a small restaurant overlooking the sea in the English port of Felixstowe. Despite her fascinating life working for the UN, she now took simple pleasure in watching the container ships sailing in and out of port. As so often happened, the conversation turned to my father, who died 17 years earlier. On this occasion, my mother told me about an event in June 1973, while she and my father were living in New York. She told the story slowly, deliberately and in great detail.

'When Daddy left for one of his secret meetings one evening, he accidentally left his briefcase behind. I noticed it by the door, so I picked it up and placed it on the settee. I sat next to it and stared at it for ages, not quite sure what to do.'

Although diminutive and from a humble background, in 1973 my mother was a beautiful, intrepid and elegant woman in her late 40s, with an innate sense of style well suited to the lavish lifestyle she enjoyed with my father. But since the day they married, he had been secretive, erratic and unfaithful. My mother came from a generation of women who had been persuaded it was their duty to support their husbands through thick and thin. There was an unspoken understanding that men, particularly in positions of power, had affairs while the 'little lady' stayed at home and took care of the children. My mother's problem was that while she did feel a sense of duty, she knew she was capable of so much more. Her intellect was easily the equal of my father's and she had a real thirst for knowledge. Whatever my father's failings, she loved him deeply. It was through his contacts that she was working as a volunteer for UNICEF, at the UN complex in New York.

Twenty-five years into a marriage which had brought her both immense happiness but also total despair, in front of her was a briefcase that might reveal all kinds of secrets. Should she open it?

'I really didn't know what to do,' she said. 'A part of me felt it would be a betrayal to take a look, particularly as we knew he had secrets from his work that no one was to know, and I respected that. But the other part of me wanted to know.'

She paused.

'Well?' I said, waiting impatiently for her to finish her mouthful.

'For a while I just kept staring at it. In just the same way that a man looking inside a lady's handbag is considered a sin, that's how I felt about the briefcase. What's the difference?'

'So, you didn't open it?' I was starting to lose interest.

'No. I did open it.'

'And?'

'It was almost unbearable. I kind of looked through squinted eyes in case I saw something that frightened me, or I didn't like.'

Suddenly, I saw her as old and vulnerable, no longer the strong and reassuring mother she had always been. Evidently, the memory was still raw. She was tearful, but slowly continued. 'At first it didn't appear that bad – just business papers and letters. So, I picked a few up and then a picture dropped out and my heart sank. It was everything I'd feared.'

'What was it?' I was almost too scared to hear the answer.

'It was a picture of a beautiful young woman.'

'Well, there's a surprise,' I said sarcastically, and a little relieved, 'Presumably you didn't recognise her?'

'No. I can't even really remember what she looked like. Only that she was beautiful – young, blonde and slim.'

I had a sneaking suspicion I knew who the woman was, but I wasn't about to say.

'Anyway,' my mother said, 'I couldn't wait to find out who it was, so I decided to call him.'

'What? At his secret work?'

'Yes. He always left me an emergency number for life-or-death emergencies. I knew it wasn't an emergency, but I used it anyway, even though it was late in the evening. I wouldn't have been able to sleep without knowing.'

'Did he answer?'

'Yes. And quickly!' She chuckled. 'I told him he'd left his briefcase behind. He was relieved to say the least! He thought he'd left it in the cab.'

'Did you tell him what you'd found?'

I knew the answer already. My mother would have gone straight for the jugular.

'Yep. I just asked, "Who's the girl?"

'He said, "Which girl?"

'And I said, the one in his briefcase. I think he was pretty stunned. But not as stunned as I was by the answer.

'He said, "It's someone we have to get rid of."'

By that stage, I was seldom shocked by anything I heard about my father, but 'get rid of' did surprise me.

'"Get rid of"?! What did he mean by that?'

'Your guess is as good as mine. What do you think?'

I was lost for words for a moment. The term has any number of connotations, but, given his secret work and aspects of which I had discovered but not told my mother about, I believe he deliberately gave the impression that it meant 'kill'.

'Mum, I really don't know. It was probably someone they were going to fire. Didn't you ask him?'

'Yes. But he just said he would explain the next day. Then he put the phone down. The following day he said he was unable to discuss it, and we had to leave the matter alone. The thing is, I remembered a discussion we'd had years prior to that, when he'd asked me what I would do if he murdered someone. I told him I didn't know and that I might tell someone because he would need help. I didn't take it seriously at the time, but when that briefcase thing happened in New York, I started wondering.'

'Mum, I really wouldn't worry. I know Dad had many faults, but he was a gentle person whose biggest fault was loving too much – he couldn't even kill a spider. I'm quite sure murder was beyond his capability.'

She hesitated for a second. Then said, 'But Jeremy Thorpe once told me Daddy had killed someone.'

For a moment I was speechless.

'I wouldn't believe anything Jeremy told you. What a nasty thing for him to say to you.'

For a while we said nothing. Then it was as if something suddenly dawned on her. She blurted out, 'Of course he was homosexual, you know?'

'Yes, I know. Everyone knows that.'

'They do?!' She was astonished. 'How did they find out?!'

'What are you talking about? He was tried for conspiring to murder Norman Scott. Of course everyone knows he was gay!'

'No, not Jeremy, your father. Your father was homosexual!'

'Dad?!'

I was startled. Why, after all these years, would she suddenly say that? Perhaps she had allowed herself to believe it, to explain issues in their relationship. I told her that, given his evident attraction to women, I thought it was unlikely. But her pain and confusion were palpable, and had been ever since he had left her. Her search for some kind of salvation from the agony of loving him while knowing he played around was unending. My mother was telling me about a photograph of a beautiful woman she'd found in my father's briefcase many years ago, yet she could only accept that her relationship with him had failed because he was homosexual. My father's indiscretions with women were well publicised over many years, yet there had never been mention of any men.

When I told my sister, Paula, she thought our mother was naive about sexual terminology and had probably muddled 'homosexual' with 'heterosexual'.

My mother's anecdote also made me wonder if my father had worked for an organisation that 'got rid of' people.

To make sense of my father's life, I would have to go back to my earliest memories.

X

Like most children, I was largely unaware of my family's social standing until I reached the age of about eight, in 1960. Gradually, it dawned on me that my father was out of the ordinary, that his attempt to become the MP for South East Cornwall for the Liberal Party was an uncommon ambition.

Whilst not particularly good-looking – skinny, about 5ft 9ins, with a full head of black hair, combed back, and a face once famously described in the *Daily Mirror* as 'ravaged' – my father had presence. Always immaculately dressed in tailored suits from Savile Row, his nails were perfectly manicured and, to complete the look, he had a small, gold filling, which was briefly visible whenever he smiled. He was well-spoken, with a deep, gravelly voice which exuded authority. It didn't matter what he told you, you simply believed him – not a bad quality for a politician, and an excellent one for someone who might not always want to tell the truth. Couple all this with a wicked sense of humour and it's not hard to see why women were drawn to him – even my girlfriend at school had a crush on him. My mother must have been well aware of his appeal to the opposite sex – after all, she had fallen for it herself – but it can't have been easy for her.

At this time, I had no idea of the various trials and tribulations he had faced. All I knew was that, in 1959, we had moved into a glorious dower-house named Polraen – pronounced *Polrain* – near the fishing village of Looe, in the prettiest of Cornish valleys. I was aware we were rich, that my father was campaigning to become an MP and a local celebrity and that the boarding school I was packed off to was expensive. My sister and I led an idyllic life filled with gardeners, maids, Bentleys and jets.

For teenagers, the 1960s was a utopian decade; but for parents brought up in the austerity of the Second World War, they were a nightmare. Parents in all parts of society found themselves unable to understand what was going on in their children's minds. Society changed beyond recognition in just a few short years, not least due to 'the pill' allowing women finally to gain control over their own bodies. The Beatles changed everything, ushering in long hair, rock music, free sex, psychedelia, marijuana, peace and love – all of which were mystifying to the previous generation.

The 1960s may have been one reason why my relationship with my father was a bit distant. I didn't feel any lack of love, but because of his lifestyle as a politician and international businessman, I simply didn't see that much of him. While he was taking on the world, I was at a co-ed boarding school in Saffron Walden, in Essex. Our communications were brief, few and far between, usually a letter from me asking for money, which he always sent.

But in the summer of 1969, I received an unusual letter; he wrote that he planned to visit me that coming Sunday. In all the years I had been at school, this was the first time he was going to visit. Something must be seriously wrong.

In 1969, I was 17 years old and already a full-blown hippy, with hair down to my shoulders, a psychedelic wardrobe and a taste for black Afghan marijuana. In opposition to the school's Quaker principles, I joined a rock band, curiously named Booker T Peanut and the All Stars, which was banned by the headmaster at one point for 'promoting hero worship'. Becoming immersed in a world of rock music and girls wasn't conducive to a top-level education. I was going a bit off the rails and now, my father was coming to visit me out of the blue. I was scared I had been found out.

That Sunday morning, I waited by the Victorian entrance to the school. My father duly rolled up the drive in his Bentley. I was excited to see him, but also nervous. The nature of our relationship meant there was no hug, he just wound down the window and told me to jump in.

'Hello, Dad. This is a surprise!' I was fishing for a reason for the visit.

'Well, it's been too long since I've seen my son, and we should spend a little time together. I thought we might take a drive to Cambridge and find somewhere to sit and chat.'

'Sounds good to me.' I wasn't convinced, but getting out of school for a few hours was always a relief.

What I didn't know then, but have since discovered, was that my mother had expressed concerns I might be gay (the long hair) and that I lacked ambition and had become, basically, a miscreant. He had been sent on a mission to discover the truth and to report back.

The half-hour drive was not particularly memorable, and my father and I then strolled along the narrow streets between limestone buildings, engaging in general chit-chat. Eventually, we found a park bench and he suggested we sit and talk.

'Here it comes,' I thought, 'I must be in deep trouble.' No doubt he had been preparing for this moment for some time.

'We've never spoken about growing up,' he began.

'Oh god,' I thought, 'here we go.' I feared we were going to have a repeat of a conversation I'd had with my mother a few months previously. While driving past a field of cows, she'd suddenly blurted out a question about whether I understood how they reproduced. I assured her I did. That, as it turned out, would be the sum total of my sex education from my mother. My worry now was that my father was about to expand on the issue. Had he done so, it would have been way too late. But the conversation took a different turn.

'I've never had the opportunity to tell you about my own upbringing,' he continued. 'It may not seem important to you, but there were aspects of it which may well affect you now.'

'In what way?'

My father often told stories of his early teens when, with his friend Hayden, he had started a business shovelling horse manure off the streets of his hometown of Bath – using his grandmother's best brass coal scuttle and shovel – and selling it as garden fertiliser. They were amusing anecdotes, but on this day he appeared serious.

'When war was declared, I became an ambulance driver. Then I joined the Ministry of Information as a lecturer.'

'A lecturer? Lecturing on what?'

'Music. Specifically, classical music, to American troops, who were stationed in the area prior to the Normandy landings. It's through them, such wonderful men, that I gained my affection for all things American.'

I wasn't sure where this conversation was leading. 'How did you become involved in that?'

'Well, that's the point, and it's one of the reasons I wanted to talk to you. I was approached because my father did similar work. But it wasn't all about lecturing; much of the work was secret.'

'Secret?'

'Secret government work. I can't elaborate more than that.'

I was a little taken aback, so didn't respond. He continued.

'The point is that this tends to run in the family. They approached me because of my father's involvement. It's more than reasonable to expect they will do likewise with you at some time in your life. I hope they do. It's an honour.'

I was floored. I had to assume this was something to do with the intelligence services. I can't deny it made me feel a little special, but I still couldn't understand why he was talking to me about it. And I had a lot of questions. Which government was he talking about? The British government? The Americans? The German government?! What was all this about?

'How will they approach me?' I asked.

'Usually out of the blue. Someone will come and talk to you.'

All this was starting to sound like James Bond, and a little frightening. But my father's normal air of authority left me with no reason to doubt him.

'Of course,' he continued, 'I don't think they'll be recruiting hippies. They're very specific about the background of their employees and do thorough checks.'

The penny dropped. This was his way of expressing displeasure at my life choices so far, the implication being that I was, in some way, letting him down. I had absolutely no reason to doubt anything he had said, but the truth or otherwise of his secret work was to become central to my attempts to understand his life. As I grew up, other stories about his childhood emerged piecemeal.

My great grandmother, for example, whom he loved and with whom he'd lived after his parents separated when he was still young, was supposedly the creator of Rupert Bear. There is a document in his papers explaining how Rupert came into existence through her making up short stories, featuring a little bear, to tell her regularly bed-ridden son, Joseph, my grandfather, who suffered from severe asthma.

My father explained that she sold these stories, for a paltry sum, to *Express Newspapers*, who ran them as daily cartoons. This was something he told us many times. Rupert Bear became almost as famous as the creations of Walt Disney in the UK, and the newspaper always said he was created in 1920 by Herbert Tourtel and illustrated by Tourtel's wife, Mary.

In the early 1970s, when my sister worked as a personal assistant to John Junor, the editor of the *Sunday Express*, she asked him about Rupert Bear. He angrily denied my father's claim.

Joseph, who I never met, was supposedly a Brooklands racing driver and the inventor of the windscreen wiper.

Being a Brooklands racer was a daring undertaking. The Brooklands motor-racing circuit has legendary status in England. Opened in 1907, it was the world's first purpose-built 'banked' circuit, 30ft high and with no crash barriers to stop wayward racing cars from disappearing over the top to crash, often fatally, into the trees beyond. It was a circuit for real daredevils. Brooklands racing drivers, who were often counts or princes, were considered heroic. The track conjured the most romantic images of my grandfather. I grew up in awe of him. It made me feel special to know that he had also been some kind of secret agent.

Joseph died at the beginning of the Second World War, serving as a lieutenant in the army. While tragically young, his death seemed fitting for such a glamorous man.

While I knew something of my father's background, I knew hardly anything about how he had felt about his mother leaving home or his time at school, where he was bullied. On that Cambridge bench, he was cleverly feeding me a little more information about himself in order to delve into my own psyche.

'How's Jane?' he asked. It was an embarrassing question for a 17-year-old. Jane was my girlfriend, and one didn't discuss such things with one's parents.

'She's fine,' I said,

'She still your girlfriend?'

'Yes!'

'I spoke to John Woods about you a few days ago.' John Woods was the headmaster, so, naturally, I was horrified.

'What? Why?!'

'He's concerned about you. He said you were caught smoking again, that he thinks you lead Jane astray, and your schoolwork is poor.'

My instincts had been right. I was in trouble. But I did what teenagers always do when they've been caught out: I expressed indignation.

'What business is my relationship with Jane of his?!' I got up and walked away. My father followed.

'He told me he would have to suspend you as it's the second time you've been caught smoking.'

'So, is that it? You've come here to take me home?'

'No. I told Woods that suspending you would be pointless, that if he sent you home, I would give you a carton of cigarettes and you would spend the whole time smoking.'

I stopped walking and looked at him. I burst out laughing.

'You must understand that having a suspension on your record would not look good. I wasn't about to let that happen. So, he agreed to put you on "suspended suspension". You need to behave or at least not get caught for a while.'

Years later, I discovered he had also made a small 'contribution' to the school coffers in return for Woods not suspending me. His message to me that day was clear: he would protect me beyond what was reasonable for a parent, on the understanding that I would clean up my act.

By the late 1960s, I knew my father worked for some secret organisation, as had his father; that he had worked as an ambulance driver and a lecturer in the Ministry of Information during the war; and that his childhood in Bath was essentially a happy one. What I didn't know then was that this was only part of the story; there were some glaring omissions and exaggerations.

Who could possibly blame my mother for looking in his briefcase?

CHAPTER TWO

SEX AND WAR

SEX ENTERED MY father's life early, and unexpectedly, in a very welcome way, despite it being completely at odds with his other great passion, religion. Around the age of 16, he became deeply involved in the work of his church. His belief in God and the teachings of the Bible was steadfast. He went to Sunday school and attended church services twice every sabbath. Although his father, Joseph, was broadly supportive of this religious inclination, he was also a man who believed in moderation, so he had some misgivings.

One evening in 1938, over supper, Joseph surprised my father with an unexpected announcement.

'Son, I've been thinking. A few years ago, I was in Paris and visited the great cathedrals of Notre Dame and Sacré-Cœur. I think you would do well to spend some time there. It might help to broaden your outlook.'

'Paris?' my father said, 'How on earth will I do that?'

Paris was not the quick one-hour flight from London that it is today; it was a major undertaking, entailing significant expense, on trains and a crossing by ship.

'I'll take you,' said his father, 'I know you'll love it, and it's worth the expense.'

'Yes! Thank you! Thank you! I would love that.'

A couple of weeks later, my father found himself alone on a boat train from London due to arrive at Gare du Nord at 9am. At the last moment, Joseph changed his plans, and my father had to travel solo – quite daunting for a 16-year-old in the 1930s. He knew barely any French and the prospect unnerved him.

The excitement and awe he must have felt as he stepped out of the station into bustling, romantic Paris, so very different from his provincial home city of Bath, would have been tangible. He had enough money to pay for a taxi from the station to a small hotel off the Champs-Élysées, where his father had booked a room. Surprisingly, everyone spoke English, including most of the guests – many of whom, again unexpectedly, were of a similar age to my father. He spent that first day visiting Sacré-Cœur, but was left unmoved. As a Congregationalist, used to a humble church, the rituals of the high mass, with its pomp and ceremony and ubiquitous gold, were things of which he strongly disapproved.

That evening, he had supper at the hotel and went to bed early, determined to make full use of the next day. Just as he was dropping off to sleep, though, there was a tap on the door. When he opened it, he was confronted by an astonishingly beautiful girl, with jet-black hair.

In a strong French accent, she asked, 'Is your name Peter?'

My father rubbed his eyes. At first, he thought she must have knocked on the door of the wrong room, but this heavenly aberration knew his name.

'Yes,' he said, 'but–'

Without waiting to be asked, she entered the room, signalling for him to close the door. She placed the small case she was carrying on the bed and opened it, producing a half-bottle of champagne and two glasses, which she matter-of-factly placed on the table.

'My name is Marie,' she said, popping the cork of the champagne bottle. She filled the glasses while my father, still in his pyjamas, stood watching her in total bewilderment.

Marie smiled. 'I think maybe you weren't expecting me,' she said, 'I've known your father for a long time. He told me I should visit you in case you were lonely and confused in a strange city.'

She sat at the table, took a sip of her champagne, and signalled for my father to do likewise. He put on his dressing gown and sat next to her.

'I don't drink alcohol – my beliefs won't let me.'

'Really? I think we need to work on some of your beliefs!' she said, laughing.

She slipped her coat from her shoulders, revealing a low-cut dress and releasing a distinct puff of perfume. She let her hair fall as she pushed my father's glass towards him. He took a sip, then another. As he wrote, some years later:

> *When I drained the glass, and another, I became filled with alcoholic conceit and convinced myself that she had found me the most attractive male in Paris, if not the whole of Europe. I'm not sure how it happened that we were both standing and she was in my arms or quite why I kissed her. It was a remarkable kiss and put me among the relatively few Englishmen who learned the art of French kissing from a Parisian.*

Joseph's intention of broadening my father's outlook was clearly proving successful. My father's account continued:

> *There is no doubt she was a superb seductress with unsurpassed equipment. I can still feel my heart pound slightly at the memory of her when she had slipped off her dress. She was wearing that most seductive of all female lingerie, cami-knickers, and the sight of her bare thighs between them and the top*

> *of her black stockings made the blood rush to my head. Apart from her hair, her most beautiful feature was her legs, and as I discovered within the next hour, these exquisitely sculpted pillars led to a heavenly paradise that had no connection with theology.*

A little later, Marie got up and left, leaving my father confused and naively asking if he could see her the next day. Unsurprisingly, she made no promises.

A few minutes later, there was another tap at the door. Opening it, this time my father was confronted by an elderly night porter, holding a bowl of purple liquid, with a towel draped over his arm. He bowed politely, and indicated that he wished to enter the room. Once the door was closed, the porter beckoned my father, deftly undid the bow of his pyjama trousers and, with the air of a trained nurse who had done nothing else his entire life, proceeded to wash his genitals in what turned out to be a potash solution. The porter explained, in very broken English, that this was to prevent him catching a venereal disease, or, in my father's words, 'le clap'. He later wrote:

> *Marie brought her profession's good taste and supreme artistry. I often wonder how many frustrated brides and bridegrooms, whose clumsy attempts at lovemaking on their wedding nights have caused frustration, would not have found sex a much more delightful experience if the male half of the partnership had been inducted as I was by a gentle expert.*

As he thought about his experience, he found it hard to believe that anything so beautiful could be wrong. In this way, his addiction to the charms of women was born – it was an addiction ultimately destined to shape every corner of his life.

Just 18 months later, war broke out in Europe.

My father told me he worked as an ambulance driver during the Second World War. I assumed that either this was his choice, or he hadn't enlisted in the army for health reasons.

But a couple of years before my mother's death, I asked her idly, 'What did Dad do during the war?'

'He was a conscientious objector!' she said, with a tone of voice and a facial expression which implied surely I had known that. I hadn't. I was shocked. Why did he keep that secret his whole life?

Being a conscientious objector (CO), when the Nazis were overrunning mainland Europe and threatening to invade Great Britain, was not an easy option. COs were seldom respected. Given the derogatory name of 'conchies', they often faced hostility from soldiers, members of the public and even their own families.

The transcript of his Conscientious Objectors Tribunal, in which he requested complete exemption from military service gives an idea of the humiliation he would have endured as a CO. The Tribunal was reported in the *Bath Chronicle and Weekly Gazette*, on 3 May 1941, as follows:

Bath Man Must Work on Land

That he was helping the Nazis to destroy civilisation, and he was doing it in the name of Christ, was the description given by Judge Wethered, President of the South-Western Conscientious Objectors Tribunal at Bristol, of the attitude adopted by Peter Joseph Bessell of Pierrepont Street, Bath, who asked for complete exemption from military service.

Applicant, who is 19 years of age, belongs to the Congregationalists. He carries on business as a tailor, on his own account, doing a large repair business.

He said it would be against his conscience to have anything

> *to do with the war. He believed that Christ would renounce any war, and therefore, if he did anything to assist the war it would be a denial of Christ.*
>
> *Bessell was retained on the register on condition that he undertakes some form of work on the land – agriculture, horticulture, forestry or land reclamation.*

This description of the hearing in the newspaper doesn't entirely match my father's account, him saying only that, a year before the outbreak of war, in 1938, his strong religious beliefs were leading him towards the pacifist theology of the Society of Friends, also known as the Quakers. He later sent both my sister and me to Quaker boarding schools.

His conversion to this theology caused him to register for National Service as a CO in 1940 but he later claimed he regretted the decision because the Nazi invasion of Europe and his own experience as a civil defence worker led him to try to enlist in the armed forces in 1941. He said he was rejected because of his earlier registration as a CO. This is simply not true, though. Far from attempting to enlist, my father sought successfully to reconfirm his registration.

He later wrote about how it took until 1943 to sort out this 'bureaucratic absurdity', during which time he undertook various forms of war work, including the 'unheroic task of playing nanny to 400 pigs for a few weeks' – the agricultural work he was ordered to undertake by the judge at the hearing. There is no doubt in my mind that he felt a degree of shame about his war record, not because he thought it was wrong to be a CO, but because the moral attitudes of society at the time demanded it. Many COs kept their status a secret throughout their lives.

By 1943 he had been appointed to the Ministry of Information as an official lecturer to British and Allied forces. As he'd told me in Cambridge, most of this lecturing was to American GIs and it was through those tough, unassuming men, as he described them, that he formed an attachment to the United States. When my father first told me about how he drove an ambulance during the war, I assumed he meant on the battlefield, but his civil defence work was around his home in the small, quiet city of Bath. Nearby Bristol, a busy port and a centre of aircraft manufacturing, was regularly the target of heavy bombing by the Luftwaffe, suffering terribly between 1940 and 1944, but Bath was largely spared, apart from stray bombs hitting the city as the bombers passed overhead in the dark on their way to and from Bristol.

There was one horrific weekend, though, 25 to 27 April 1942, which became known as the Bath Blitz. In retaliation for British attacks on German cultural centres, Hitler decided to seek revenge with what came to be known as the 'Baedeker raids' because they focused on cities of significant cultural and historical value. Bath, a city containing many Roman ruins and fine Georgian buildings, became a prime target. The raid caught residents completely off guard. They heard the planes approach, but assumed they were making their usual sorties to Bristol, so people did not seek shelter. More than 400 were killed and another 1,000 injured.

Thirty-seven years later, on 3 September 1981, my father wrote to a friend as follows:

> *Forty-two years ago, Britain and France declared war on Nazi Germany. The declaration was delayed while the British tried to persuade the frogs to pluck up their courage – just as the frogs had been compelled to wait upon the British in August 1914. I was living in Bath and was 18 years old. I spent the day fixing up black-out curtains etc. in our house. It was quite easy 'cos the house was of Georgian vintage and had wooden shutters to all the main rooms. They had not been used for decades,*

possibly more than a century, and had been painted over many times. But once restored they provided a perfect black-out plus protection from shattered glass. I was glad of that because three years later when Bath was blitzed, I was on leave and took refuge in the cellar while the bombs whistled around me. One very near miss did indeed shatter every pane of glass. But just after that I had to go out on air raid duty. It was an awesome sight, the old city enveloped in flames and the bodies we dug out were an awful sight. Now it seems so long ago, as indeed it is, so remote from my present life, as indeed it is.

I still felt I needed to confirm his ambulance work. I managed to find a newspaper article, which appears to do so, but it was not what I had expected. Dated 16 May 1942, it is headlined 'Ambulance Workers' Petrol Offences'. With fuel in short supply, only vehicles used for the war effort – like ambulances were allowed coupons to buy it.

The article in the *Bath Chronicle*, referring to a day's session in the local courtroom, read:

Victor Penny, 23, Malvern Buildings, Bath, was summoned for accepting a petrol coupon from Peter Joseph Simons Bessell … Peter J. S. Bessell of 10 Pierrepont Street, Bath, for transferring a petrol coupon to Victor Penny was fined 10 s. and 10 s. 6 d. Costs.

I was disturbed the proof that my father was an ambulance driver during the war came in the form of an article outlining how he was prosecuted, and fined, for apparently stealing coupons for much needed, rationed, petrol, which should have been allocated to ambulances.

My immediate reaction was that it revealed my father to be a wartime spiv – someone who not only managed to avoid national service by claiming to be a conscientious objector, but who also gained personally from selling illegal items on the black market. While many people used spivs to obtain extra food, clothing or luxury items not generally available, they were still regarded as the lowest of the low for profiting from people's desperation. To think of my father as a spiv was upsetting. But when I looked at the article again, I registered that the court report language is quite specific: 'Peter J. S. Bessell of 10 Pierrepont Street, Bath, for transferring a petrol coupon to Victor Penny'. He was 'transferring' the coupon – nowhere does it say he 'sold' it.

Two days after I'd found that article, I came across another, again reporting the petrol coupon court case. In this second article it was clear that Victor Penny and my father both pleaded guilty and that Penny had used the coupon to fetch his sick mother. My father had pointed out to the court he had not done it for personal gain. Both were given small fines with costs.

My father had been trying to help a friend, yet I had been all too ready to damn him for being a spiv. During the war, he was also falling in love. In January 1943, at the age of 21, he married Joyce Thomas, at Argyle Congregationalist Chapel in Bath, an austere, yet pretty church just a few yards from his home.

Despite a humble wartime wedding, Joyce and my father appeared to be reasonably well off, moving into their marital home in well-to-do Wellsway, Bath. Their marriage was a happy one, but the cruellest of fates was about to befall them. Just as the war was ending, and the world around them was celebrating, Joyce contracted tuberculosis. For three years she battled the disease, even spending time in Switzerland, where the air was cleaner, but it was a battle she lost. On 5 February 1948, Joyce died at the age of just 27. I can only imagine my father's agony as he watched his young wife deteriorate. He spoke about Joyce maybe twice in my whole life, saying no more than that his first wife had died of TB.

Then, just three months after Joyce's death, on 13 May 1948, he married my mother, Pauline. My parents first met, in 1946, through Joyce, who worked with my mother at Fry's chocolate factory at Keynsham, near Bristol. My mother described him as 'an interesting man, a prominent businessman, music lecturer, Congregational lay preacher and very well reported'. He was glamorous for the time; he was well off – his tailoring business, which he had inherited, was expanding into several branches; he drove a Jaguar convertible; and he had a romantic turn of phrase – there's no doubt he had the ability to sweep women off their feet, my mother included. But she was then engaged to another man and my father was still married to Joyce, so that was that. My mother had strong morals, and nothing was allowed to develop between them, so, at the time, she wasn't inquisitive about his background and upbringing. Ultimately, however, my parents succumbed and their courtship was brief, but intense. They married in secret, eloping to the seaside town of Torquay for a honeymoon.

Within hours, though, it was all going to go terribly wrong.

CHAPTER THREE

THE PHILANDERER

MY MOTHER, PAULINE, was an attractive woman. She was chic and, as her sister Anne put it to me, 'She had men queuing at the door – we couldn't get in!'

My father was similarly handsome. Given their comparable intellects, it's not hard to see how they were attracted to each other. My mother's humble and fairly staid upbringing was a complete contrast with the flamboyant style of my father, who drove fast cars and had very big dreams, which my mother came to share. Her parents thoroughly disapproved of the relationship, which is why the couple had married in secret. That would have been a very big deal for my mother, as she would have known she risked tearing her happy family to shreds. The secret wedding and honeymoon must have been thrilling, but their marriage couldn't be kept hidden forever.

Straight after the ceremony, the newly-weds drove to Torquay, to spend the first night of their honeymoon at the Queen's Hotel. How wonderful that day must have been for my mother, eloping with the love of her life, driving through the Devon countryside in my father's Jaguar with the roof down in the spring sunshine, wearing her Dior New Look clothes, much prized in the post war-era. Her future looked very bright right then.

The happy couple's first night was blissful. In the morning, when my mother woke, she saw her new husband standing by the window with his back to her, gazing out to sea. She smiled.

'Good morning,' she said.

My father didn't turn around. 'Good morning,' he replied, flatly.

'What a lovely morning,' she said. He didn't answer.

'Peter? Are you alright?' Again, no answer. 'Peter?'

He turned to look at her, his face ashen. Out of the blue, he said, 'I must be honest. I have had a girlfriend in my first marriage.'

The declaration was so blunt and unexpected my mother thought she must have misheard. 'What?'

'I had a girlfriend in my first marriage.'

She still didn't believe what she was hearing. 'What do you mean?'

'Joyce was physically incapable for a long time. I had an affair.'

My mother's face fell; the room spun. Surely this was a bad dream. Such happiness could not be undone within the blink of an eye, could it? She wrote later, it 'made me sick'. She came from the generation that believed sex before marriage was improper, and she had saved herself for one man. Having done that only to discover the man she had saved herself for had committed the ultimate sin in the course of his previous marriage left her 'desolate'. The fact he had failed to tell her before their marriage, thereby allowing her to make her own decision, made it even worse. Now, she felt trapped. What on earth was she to do? She tried to pull herself together.

'No! Why would you do such a thing? You're not a bad man, you're not sinful. Why are you saying such an awful thing to me?'

'Because it's true. I did. And now I must live with it on my conscience. I had to tell you, to be honest with you. I couldn't keep it a secret for the rest of my life. I want you to believe in me and know I always tell you the truth. I'm telling you for our sake,' he pleaded.

She started to get angry. 'For *our* sake? For OUR sake? You waited until after I had given myself to you, the first man in my life, the man for whom I spent all my life saving myself! And you wait until *after* the event to tell me?' She took a breath, trying to calm down. 'My god, I realise now. You see our physical relationship in a totally different way to me. To me it is the ultimate expression of our love. To you, it's just ... *sex*.'

It's no wonder my father's confession left my mother desolated.

It appears, bizarrely, that Peter had not anticipated her response. He presumably hoped he could clear his conscience and be forgiven. He thought his openness and honesty would be the best thing for their relationship, that it would establish trust that he would keep no secrets. My mother would not have held back in letting my father know what she thought of his behaviour. Such was her response that 'he prepared to drown himself'.

Eventually, though, in a true case of love being blind, she chose forgiveness. She preferred to be with him, even given what he'd said, than not be with him at all. In years to come, she would refer to these events as her 'first disillusionment'. Pauline now had to face telling her parents she had married this man, who deceived his previous wife. If her parents had ever found out, they would have said, 'Well, we told you so!'

Following his marriage, my father offered to resign from his preaching duties at the church, presumably because his new marriage followed uncomfortably swiftly on the death of his previous wife. The offer was rejected.

In July 1948, two months after their marriage, my father's tailoring and dry-cleaning business was registered as a private company, naming him and my mother as directors. The business was initially okay, but then began to fail – probably because my father had borrowed more than the company could afford. In the end, the business did fail and, by 1950, a year after the birth of my sister, Paula, our parents moved from Bath to Torquay, to make a fresh start.

Once there, my father worked in a women's clothes shop. But his dreams were way too big to ever settle for that. It became the overwhelming feature of his life that he had something to prove to the world, whatever the true cost to his inner wellbeing. He sought fulfilment in wealth, success and, yes, women. It wasn't long before he started another tailoring and dry-cleaning business. He was highly educated in classical music, so he quickly became involved with the local music society, and then, gradually, the dramatic society, too. Within a short space of time, he had become a bit of a local celebrity. He was on the way.

I was born on 6 June 1952 and, at the insistence of my father, was named Paul. The family was then Peter, Pauline, Paula and Paul. I read a YouTube comment recently which referred to my family's names as proof we were weird, but I had always assumed people would think it was a nice idea!

Life in Torquay allowed my mother to try to forget her 'first disillusionment'. My parents now had two children, my father a new business and he was very active in the local community. Home life wasn't perfect, in part because of tension with their landlady, who did not have children.

But then, a fresh shock. Peter had been in someone else's bed again, this time with the local jewellery store assistant, Shirley. My mother referred to it as my father's 'seven-year itch'. She found letters, presumably while doing his laundry, containing lines like 'I can't live without you', 'Too big for us both …' and 'I can feel your heartbeat'. She tore them up, and waited for my father to get home. He thought better of trying to deny it. Apparently, he had been dining at Shirley's each night before his music and drama evenings. My mother now had confirmation her husband's indiscretion in his previous marriage wasn't a one-off aberration; it was a compulsion. Should she blame herself for not being the perfect wife? She needed time to think.

She left my sister and me with Gran, my father's mother, and went to London to stay with a friend while she took that time to think about what to do.

Her situation was probably no different from millions of women in the 1950s, who found their husbands had been unfaithful. Then a divorced single mother received only what the essentially misogynistic courts could squeeze out of fathers, who went out of their way to avoid paying anything. The prospects for a divorcee was poverty and being regarded as a social pariah. As a result, millions of couples stayed together 'for the sake of the children'.

But whereas unfaithful husbands were usually despised by their wives, my mother was still deeply in love with her husband. Her confusion, disillusionment and deep hurt must have been heartbreaking.

As she wrestled with what to do, she wrote many letters to Peter, which are truly pitiful to read, not just with regard to her, but to the many other women trapped in similar situations. They reveal clearly the awful sexism of the day:

> *I know now where I went wrong. It was right at the beginning. From that time, I should have realised that our love was the same as everyone else's. Or at least yours was. I should have done what 999 wives out of 1,000 wives have to do and sympathised with you. As you say most successful wives do this and make a 'success' of their marriage although I firmly believe that in the end, they have secret contempt for each other, even if it's never admitted... But I have been so hurt by your attitude which has been so consistent for years... My whole world is completely shattered. This isn't idle talk... I just cannot believe still that all this has happened. I have always had such faith in you and your love for me as in mine for you... I have loved you with a love that you cannot understand and I have expected*

the same in return, which was too much to hope for, I should have realised... What a fool I've been!

My mother's bitterness is evident, yet, still, her love for my father didn't die. I think she couldn't bring herself to send that letter. The next letter was the saddest of all. She thanks him for all he has done for her; she feels remorse at her previous feelings and needs to make up for them, to make him feel better:

My dear,

This is a cowardly thing to do really and yet shyness is my excuse and since this is probably the only time in my life when you will be able to believe what I'm going to say, I must do it now. If I leave it until I come back you will think it either politeness, or gush, depending on whether we stay together or not.

It is just to say 'Thank you' to you. Not thank you for being happy or miserable, but thank you for all you have done for me during the years. It's time, my love has changed since we were married but that early love was a poor thing compared with the one that has grown since. It was then very unappreciative – it is now one which recognises in you a fundamental goodness which has helped me so much and taught me such a lot. I am, because of you, a far, far better thing than I was seven years ago.

Worldly success doesn't really bother me – oh I should like a big car etc. as you would, but I have never blamed you for not having one. I never considered you either a success or a failure – just you. And even if you had been the biggest failure, or success for that matter, my respect and admiration for you would not have changed. I have been happy for you when things have gone well and miserable for you when disaster loomed.

I have felt a true and deep love for you and with all my heart wish that you could or would have found it sooner.

Perhaps we are not too late.

Always yours.

Like millions of other women have been compelled to do by circumstances, she caved in, appearing to accept the blame. She didn't need a big car. He wasn't listening.

CHAPTER FOUR

POLITICS AND BANKRUPTCY

ON A WARM June night in 1952, the sound of fire engines filled the air in the quiet coastal town of Torquay. My father, who hadn't been home long and just crept into bed, got up and went to the window to see what was going on. In the distance, towards the town centre, the red glow of a substantial fire lit up the surrounding buildings.

'That's quite a sight,' he said to my mother, 'I wonder which building it is.'

The noise of the sirens had woken her, too. She got out of bed and came to the window. 'Can't be far from your business,' she said, 'It's the right direction.'

My father paused for a moment. 'You're right,' he said anxiously, 'Actually, it must be very close. Maybe I should go down and make sure everything's alright.'

My mother put a comforting hand on his arm. 'I'm sure it is, but it might not be a bad idea to take a look.'

My father pulled on some clothes, ran out, jumped in the car and drove as fast as he could to his tailoring shop. As he turned the corner, he could see that everything was far from alright. The building was engulfed in flames, with two fire engines and several firemen working furiously to douse the fire. He got out of his car and stood there, helplessly watching his livelihood burn before his eyes.

It was dawn before he could pull himself away and head home to tell my mother. The cause of the fire was unknown, but my father's solicitor had to write to the local newspaper threatening prosecution of those suggesting there might be something suspicious about it. The fire destroyed all the equipment in my father's shop; it had also destroyed all the financial records. There was an insurance policy in place to cover the losses, but the equipment and premises had been bought and rented through an individual investor, William F. Amery, and the debts to him were a problem. My father was shattered.

Prior to the fire, the business was not going well. As the financial records had gone up in smoke, Peter had to outline them in an extensive document he prepared to explain the situation to William Amery. The bottom line was that he had been trading at a loss for several months and was now effectively bankrupt. In the document, my father claimed he had suspected for a while that the business was not profitable, but it was only when he sat down to do the figures after the fire he realised how serious the situation had become. At best, it was negligent of the owner of a business to be unaware of its financial position; at worst, there is cause for darker suspicions. As it is illegal to run a business knowing that it is insolvent, he proposed to Amery two possible courses of action. The first was to hold a meeting of creditors and reorganise the finances to allow debts to be paid over a period of time. He considered this unlikely to be accepted.

His second proposal was to declare bankruptcy. As he wrote:

> *File my petition of Bankruptcy forthwith. This seems the most probable course even though it means personal ruination*

and leaves me in the greatest difficulty to support myself and family due to my being unable to take anything other than a managerial or non-physical job of work through health reasons. These sorts of jobs are not open to undischarged bankrupts as a rule, although someone may take pity on me. My idea, which I have considered in the past, of accepting the post of a paid carnival organiser is out on three counts. Firstly, the carnival committee is in a grave financial position and there would be no guarantee of ultimate payment for the work. Secondly, it is forbidden by the doctors on the grounds of prolonged physical and mental strain during Carnival weeks. Thirdly, I should not get the appointment in any case as an undischarged bankrupt because of public opinion.

There was much more social stigma associated with bankruptcy in the 1950s than today. Was my father making an emotional appeal to Amery, who appears to have been a decent person? Despite his claims of ill health in writing to Amery, my father would maintain that he had always been blessed with good health until the late 1970s, when he contracted terminal emphysema. He treads a fine line between playing on Amery's emotions in the hope the debt might be forgiven, or at least deferred, whilst not giving the appearance of trying to take advantage of Amery's good nature. The document also includes an explanation for the disappearance of the insurance funds, which might well have recouped a large percentage of Amery's investment:

Statement of Position Regarding Insurance

The worst shock is contained here. It is useless to make excuses, and I can only explain what happened and you must reach your own conclusions regarding my stupidity, negligence and sheer foolishness. To say I am sorry is totally inadequate although I do say it sincerely. One thing I wish to state even though you may disbelieve me. At no time have I wilfully misled you on this or told you other than what I honestly believed to be the entire truth on the subject.

My father went on to explain, in detail, how there had been a misunderstanding over the payment of the insurance funds for the fire, resulting in him 'inadvertently' spending it. He concludes: 'I understand what a shock this will be to you, and I do not propose to labour what a terrible blow it was to me when I learned the true position.'

Then there was a letter to Amery which accompanied the document. It begins:

Here are the figures and they will be an even greater shock and blow to you than they have been to me. I cannot even begin to guess your reaction. I will say nothing about mine beyond the fact that since getting them I have put in hours and hours to solving the problem and trying to see daylight. I have realised for the last couple of months that all was not well but never appreciated how far things had gone.

It is useless to ask forgiveness for such a situation or to try to make excuses. Only one thing I ask you to remember, that desperately serious though this is for you, you should recover at least half your investment through the bankruptcy Court. I, on the other hand, am utterly ruined and on top of last month's news it is the crowning blow for us all.

It's a begging letter and the bottom line is simple: there had been a fire at the premises; and he had spent the insurance money. It's not difficult to reach uncomfortable conclusions.

Incredibly, despite all this, he did manage to save the business, and, ironically, it might have been the fire that helped him to do it. His public plight after the disaster appears to have garnered sympathy from many quarters and, perhaps realising they were likely to lose their money anyway, his creditors agreed to forgo money owed to them, provided the company stayed afloat and they continued to supply services. Furthermore, his clients came to the rescue by promising to put as much work his way as they could. Somehow, my father managed to persuade Amery not to foreclose on him – presumably on the basis that there was nothing to be gained by doing so.

In the early 1950s, my father found himself with a young family, a wife who was not working and who was on the verge of leaving him because of his indiscretions, and a business which was very publicly on the point of falling to pieces. Over the next couple of years, he became so poor we could no longer afford a house of our own and we lived in the spare rooms of one of his employees. But he wasn't beaten and, although his tailoring business in Torquay eventually failed, he had in the meantime started another similar business in London. Because of the distance, over 200 miles, he had to live in London during the week, visiting his family at weekends. This was hardly ideal for my mother, but it was a pattern that would persist for the next 20 years. On one occasion she visited him in his rented room where they 'made love', but then had to secretly leave the building because he owed rent.

The remarkable thing about my father is that no matter what he did or the trouble he got into, everyone still loved him. He was immensely popular, even with those who hardly knew him. Never has the description 'loveable rogue' applied more fittingly. Despite all his mistakes, everyone was willing him to win, even those who lost as a result of those mistakes.

In the midst of all this, there was one silver lining for my father, the

Paignton Pageant, in honour of the Coronation of Queen Elizabeth II, which he was organising. The pageant – a procession of people dressed in historical costumes and an outdoor performance of an historical scene – was quite a challenge to pull together.

As the creator and producer of the event, my father had to encourage over 40 organisations to take part, then coordinate over 1,000 individual participants. Its success made him a household name in the area. At a time when telephones were not common and there was no email nor mobile phones, the stress of organising the pageant was enormous, particularly when his tailoring and dry-cleaning business was struggling. But the Paignton Pageant changed my father's life by bringing him to the attention of the local Liberal Party who were seeking a parliamentary candidate for the Torquay constituency.

The Liberal Party had been suffering a catastrophic national decline for a number of years. In Torquay in particular, they were running a very poor third and there was no chance of their candidate being elected to Parliament. Even finding a good candidate was proving a challenge. But, having seen my father's local popularity, knowing him to be a staunch Liberal and being aware of his background in public speaking as a lay preacher, they completely ignored his business 'difficulties' and asked him if he would stand for them in the next election.

With all his responsibilities and his regular commuting to and from London, my father was reluctant to take this on, particularly as there appeared to be little chance of success. But his fervent belief in Liberalism led him to take up the challenge, soon spending his spare time cycling around the constituency to get to know as many people as he could on a one-to-one basis.

The 1955 general election saw the Conservative candidate, Charles Williams, re-elected with 60 per cent of the vote; Labour ran a poor second; and the Liberals, with my father as their candidate, ran an even more forlorn third. But soon after the election Charles Williams died, and a by-election was held. Predictably, the Conservative candidate, Frederic Bennett, was elected, but nowhere near as convincingly. He lost almost 10 per cent of the vote and the swing was entirely to my father. The national headquarters of the Liberal Party sat up and took notice. Could Peter Bessell really be capable of achieving the impossible and getting himself elected as a Liberal MP?

My father's campaigning was relentless, even in the fairly certain knowledge he would not win. At one point, he invited another up-and-coming candidate from a nearby constituency, North Devon, to support him canvassing on the streets of Torquay. Campaigning in those days was very different. Candidates literally moved from one street, or town, to another, setting up a microphone and inviting people to come out of their houses, or shops, to listen to them. The ability to stand on a soapbox and engage passers-by was crucial to becoming an MP. It was a skill my father had learned as a preacher. The support of an equally adept candidate was a great help and, in this case, that candidate was Jeremy Thorpe. The first time they properly met was when Thorpe arrived while my father was speaking on a Torquay shopping street. It would prove to be a fateful meeting, setting them on course for disaster, but at the time, it felt exciting and filled with promise. Thorpe arrived like a whirlwind, leaping from his car, grabbing the microphone from my father and waving his bowler hat to a few bemused bystanders, as if he were waving to a multitude.

'Good afternoon, everyone!' he bellowed, 'My name is Jeremy Thorpe, and I'm here to support my old friend Peter Bessell, your Liberal candidate in this vital by-election!' There was a smattering of applause as a few more shoppers stopped to see what was going on. Thorpe then shook hands vigorously with my father, grasped his arm and shoved him into a shop doorway.

'Tell me, have we ever met before?' he whispered urgently. My father explained they had previously met only briefly, at a Liberal Party conference. But that was good enough for Thorpe and he went on to enthral the now rapidly growing crowd with tales of the men's close friendship and how the Liberals would conquer the world.

X

About 50 miles from Torquay, in neighbouring Cornwall, lay the beautiful Parliamentary constituency of Bodmin. For most of the later nineteenth century and the first years of the twentieth, it was held by the Liberals. After the First World War, its MP Isaac Foot became a kind of Mafia Godfather of the Cornish Liberals. Little was done without his approval. He was the founding father of a British political dynasty. His sons went on to become MPs and Lords, including Hugh Foot, who became Lord Caradon, the Permanent Representative of the United Kingdom to the United Nations and the last governor of British Cyprus, and Michael Foot, leader of the Labour Party from 1980 to 1983. But in 1935, Isaac Foot lost Bodmin to the Conservatives. Then, for many years, the Conservatives had an iron grip on the seat, later in the person of Douglas Marshall, whom my father called 'No-neck', as his shoulders appeared to meet his head somewhere around his ears. He later named our tropical Plecostomus catfish Douglas due to similar characteristics.

But unlike Torquay, Bodmin was a constituency in which the Liberals always came second, and not too far behind. There was a feeling that even if the seat wasn't actually winnable, it might be possible, with the right candidate, to run the Conservatives close. Following his strong showing in Torquay, my father was invited to meet Isaac Foot. He clearly impressed Isaac as he was offered the

Bodmin candidacy. My father knew this would mean uprooting his family to move to Cornwall. My parents were so poor, it was a colossal decision which, if it turned out to be wrong, would leave them in dire straits.

But they did just that. Risking what little they had, they packed a small car, put their children in the back and headed off to Cornwall to seek their fortune. This remains one of my strongest memories: in 1957 lying on the back seat of our car as we drove away, saying to myself, 'I'm going to remember for the rest of my life the day we moved to Cornwall.'

CHAPTER FIVE

THE ENTREPRENEUR

IN THE 1950S, the United States was still very much the New World. With true entrepreneurial spirit, my father was not slow to realise it genuinely was a land of opportunity. History fascinated him and he took the words inscribed on the tablet at the base of the Statue of Liberty to heart:

> *"Give me your tired, your poor,*
> *Your huddled masses yearning to breathe free,*
> *The wretched refuse of your teeming shore ..."*

He too believed hard work and original ideas could bring wealth and prosperity to individuals who were prepared to take risks. At the same time that he moved his business to London and his family to Cornwall, he invested all his meagre resources in a first trip to America, aboard the *Queen Elizabeth*. As he stepped off the ship in New York, he was overawed. It was, he later wrote, like 'coming home'.

What he found was an exciting world of multi-lane freeways, big cars, soaring skyscrapers, and similarly ambitious ideas. The buzz of New York in particular was irresistible to a man brought up in provincial Bath. His English accent garnered attention wherever he went. Curiously, it was an accent Americans felt they could trust. My father quickly made many business contacts and it took him to the highest reaches of society. The contrast between New York and his quiet family home in a tiny Cornish fishing village could not have been greater. Most importantly, though, he used his trips to look around for new ideas to bring to the UK, which was trailing far behind in innovation. The staid British tended to regard the Americans' overt displays of wealth as brash, but my father was quick to see the opportunities the coming cultural shift would offer. As well as making many business and political contacts in New York, he brought back several innovations, all of which proved profitable.

The first of these was to open, with a partner, the first chain of coin-operated launderettes in London. Called Coin-Op, it was a great success, though the idea couldn't be patented, so it wasn't long before self-service launderettes were popping up all over the country. The second was the felt-tip marker, then unknown in the UK. My father opened a small factory, Manhattan Equipment, in Cornwall, which manufactured felt-tip markers for many years, while providing employment to some of his constituents. In just a few years, these ideas fresh from the United States would transform him from being practically a pauper, without a home of his own, into a successful, wealthy businessman.

X

Eleanor Roosevelt was arguably the most dynamic First Lady in United States history. Her husband, Franklin D. Roosevelt, was President for four terms, and was in office during many of the most critical years of the Second World War, until his death in 1945. Eleanor was much more than simply a First Lady; she was a politician, diplomat and activist in her own right. She later served as a United Nations delegate whose dynamism was loved, and feared, by all those who worked with her.

By the late 1950s, my father's increasingly successful businesses led to him making many trips to New York. On one such trip, the Liberal Party made arrangements for him to meet Mrs Roosevelt on behalf of the party. As it was put to him, 'If Mrs Roosevelt likes you, she can open every door for you, and will do so.' A letter of introduction was sent ahead as he crossed the Atlantic. As soon as he entered his hotel room, the phone rang.

'Hello?' said my father, wearily.

'Is that Peter Bessell?' The woman at the other end didn't announce herself and my father was a little confused.

'Yes … yes, it is.'

'Are you tired after your crossing? Or was it a good one?' she asked.

'No, I'm not at all tired, thank you. It was a most pleasant and refreshing crossing.'

'That's good. Do you have any immediate appointments?' the woman asked. My father still had no idea who he was speaking to.

'Er, no. I've allowed myself a couple of days to get my bearings.'

'Good. This is Mrs Roosevelt. Would you care to have tea with me tomorrow afternoon?'

'Yes, of course. I would be delighted.'

They agreed a time and my father put the phone down, feeling a bit overwhelmed. An ex-First Lady had called him, personally, and she wasn't just any ex-First Lady; she was Eleanor Roosevelt. He, on the other hand, was a man she didn't know, who, at that time, was a nobody on the world stage.

The following day, my father arrived at Eleanor Roosevelt's 62nd Street apartment at the appointed time. He was met by her German maid and escorted to the drawing room, where she was standing with her back to the door, reading. On hearing him enter, she turned, and he immediately got the feeling that here was someone of enormous strength and, surprisingly, because she was widely considered to be 'plain', of 'extraordinary beauty'. He considered her, even in her 70s, to have a sensual quality which was not conveyed in press pictures. He was not surprised the very handsome young Franklin Roosevelt had found her irresistible.

The meeting lasted over an hour and a half, during which time tea was served in the English fashion and Eleanor devised a programme for my father's stay in America. Once or twice, she paused, taking off her heavy-framed glasses, which concealed her hearing aid, and said almost to herself, 'I think I had better take you to see him or he'll fob you off with one of his staff.' Or, 'of course, he's difficult to meet, but I'm sure he'll see me.' My father found himself privileged to have a very special guide and mentor in the United States. Eleanor was fascinated by every aspect of my father's life: his family, hobbies and political ambitions.

For the next two years, Eleanor and my father saw quite a lot of each other and he often visited her for tea.

She taught him a great deal about American and international politics, the United Nations and, most importantly, how to win an election.

While he was living the high life in New York, my mother was becoming increasingly isolated in Cornwall. Despite the success of his London business, we still had very little money. Travel between the capital and Cornwall in those days, an arduous drive of 250 miles, regularly took at least eight hours, often much longer if traffic was bad. The Great Western Railway steam trains were a little faster, but they were expensive. All of this had a major impact on the family.

My father would leave Looe early on Monday morning, arriving in London in the late afternoon; he would leave London on

Friday evening, arriving in Looe in the middle of the night. It was exhausting for him, especially during the cold, dark winters. As for my mother, she had to spend every week alone with her young children in a strange town, with little or no money, not really knowing where her husband was or what he was doing. This must have been unbearable for a woman whose husband had already proved himself capable of straying. While my sister and I were at school, she would wander the streets of Looe just to pass the time. There was no telephone in the house, so any calls with my father had to be pre-arranged, but she could hardly afford to make such calls in any case. In the early days, we had so little that one day, when my mother had no money for the electricity meter, she, my sister and I just sat on the stairs in the cold and dark until my father got home from London with enough change to provide some light and warmth. As a young child I saw nothing wrong with that, and I think my mother saw it as the price that had to be paid for the opportunity of a brighter future.

Weekends were very special, when my father came home, bringing colour and excitement into our lives. For my parents, those weekends were spent establishing him as the Liberal candidate, preparing to fight the Conservatives at the next general election, due to be held in 1959.

The Cornish people have their own culture and regard anyone not born and raised in Cornwall as a foreigner. My father was not Cornish. He was born in Bath, a good hundred miles away, in Somerset. When we moved to Looe, he was introduced to his constituents as a 'foreigner', of whom they would naturally be suspicious. He always claimed, with affection, that the Cornish would not accept you until you had lived there for at least 20 years and, at the time we moved there in 1957, he had a mere two years until the next general election in which to convince them he was a man worth voting for. This is where his ideas gleaned from his trips to the United States and his meetings with Eleanor Roosevelt were to become invaluable.

Back then there was no internet and no social media; even local television was in its infancy. There was only one way for a politician to connect with the electorate. As in Torquay, he would have to slog around the constituency, knocking on thousands of doors and talking individually to as many constituents as possible. This was time-consuming and exhausting, particularly in rural areas where there were literally hundreds of very small villages. Every weekend, my parents would drive around the constituency, knocking on doors and speaking in local halls, sometimes to no more than four or five people. And on Sundays, my father would preach at the local churches. There was no respite for him. Work in London all week; then slog around the constituency at weekends. It was physically impossible, of course, to knock on the door of each and every constituent, there being a good 50,000 of them, so door-to-door canvassing had its limitations.

But what my father had learned in the United States was that electioneering was no time for the usual British reserve. It was a time to market yourself through any means available, to put on a show. The way to get himself known, as he saw it, was not to traipse timidly round the constituency as a small-time, broke candidate from Torquay. He had to behave in a way that gave constituents the impression that he was already hugely successful, and was inviting voters to share in that success.

When we first moved to Looe, we lived in a tiny fisherman's house, Smuggler's Cottage, in the centre of town. We soon moved to a slightly larger bungalow overlooking the harbour. But once my father was formally adopted as the Liberal candidate, he felt we needed something more impressive and, if there's one thing being a parliamentary candidate gives you, it's useful contacts. One of those contacts, Robert Kitson, a local landowner, shared my father's view.

Kitson owned the large Morval Estate close to Looe, where he lived in a grand mansion, Morval House. On the estate was a large dower-house, Polraen, in the Looe valley next to a beautiful salmon river. It was not too flashy, but sufficiently impressive to project an image in keeping with my father's ambitions. Kitson rented Polraen to us at an 'advantageous' rent. It was a very beautiful home, which was to be the scene of the happiest years of our lives, particularly my mother's. It was also my father's refuge in times of difficulty.

He also realised that pootling around in his Austin Cambridge was not going to impress anyone and his trips to the United States had given him a passion for big American cars. With the growing success of his London business, he bought first a 1955 Pontiac, then a string of Cadillacs, one after the other, a gigantic black Fleetwood and a white Coupe de Ville among them. Cornwall was a remote, rural county with tiny, single-lane roads lined with high hedges. American cars of the 1950s and 1960s were gigantic by any standard, certainly compared with the tiny British cars of that era, and would literally fill the Cornish roads. They were also rare, so crowds of onlookers would flock to wherever my father parked up.

My father also introduced a new method of campaigning – the poster. At that time, UK election posters were very discreet with supporters placing an A4-size poster in a window of their home or perhaps an even smaller one in the rear window of their car. The tagline was often simply a generic 'Vote Conservative' or 'Vote Liberal' Occasionally, it might have a photograph of the candidate along with a similar tagline. The intention wasn't so much to influence the person seeing the poster as to indicate who the person displaying it supported. The assumption was that the electorate tended to vote for a particular party, rather than an individual candidate. It could be difficult to persuade people to put political posters in their windows, as the tradition of keeping your voting intention secret tended to be sacrosanct in the UK.

But my father had very different ideas. In the UK, people vote by placing a single X next to the candidate they wish to vote for. Cornwall is very hilly, with deep valleys, and many of the hills are laid to grassy fields for livestock or crops. My father paid farmers to place enormous posters on the tops of hills on their farms, with a black background and bright green Day-Glo lettering, reading simply: Bessell X

His hilltop posters could be seen for miles and all the other Liberal posters, for windows and cars, used the same colour and typeface and carried the same message. The bright lettering was like a beacon, even in dull weather. What my father had learned from Eleanor Roosevelt proved to be fantastically effective, leaving his opponent Marshall floundering in his wake.

The change in my father's image in just a few years was astonishing. From a poor, failed tailor, with seemingly questionable ethics, he turned himself into a wealthy local celebrity and international jet-setter.

One might assume the ostentatious nature of my father's image and campaigns bred a great deal of resentment amongst the Cornish, but that would be to misunderstand their nature. They understood that, beneath the brash showmanship, was a man who was genuinely dedicated to their well-being and who had quickly come to love them. The Cornish Liberals embraced him with open arms, which he reciprocated. Our family's home would always be Polraen.

During the 1950s, Bodmin was a safe Conservative parliamentary seat. But in 1959, my father's first attempt to win the seat, it was a completely different story. Marshall hung on, but his majority was slashed to under 3,000 at a time when, nationally, the Conservatives were polling very strongly, having increased their majority of MPs in the House of Commons. The Liberals, with only six MPs out of a total of 630 seats, made no impression at all. My father's result flew in the face of everything happening nationally. It was considered a stunning result, even though he hadn't won. It gave real hope that at the next election in five years' time, the Liberals had a genuine chance of winning. Five years felt like an eternity, but immediately after the 1959 election, my father set to work planning his campaign for 1964.

Even more impressive, was the 1959 result in the nearby constituency of North Devon, where Jeremy Thorpe took the seat for the Liberals from the Conservatives by the tiniest of majorities – just 362 votes. As their constituencies were so close to each other, it resulted in the pair being drawn ever closer together. As a sitting MP, Thorpe made many visits to Cornwall to boost my father's attempt to take the seat in 1964.

The next five years of my father's life were filled with relentless campaigning and with work. He and Thorpe became utterly driven in their quest to see another Liberal voted into the House of Commons. I seldom saw my father, particularly after my sister and I were packed off to boarding schools.

The Conservative government elected in 1959 had a substantial majority. But, as the 1964 election loomed, amongst several other crises, the Conservatives became embroiled in the Profumo Affair, a scandal involving the Secretary of State for War, John Profumo, and his illicit relationship with a young model, Christine Keeler. The mishandling of the affair all but destroyed the credibility of the Prime Minister, Harold Macmillan. As a result, when the election came, it was all to play for between the second biggest party, the Labour Party under Harold Wilson, and the Conservatives. The Liberals were no more than a sideshow.

Polling day was set for 15 October 1964, with campaigning beginning in earnest about a month beforehand. My father's huge posters were everywhere in the constituency, and he set out to speak at every village and tiny hamlet. It was a demanding undertaking which required my mother to drive him everywhere, along with a cavalcade of several other cars, all adorned with posters. They were accompanied by a Land-Rover with a specially constructed platform and loudspeakers on top so that, when they stopped in some suitable place, my father could climb up on top and speak briefly, sometimes to hundreds, sometimes to just two or three mildly curious onlookers, before moving on to the next village. My parents were understandably exhausted by all this. One evening, as they were driving over dark, deserted moorland, my mother suddenly stopped the car and slumped over the steering wheel.

'I simply can't do this any more,' she declared.

My father, who would use the drives between villages to catnap, took over while my mother slept. But, the next morning, she was up again, supporting her husband's campaign, driving countless miles between villages once more.

When the polls closed at 10pm on polling day, the ballot boxes were sealed and transported to the town hall in nearby Liskeard. The counting began early the next day. My father was hopeful, but was taking nothing for granted. In the morning, we left Polraen and drove the eight miles to the Liberal headquarters, just across the road from where the count was taking place. Once inside, my parents left my sister and me with friends and went to the count. As the morning went on, a large crowd gathered in the town square, waiting for the declaration.

Eventually, an upstairs window at the town hall was opened and the returning officer, who oversees the count in each constituency, leaned out with a megaphone and read out the election result for Bodmin.

'Peter Joseph Bessell – 18,046. Douglas Marshall – 14,000…'

Before he could finish reading Marshall's total, a huge cheer erupted, drowning out his words. My father had won! When he and my mother appeared from inside the building, there was a scrum of people waiting for them, pushing and shoving to get close to congratulate them. Both my parents were lifted shoulder-high on wooden chairs and carried precariously through the crowd to the Liberal Party office, where my sister and I were waiting. As soon as my father saw me, he rushed over and gave me a hug so tight I could hardly breathe.

'We did it, my son. We did it!' Words I will never forget. At the time, I thought the word 'we' meant him and me.

It was the first – and last – time in my life my father hugged me so tightly, and it was also the first time in my life I found myself crying – with happiness. It was an emotion that, as a 12-year-old, I was entirely unfamiliar with and felt I should stifle. The family went onto the balcony and waved to the crowd. We felt like royalty. I guess, in our local area, we almost were. But however other people perceived us, it was undoubtedly the happiest day of our lives. I was so proud of my father and proud to be his son because he had achieved so much from such an unpromising start. He was now a Member of Parliament.

That morning, we left Polraen as ordinary mortals. In the evening, we returned with my father now a local celebrity, with the police stopping the traffic to let us through. This was the fulfilment of the dream the Peter Bessell writing letters in an attempt to escape debts in Torquay just a few years earlier had prayed for. Yet, just a few miles away in North Devon, clouds were gathering for Jeremy Thorpe.

CHAPTER SIX

A PAIR OF OLD QUEENS

JEREMY THORPE WAS educated at Eton, a school for boys only, intended to educate the sons of members of the British establishment and prepare them for an elite life, governing the country and running the media and business.

Despite having been an unexceptional pupil at Eton, Thorpe secured a place at Trinity College, Oxford, in 1948, reading law. In other words, he was the epitome of everything considered to be the 'British establishment', very much a member of the elite club of men into which it was impossible for an outsider, or a woman, to gain access.

It wasn't just about being rich, it was about one's family being historically deeply embedded in the ruling class and landed aristocracy, as well as having the right accent, education and background. This was the club that ruled society in the 1950s and early 1960s. There were very few doors that would not open for him.

Although not classically attractive, with a narrow face and a comb-over of prematurely thinning black hair, Thorpe was a flamboyant, larger-than-life character, never slow to let his feelings be known. Not always popular, he was admired as a brilliant debater at Oxford, becoming President of the Oxford Union, a position often held by those who would go on to fill the highest positions in the country.

Thorpe's heritage was staunchly Conservative, but the young Jeremy had a rebellious nature and became a committed Liberal centrist. With his background, a desire to enter Parliament was almost inevitable, and any vacant Conservative – or Labour – seat in the country would have welcomed him with open arms. No doubt a place in the Cabinet would have followed and he may well have been a future prime minister. He certainly had all the credentials. But Thorpe decided he couldn't betray his beliefs and, even though it was almost impossible to become an MP as a Liberal in the 1950s, that was the route he chose. Thorpe could pick just about any constituency he wanted. Shrewdly, he chose North Devon.

Thorpe was the antithesis of everything the constituents of North Devon were looking for. No family connection with the area, he wasn't a member of the local aristocracy, gentlemen farmers or a professional firmly rooted in the West Country. He was an outsider, and his eccentric style of dress and establishment background, coupled with his aristocratic accent, were completely at odds with the local Liberal Party.

But in the same way that south-east Cornwall accepted the extravagances of my father, so North Devon did with Thorpe. His apparent disadvantages were superficial. He may have had a penchant for Edwardian suits with outdated collars and a liking for exaggerated gestures, but he had a warm, outgoing personality, which the Devonians quickly took to. They understood and responded to the sentimentalism of the flamboyant extrovert in a brown bowler hat, and he quickly returned their love, for having accepted him. Before long, he was known in the constituency as 'Our Jeremy'.

There were significant parallels between my father and Thorpe, with regard to their characters and constituencies. They had totally different backgrounds but as personalities they appealed to their West Country constituents in exactly the same way. Their overt sentimentality and care for those around them were quickly recognised by local voters. They also shared a similar sense of humour, deep Liberal convictions and an enthusiasm for showmanship. They became close friends, Thorpe creating nicknames for my father – Beseli and Pedro.

Thorpe's first election campaign in 1955 was nothing short of astonishing. He didn't win, but he almost halved the Conservative majority, pushing Labour into third place. Overnight, North Devon was transformed from a lost cause for the Liberals into a winnable seat. And the 1959 election did not disappoint. Despite a strong swing to the Conservatives in the rest of the country, Thorpe managed to win, an incredible achievement that won him instant national fame.

But Thorpe was gay at a time when it was illegal. Catastrophe lay ahead.

In 1960, he visited a wealthy friend, Brecht Van de Vater, at his stables in Oxfordshire. Van de Vater was the self-made son of a miner and had recently employed a young stable boy who Thorpe found in one of the stables. As he wrote to my father a few years later, 'He was leaning over a stable door. He was simply heaven …'

Thorpe and the stable boy talked briefly. Thorpe told him he was a newly elected MP and suggested that, if he could get away for a day, he might like to come to London and meet him at the House of Commons for dinner. The boy's name was Norman Josiffe, but he later changed his surname to Scott.

Thorpe's lack of discretion in inviting his new young friend to the House of Commons was typical of him. Over the years, my father became increasingly frustrated with Thorpe's propensity to find young men in the most public of circumstances. He would seek out male sex workers on the King's Road and was once spotted holding hands with a boy outside the House of Commons in Parliament Square. And he did all this at a time when simply being gay was enough to end a man's career or see him facing a prison sentence.

The London gay scene in the 1950s and 1960s was very different from today. Homosexuality was illegal until 1967 (in England and Wales). Being openly gay was not an option. Gay men were viciously ridiculed and even in areas known for having a 'queer' scene, such as parts of Chelsea, the pubs and coffee bars were regularly raided by the police. It is against this backdrop the Thorpe affair emerged.

X

When my father was elected in 1964, the House of Commons was a white gentlemen's networking club and, despite there being several secretly gay MPs, it was generally homophobic, also misogynistic. Much of the culture derived from private schools, while its many traditions, such as the State Opening of Parliament, are deeply embedded in the long history of British democracy.

Being a new boy or new girl had its trials in the Commons, just as at school. A new MP, like my father, was joining a clan, many of whom had been MPs for many years and were as familiar with the Commons as they were with their own homes. But Thorpe looked after him. There was also generally a honeymoon period for new MPs when they could speak in the Chamber with little interruption or heckling, and their ignorance or misunderstanding of some traditions was quietly tolerated.

By spring 1965, my father was coming to the end of his Commons honeymoon, but, despite having been a Member for six months, he was still in awe of the institution, its traditions and even the building itself. Sometimes, late in the evening, when most MPs had long since departed, he would wander those corridors of power alone, just to soak up some of the history and enjoy the privilege of unfettered access. One evening, as he turned a corner, he bumped into Thorpe.

'Have you eaten, Peter?' Thorpe asked.

'No,' my father said.

'Alright, come on!'

The Members' dining room was almost deserted. The two men ordered their meal and chatted about the expected imminent retirement of the Liberal leader, Joe Grimond. The rules of the party meant the new leader would be chosen from one of the very few Liberal MPs, and only those MPs would have a vote. My father had an inkling that Thorpe would make a leadership bid, but he had yet to make up his mind who to vote for. For my father, Thorpe's sexuality was an issue because if he became leader and his indiscretions came to light, the fragile party would become embroiled in a scandal from which it would be unlikely to recover. So, this quiet dinner presented itself as the ideal opportunity for him to draw Thorpe out. He suspected Thorpe was gay, but needed confirmation.

Just a few weeks earlier, my father had been dining with his secretary, Diana Stainton, in the Strangers' Dining Room, where members of the public can dine with an MP. Thorpe was seated at a nearby table, in animated discussion with a fair-haired man, many years his junior and, as Diana had not yet met Thorpe, my father pointed him out to her. According to my father, she watched Thorpe closely for a few moments, then said, 'You didn't tell me he was homosexual.'

My father looked at the two men again and realised that it was indeed obvious they were gay and, even worse, Thorpe appeared oblivious to the risk he was taking. Now, during this late dinner with Thorpe, in a nearly empty dining room, he was acutely aware he had an opportunity to draw him into his confidence. I think my father also wanted Thorpe to see him as a friend who could be trusted. He was setting out to create a special bond between the two of them. After all, if Thorpe did become the leader of the Liberal Party, being his closest friend could have its advantages. This was a chance that might never be repeated. But how to do it? Then it occurred to him that, despite their already close friendship, they had never discussed sex. If he were to drop his own defences, perhaps Thorpe might feel sufficiently comfortable to do likewise.

By then, Thorpe had met Diana. My father asked him what he thought of her. It was an odd question to ask another MP – why should Thorpe care? He was evidently not particularly interested and gave a stock response.

'Is she any good?'

'Yes,' my father replied, 'particularly in bed.'

Thorpe was stunned. He stared silently at my father. Then he burst into laughter and said he'd always thought my father had a happy home life.

'It's nothing to do with Pauline. She's a wonderful wife and mother, and I certainly couldn't have become an MP without her,' he said.

He went on to explain to Thorpe that it was simply a matter of sex, of always needing more than one woman.

'Have there been others – apart from your secretary?' asked Thorpe.

'There have.'

'Does Pauline know?'

'I think so. I don't really know.' This, of course, was not true. She knew of his previous indiscretions but she did not know about Diana.

Thorpe was evidently interested, but unforthcoming about himself. My father had to push it further.

'I suppose you might call it a hobby. Some people collect stamps, play golf or breed horses. I like screwing.'

Thorpe was amused and asked one or two more questions, then the conversation flagged. How far was my father going to have to push this to get anything out of Thorpe? He tried again.

'Of course, when I was young, it was more difficult. Nice girls didn't get into bed with you unless you married them!'

'So, what did you do?'

He could have answered honestly, but instead he lied, in a final attempt to draw Thorpe out. 'In those days, I still had homosexual tendencies,' he responded casually.

Thorpe's attitude changed instantly.

'Did you? Tell me about that.'

Offhand, he couldn't think of anything, but then he suddenly remembered an event in a Vienna nightclub a few years previously. He had been an observer rather than participant, but he recounted the story in such a way that roles could have been interpreted either way. Thorpe was delighted.

'Peter, this calls for a drink! What'll you have?'

'Port.'

'Couldn't be better. I'll have the same.'

As the conversation continued, Thorpe gradually loosened up and confessed to previous gay tendencies while at Oxford, but he was still a little reticent. After all, my father hadn't admitted to anything of substance. Then my father said, 'I suppose people like us never quite lose it, do they?'

That was the remark that broke through. Suddenly, Thorpe relaxed and leaned in towards my father. In a half-whisper, he said, 'Peter, we're nothing but a pair of old queens.'

My father recounted that episode in his book about the Thorpe affair, *Cover-Up*. The scene was subsequently used by John Preston in his book *A Very English Scandal*, and again by Russell T. Davies for the screenplay of the TV drama of the same name based on that book. Rather like Chinese whispers, by the time Davies finished with it, my father's declaration was taken completely out of context as a straightforward admission that he was bisexual.

The Members' Dining Room episode drew my father into a closeness with Thorpe which was to prove disastrous. Thorpe now saw him in a different light, as someone to turn to in times of trouble. My father couldn't have known then what trouble lay ahead.

CHAPTER SEVEN

SECRET LIVES

ON 19 JULY 1966, at the end of the school term and aged 14, I travelled by train from my boarding school, in Saffron Walden, Essex, to my home in Cornwall. It was a 300-mile journey, which entailed taking a train into Liverpool Street station in London, taking a taxi across town to Paddington station, and taking another train from there to Liskeard, where my mother would meet me. At least, that was the usual arrangement, but, on this occasion, my father met me at Liverpool Street for the drive to Paddington. He had some news.

Harold Wilson, then Prime Minister, had offered him a position in the Government as President of the Board of Trade, a senior Cabinet position, if he would agree to leave the Liberals and join the Labour Party. It was quite an offer. He needed to contact my mother secretly to get her opinion urgently, so he gave me a letter to give to her when I arrived home. The envelope was addressed to 'Mummy'. Written on House of Commons paper and dated 19 July 1966, it read:

My dearest love,

Paul will fill in the details, but, in short, the PM sent for me after Question Time and offered me the Board of Trade to take effect almost at once.

We cannot discuss this on the phone for it is secret under the Official Secrets Act and you should burn this letter once you have read and understood it. On the phone we will talk about the house I am thinking of buying… I will phone you in the morning.

I should have to join the L. (Labour) Party at once.

Simultaneously I should be appointed President.

The reason given would be the economic crisis – in short, a genuine justification.

I should get a safe seat next election.

I should have to continue to sit for Bodmin as a Labour member – in this crisis there is no time to mess about with by-elections.

I should have a free hand at the Board of Trade.

I become a Privy Councillor at once.

I step out of the Rhodesian affair next week.

I have to give my decision next Tuesday.

All the love in the world,

My immediate reaction was to wonder what all this stuff about 'the Official Secrets Act' and 'burn this letter' was for. Perhaps he was simply being prudent. Offering a Liberal a Cabinet position in a Labour Government would certainly have been headline news, and an embarrassment to Harold Wilson, but hardly a threat to national security. Was it just a fantasy on my father's part? After some consideration, my father felt he couldn't betray the Liberals, so he turned the offer down. But I have to wonder now, had the offer actually ever been made?

My father had continued to find his attraction to women impossible to resist. This time, the object of his affection was his secretary, Diana Stainton, as he had already let Thorpe know.

Finding a good secretary was one of his first tasks upon entering Parliament, it was a must if he was going to do justice to his constituents and their problems. But finding a good one was not easy; he interviewed many applicants with no success. Evidently his expectations were too high, or his requirements too specific.

When Diana came to the House of Commons for her interview, it seems my father reacted in the same way Jeremy Thorpe had done to young Norman Scott. Not only was Diana well qualified for the job, but had, as my father put it, 'a beautifully shaped thigh'. She got the job.

It wasn't long before he invited her to dinner at the House of Commons. He took her home and she invited him in for a drink. She was in her 20s, with medium blonde hair with 'striking brown eyes and an expressively sensuous mouth'. As they chatted in her flat, she showed no desire for him to leave. Suddenly, my father blurted out, 'Diana, would you come to Paris with me?'

My father did at least seduce women with a modicum of style. A weekend in Paris with him would not have been a cheap dosshouse and a stroll down the Champs-Élysées taking a few photos. It would have been the Hotel George V, champagne, caviar and the opera – even if he couldn't afford it. Diana would have found it difficult to resist such a tempting offer from a man she was evidently attracted to, despite him being married with a family. She turned away to consider the invitation.

That was the beginning of my father's long affair with Diana. One might imagine a busy MP and businessman would struggle to find the time to spend with his lover as well as his family, but Diana was just the beginning.

In 1964, a few months before he met Diana, he had hired a temporary secretary, Sally, who later became his research assistant for a book he was writing, *Prime Minister or President*. Sally, like Diana, was a beautiful, intelligent young woman to whom my father was instantly attracted. The attraction was mutual. Sally later described him as a very good-looking man, not that tall, but very slender. Apparently, he hardly ate. She would make him Marmite sandwiches in the evenings because, though we didn't know this at the time, due to his significant expenses elsewhere, he couldn't afford to feed himself. Sally and Peter's liaisons quickly became romantic, and she subsequently referred to herself as a 'kept woman'. But their relationship became much more than just an affair. In 1966, they rented a Chelsea apartment together and, when my father was not at his family home in Cornwall, he lived with her. This lasted for many years, with Sally believing Peter was going to leave his wife and marry her. Given the significant age gap, Sally's father thoroughly disapproved of the relationship and had my father investigated by what Sally assumed to be the security services. Disappointingly for her father, there was no shattering revelation that he could confront her with. Sally was Peter's girlfriend at the same time as Diana Stainton, in 1964 and 1965. They were clearly unaware of each other. During the same period, my father wrote to my mother:

House of Commons, London, S.W.1
9/5/65

My dearest dear love,

I am writing this on the train for I know we shall have so little time together before I go to New York.

It is impossible for me to tell you now or ever how much you mean to me and will always mean to me. May 13th is our wedding anniversary and for me the 17 years we have had together have been the most wonderful of my life. We have shared so much, and have met disaster and triumph together.

We have two wonderful children, and all that I have achieved would not have been possible without you. My need of you my darling is greater than it has ever been, and without the love and security you give me I should not be able to do all I try to do. Thank you from the bottom of my heart for everything my love.

I was shaken and hurt last week at the suggestion that I was doing something which would hurt you. I do not blame you for thinking it might be true, and it was not this which hurt me. It was the thought that there can be people with such vile [illegible] who would do this and say things to hurt us and try to destroy the faith we have in each other.

Nothing and no one could ever come between us, and I would never consciously do anything to hurt you, my darling. But I do not think I need to say this – you know it already.

Whatever the next 17 years hold for us they will be our 17 years like the last. Don't ever stop loving me for I shall need you more and more. The children will soon leave us. I do not mind this even though you think I do. I know that the happiest times in the past have been when we have been alone together. It will be so in the future.

Our world of love is… our world and will always be so.

I love you darling Pauline

Peter

Sally knew about Pauline, but not Diana. Diana knew about Pauline, but not Sally. Pauline knew nothing of the other two women. It was rapidly becoming a mess.

Shortly afterwards, my father made a business trip to New York where he socialised with his friend Eliot Steuer. Steuer was the child of poor European immigrants who had been brought up in

New York's Hell's Kitchen, in Manhattan, close to where *West Side Story* was set, working his way out to become a highly respected New York commercial real-estate broker. When they first met in 1958, government currency regulations allowed British businessmen only a meagre dollar allowance, and for some years Steuer showered my father with hospitality. Being seen with an apparently successful Englishman at that time was very socially desirable, as well as being good for business.

Steuer lived a bachelor life in Greenwich Village. His main pursuit, chasing women, suited my father perfectly. They partied regularly with New York's social elite, for whom my father's English accent was an instant attraction. Steuer later said of my father, 'I knew I was going to be fleeced, but I enjoyed the journey.' It was a remark which deeply hurt my father, as he considered Eliot a close friend who got as much from the relationship, both personally and in business terms, as he did.

While Diana, Sally and my mother were waiting patiently for my father back in the UK, he was living the high life in New York. As more women came into his life, keeping them all secret from each other was becoming increasingly difficult.

Not only was my father's life chock-full of women, it was also jam-packed with politics. And Thorpe was about to disturb the peace.

In April 1965, when my father had been an MP for a year, he was working in his office when his private telephone rang. It was Thorpe, and he sounded worried. 'Can we lunch today?'

They settled on the Ritz Hotel, just a few yards from my father's office. It seemed a strange choice as they would usually meet at one of their clubs, but the reason became apparent quite early in the conversation. Running a couple of minutes late, Thorpe was already waiting for him in the lobby, looking distinctly edgy, his usual good humour absent. They went straight to the dining room, where they were given a quiet corner table. As soon as they had ordered, Thorpe handed my father a letter. 'Read that.'

What followed was a pivotal moment in the lives of so many people. My father often said if there was a single decision he could have changed in his life, it would be this one.

He looked at the envelope, noting it was addressed to Thorpe's mother, Ursula. It was a long letter, running to a dozen pages, written on blue paper, which made the handwriting difficult to decipher. He read it slowly and carefully. Its contents were astonishing and, in my father's view, pathetic. The letter was from Norman Scott. It gave a detailed account of his relationship with Thorpe, described how they had been lovers and stated that Thorpe had promised to look after him, but had failed to do so. Scott was now living in Dublin and wanted his National Insurance card, which Thorpe had and without which he was unable to get work. In my father's words, the 'references to Jeremy were a mixture of reproach and affection – the sort of thing an immature girl might write after being jilted by the man she loved. But although it was sad, I was instantly aware of the danger it represented'.

The worry, of course, was any chance of blackmail. The intention was undoubtedly to shock Thorpe into some kind of action. My father's first question was succinct and to the point. 'Is this true?'

'Yes.'

'And what was your mother's reaction?'

'She didn't believe a word of it.'

At this point, my father was still not quite sure why Thorpe had decided to share this with him, but he was glad he had because Thorpe had proved himself prone to rash decisions, the outcome of which in this case might have been dangerous for the whole Liberal Party. This concern proved justified when Thorpe pulled from his pocket a draft letter to Scott, from his solicitor, denying a relationship and threatening legal action if this claim were to be repeated.

This would have been a red rag to Scott. My father persuaded Thorpe that it was completely the wrong approach.

'Then what the hell am I to do?' said Thorpe.

'Start by telling me the whole story.'

Thorpe recited, in detail, his relationship with Scott and how it came about. The more he spoke, the more worried my father became. This was much more than some fling, and it involved under-age sex. He asked if the boy had evidence of the affair.

'No. It's his word against mine.'

'No letters?'

Thorpe's confidence deserted him. He hesitated for a moment, then replied slowly.

'Yes. There are letters.'

'Are they–?'

'Yes.'

He didn't show it, but my father was completely flabbergasted. How could Thorpe have left such evidence with someone who was evidently capable of behaving completely irrationally? Not only would a letter from Thorpe's solicitor probably tip Scott over the edge, but Scott also had the evidence to prove everything he was saying. My father thought for a while, then made the decision that was going to prove so catastrophic for all of us. He noticed the letter was from Dublin and assumed Scott was now living there. He thought for a moment, then said, 'Perhaps I should go to Dublin and see him.'

Thorpe responded quickly, 'Would you?'

Again, my father hesitated, but then decided.

'Very well, I'll go.'

And in that split second, any hope for a normal life for my father and us, his family, slipped away. This was the first time my father had heard of Scott, but it most certainly wasn't going to be the last.

A few days after their lunch, my father flew to Dublin to meet

Scott. Before he did so, he called Thorpe to tell him of his plans. Apparently, Thorpe was grateful and asked if my father would be inviting Scott back to his hotel.

'You should,' he said. 'You'd find him marvellous in bed!'

This embarrassed my father, but, more than anything, it reminded him of how incredibly careless Thorpe could be. He was genuinely suggesting that my father go to Dublin to threaten Scott to keep him quiet, whilst at the same time to have sex with him. My father met Scott, who was nervous and seemed run down. A mix-up over their meeting time meant they had to have their discussion in a taxi on the way to Dublin airport as my father began his journey home. The meeting didn't go as planned.

To begin with, they discussed Scott's problems and how he might be rehabilitated. Then, my father's tone became more threatening. He told Scott that, although he understood his feelings, the letter he had written to Thorpe's mother amounted to a threat of blackmail. He said that such a threat was far more dangerous to Scott than it was to Thorpe. This was, of course, completely untrue. As my father later wrote:

> *The letter did not constitute a blackmail attempt and, at worst, was only a veiled threat to expose something that was true. I went on to say that Jeremy, as a Member of Parliament, was in a strong position. He was a friend of Sir Frank Soskice, the Home Secretary, and the normal procedure for an MP who considered himself threatened by blackmail would be to go to the Home Secretary, who would take steps through the Director of Public Prosecutions to have Scott charged. This, again, was a gross overstatement.*

Despite my father's threatening tone, Scott appeared entirely defenceless. My father quickly relented. Because Thorpe had kept

Scott's National Insurance card, Scott was unable to work in the UK. As Scott sat, shivering, in the taxi, not only did my father promise to sort out his problems for him, he also gave him £5 and paid for his taxi back from the airport. He told Scott not to hesitate to get in touch with him at any time. But as he later explained:

> *As the years were to prove, however, Norman Josiffe's [Scott's] demeanour masked an extraordinary stubbornness and resilience. His letter to Ursula Thorpe was his first move in a plan of action upon which I am certain he did not consciously embark, but which he was to pursue to its disastrous climax 14 years later. A plan which, but for the remote chance of a bullet jamming in a revolver, would have allegedly cost him his life.*

Scott would go on to take my father at his word, contacting him many times for help, which resulted in my father putting him on a small 'retainer' of a few pounds a week. These were later regarded by some as blackmail payments and the fact that Thorpe was a leading political figure meant that the media treated the whole saga as a major national scandal. For my father, at the time, it was no more than an irritating side issue. He had far more pressing problems than Thorpe's romantic disasters. Yet another woman was about to enter his world, with life-changing consequences for him, for me and for the rest of his family.

In April 1968, my father was on one of his evening jaunts with Eliot Steuer in New York, when they decided to dine at the Oak Room at the Plaza Hotel. My father noticed a beautiful, dark-haired woman sitting with an acquaintance of theirs. Typically, he pointed her out to Steuer and asked who she was.

'Diane Kelly. She's a broker in another department of my firm.'

'I'd like to meet her,' said my father.

'Well, you know the guy she's with. Go over and say hello. Maybe he'll introduce you to her – though he'll be out of his mind if he does!'

My father did as Steuer suggested and the man with Diane introduced them. On seeing her up close, my father was immediately smitten, so grilled Steuer about her. She was married, but rumour had it she and her husband were having problems.

'Now she's met you, do you want me to ask her if she'll have dinner with us one evening?' said Steuer.

'Yes.'.

A few days later, he, Steuer and Diane were having dinner together. Afterwards, my father drove her to her apartment on Long Island. On her doorstep, they shook hands formally and he said he hoped to see her again on his next trip to New York. With that, he politely left and flew home to his wife – and Sally – in England.

A few months later, he returned and duly called Diane, to arrange dinner. But she was cooler and said she would find out when her husband, John, was free. This wasn't quite what my father was expecting. He later said if it had been a woman he was trying to get into bed with, he would have made some excuse to avoid the dinner and moved on. As it was, he claimed, that wasn't his intention; he was hoping to cement a friendship. So, if Diane and her husband came as a package, he was prepared to accept that. Though, curiously, he neglected to tell my mother about this friendship he was striking up with a couple in New York.

As John was a busy TV executive, they were unable to meet up as a group on this occasion, although my father met Diane with the same formality as previously. A few months later, he did meet John and liked him immediately: 'If I had intended competing for his wife's affections, a glance at his almost boyish good looks and well-developed physique would have cancelled it.'

John and Diane visited London a few months later and, in a very short space of time, things changed dramatically. Diane and John separated and she and my father became lovers. Diane fell deeply in love, and devoted her entire existence to my father.

She was a sophisticated woman, a New England Ivy Leaguer from a wealthy background. In the early 1950s, at the age of 17, she had been an American Field Service exchange student in Flensburg, Germany. During that experience she learned more about her own country, about the McCarthy hearings (Senator Joseph McCarthy was leading a witch hunt into supposed communists in the US) and cultural differences between the US and the rest of the world, than she could possibly have learned had she stayed at home. She felt part of recent history when British troops came to town. Her German host had been in an American prisoner-of-war camp, where the soldiers had stolen the Germans' watches.

'The experience changed my life,' said Diane, 'I became, if you will, a fledgling citizen of the world.' In college, she took every international course in sight and majored in political science. In America, she felt very alone in her interests.

Diane married John a couple of years after she left college. He was working the night shift at NBC TV's newsdesk in New York, so she created her own social life, mostly with colleagues, one of whom she was with on the evening she first met my father. As Diane later wrote:

> *You can imagine how interesting I found this sitting Member of Parliament, actually involved in the real world politic. He had been behind the Iron Curtain twice, had my heroine, Eleanor Roosevelt, as a sort of mentor at the United Nations, went flying around with Kurt Waldheim, before he was UN Secretary-General, on some kind of matter relating to Rhodesian independence, had meetings with Senator Jacob Javits and former Governor Nelson Rockefeller of New York*

regarding the proposed North Atlantic Free Trade Area. I once put him on a plane to Vietnam and got to hear what he thought was happening on his return. He even appeared on the NBC Evening News *when Britain devalued the pound while he was in New York.*

Then, of course, he was good-looking, with a really fine, quick mind – thoughtful, too. He was a gentle man. He loved classical music and the Great American Song Book. He introduced me to British musicals. He took me to see Marlene Dietrich on her last tour in New York. He cared about human rights, equality, justice and the environment. He used the English language as only a Brit can do – beautifully and persuasively. He had a wonderful sense of humour and could make me laugh. Also, he was from a different country and culture. I was impressed, fascinated. I was hungry to learn.

And then, eventually, there was a wonderful and incredibly romantic love poem. I was enchanted.

Before long, my father and Diane had an apartment in New York, where he would stay on his many trips to the US. My father's secretary, Diana, was about to leave the scene, so his harem would now comprise Diane, Sally and my mother, Pauline – most successfully kept secret from each other, though both Sally and Diane knew about my mother.

How did my father explain his regular, lengthy, disappearances from one woman while he was with another? In the days before the internet and mobile phones, this wasn't as difficult as it would be now. All he needed was something plausible and consistent, so he didn't have to remember what he had told to whom. The answer was his secret work.

CHAPTER EIGHT

NOT SO SWEET IGNORANCE

ALTHOUGH MY FATHER'S life was in many ways remarkable, I appeared simply to come from a wealthy family. I have very little memory of the family's years of poverty. Young children tend to know only what is immediately around them, believing that to be how the world is, for everyone. I had no idea of my mother's loneliness in Cornwall, and no conception of how my father might be misbehaving while he was away. My parents were loving and never mistreated my sister and me – in fact, I was very spoiled and wanted for nothing. When we first moved to Looe, I used to gaze longingly at a beautiful pedal car in the toy-shop window. It had a bonnet and boot which could open and a pretend petrol tank that could be filled with water. My father bought it for me. Now I know that he had so little money he could barely afford even to pay for electricity at home, but he still bought me the pedal car. This was one of his biggest problems – a complete inability to say no.

There was one stage of my childhood, though, which was complete, unadulterated misery. In 1961, at the age of just nine, my parents packed me off to a private boarding school. It was an event for which I was completely unprepared, and it came as a total shock. They had told me that I would be going to a new school, and that it would be a boarding school, but I hadn't really appreciated what that would mean. One Monday morning, my mother put me in the car with a suitcase of my clothes and drove the 20 or so miles from Polraen to Par, another coastal town. We arrived at Roselyon School, where the head teacher, Mrs Tomlinson, was waiting to receive us. She seemed very kind as she chatted to my mother for a while. Suddenly, my mother kissed the top of my head and said goodbye. She got back in her car and drove off down the long, curved driveway. I watched her go in total shock. What had just happened? Where had she gone? Slowly it dawned on me that I would be staying at the school and not going home. Mrs Tomlinson took me inside, where the pleasant manner she had shown my mother changed completely. She became cold, issuing a stern order to me to take my case, which was too heavy for me, to my room. Then she left.

I struggled up the stairs and found my dormitory. I'd never shared a bedroom with anyone before, let alone 10 or 12 other boys. I had been the first to arrive for the beginning of term, so found myself completely alone, with no idea what to do. I didn't know what these other boys would be like. I was distraught. I found my way out of the building and into the extensive gardens. I considered running away, but where would I go? I found a small, wooded area, sat down behind a tree and sobbed. I have no idea how long I was there. Eventually I was discovered by one of the gardeners, who was gentle and kind. He persuaded me to go back inside, where he left me with a teacher.

My sister was also sent to boarding school. I assume the reasoning was that, in 1961, my parents were working to get my father elected as an MP and it helped them to have us out of the way; also, in those days, sending children to private boarding schools was just something that wealthy parents in the UK did. It turned out that I was only a weekly boarder, but I was so miserable that it made little difference. Every Monday morning, when my mother drove me to school, about 10 minutes before arriving, I would start to cry – without fail. My entire life revolved around fear of going to that school; my only happy day was Friday, when my mother would pick me up. But, come Saturday morning, I would start dreading Monday again. It was a constant cycle.

Not for one second, though, did I feel that my parents didn't love me, which made their decision to send me to boarding school all the more baffling. I saw very little of my father because, as I saw it, he was important and busy. Later, of course, it became clear that for much of the time, it wasn't important things that he was busy with.

My father's letter to my mother, in which he declared his undying love for her, was written after someone called my mother and told her that he was having an affair with his secretary. Perhaps Diana Stainton, or a friend of hers or someone who knew them and had an axe to grind, made the call, but we are unlikely to find out. My sister and I were at home at the time and my mother called us to drive into Looe to do some shopping. We stopped at the local shop to buy an ice cream, and, as I was eating it, while my mother drove on, she suddenly started crying. Shocked, my sister and I asked what was wrong.

'I've just been told your father has been having an affair with his secretary.'

I felt sick to my stomach. I threw my ice cream out of the window, something my mother remembered vividly to her dying day. We decided we couldn't face driving into town, so went back home. It was a warm day and I sat in the garden – alone. My whole world had suddenly collapsed. What would happen to us now? Then the bedroom window opened, and my mother shouted down to me. She was laughing.

'It's alright! I've spoken to Daddy. Somebody doesn't like him and wanted to get him into trouble. None of it was true!'

In later years, particularly when the Thorpe affair became public,

I was often asked how I could have loved such a man. I found the question insulting. He was my father.

My father's explanation for his behaviour was explicitly laid out in his book, *Cover-Up*:

> *My relationship with Diana Stainton was by no means my first act of marital infidelity, nor was it to be my last. Like Jeremy [Thorpe], my extraordinary physical and mental energy was coupled to a desire for conquest in many things. Politics was one, although that had safe roots in ideals and principles from which I did not waiver. But it also found expression in my irresistible desire to possess, often quite briefly, sexually attractive women, and the willing response of many of them flattered my ego. By most people's standards my conduct was grossly at variance with other aspects of my life and certainly with the public image I created. Yet it would be hypocritical to pretend I regret my behaviour or that I believe it was particularly immoral. For me, women were the most beautiful of all creations, and I adored them. Nevertheless, it will be charged that by deceiving Pauline, I treated her abominably. I offer no defence. As I have stated, like Jeremy, I selfishly compartmentalised my life. I cared deeply for Pauline and my short-lived, sexually-orientated encounters with other women were unimportant compared to the significance of my relationship with her. Personally, and obviously politically, we shared much that was of infinite value and for which I am forever indebted to her.*

In fact, many of my father's encounters were anything but short-lived. On that hot day in 1965, though, just as quickly as everything had crashed, everything was alright again. My mother, my sister and I laughed about how silly it had all been. We believed my father's explanation implicitly.

CHAPTER NINE

HETHERINGTON

BY THE LATE 1960s, my father's business was struggling due to the demands of being an MP, so he announced he would resign his seat at the 1970 election to concentrate on restoring his income. Although he wasn't standing himself, he went to Cornwall for a couple of weeks prior to polling day to support his successor, Paul Tyler. He stayed at Polraen where, one evening, the phone rang.

My father picked it up. 'Hello?'

'Hello, this is Mr Hetherington.'

My father paused. The name rang a bell but, for the moment, he couldn't recall a connection.

Hetherington continued, 'I want to talk to you about Thorpe and how you've looked after his friend Norman Scott.'

With his experience of a lifetime of shocks, it took a lot to rattle my father and he remained perfectly calm and matter of fact.

'Scott? Ah, yes. He's someone Jeremy helped years ago. Jeremy's a good man, who has helped many people.'

Obviously a little miffed at not having been able to provoke a sharper reaction, Hetherington responded sarcastically, 'Did it help Scott that Thorpe turned him into a homosexual?'

'I don't know who you are, but you're making a slanderous accusation. Far from being homosexual, Jeremy is a happily married man and father.'

'Don't be ridiculous. You know very well all that is just a cover and that he ruined Scott's life,' said Hetherington, 'Norman's told me you looked after him because you were disgusted by what Thorpe had done to him.'

Suddenly, it all fell into place. About a year before, someone had called my father at his London office, claiming he was the stepfather of Scott's then wife, Susan. He complained that Susan's life had been wrecked by Scott's association with Thorpe and he believed Thorpe had an obligation to her. My father had rejected the notion on the grounds there was no truth in Scott's story.

Obviously, that in itself was not true, but despite the conversation having ended inconclusively, my father assumed that to be the end of the matter. This call, he believed, seemed to be from the same man, but now he was being much more aggressive. My father continued the conversation in an effort to find out how much the man knew.

'These are grave accusations you are making. Am I to assume you have something more to rely on than just Scott's word?'

The caller's response stunned my father.

'I have. Norman's wife has given me three letters Thorpe wrote to him years ago.'

Scott had previously assured my father he had destroyed all remaining letters from Thorpe. Had he been lying? Perhaps Thorpe's fears were well-founded.

'So, why are you phoning me?'

Hetherington became calmer. 'I have nothing against you, Mr Bessell. You befriended Scott and, now you are no longer a candidate for Parliament, there is no reason for you to remain loyal to Thorpe. I'm hoping you might help me to end his public career.'

My father's loyalty to Thorpe went way beyond that of a political ally, they were the closest of friends. But he considered the best way to deal with this man was to string him along. For a minute or two,

Hetherington raged about homosexuals in general, which gave my father a moment to think.

'What do you want me to do then?' he asked.

'I've written a leaflet setting out the facts about Thorpe and Scott. I'm going to photocopy it with the letters,' Hetherington said.

'I see. And?'

'On the night before the election I will go to Thorpe's constituency and put them into as many letterboxes as possible.'

This plan would be devastating for Thorpe. Even allowing for the fact one man could only put these copies through a limited number of letter boxes, gossip travels fast. If the man did as he had said he would, it would probably be enough to lose Thorpe his seat, and his reputation. At this point, my father wanted to establish that the caller was the same man he had spoken to a year earlier.

Hetherington continued, seemingly convinced that my father's sympathies were with Scott, 'Would you join me in distributing the leaflets?'

My father considered co-operation might be the best way of getting his hands on the letters.

'I'll tell you what I'll do,' he said. 'On the eve of the election itself, I'm busy. But I will meet you on the Monday night.'

For the moment, this seemed to satisfy Hetherington, who said he would call again to make final arrangements. The following morning he called Thorpe to let him know what had happened. Thorpe's panicked response was entirely predictable.

'Oh Christ! What can we do?'

Thorpe was due to make a brief visit to Cornwall on Monday, by helicopter, but they agreed he would have to come down by car the day before instead, and stay overnight so they could discuss in detail how to handle the situation. From that moment on, Hetherington occupied my father's thoughts almost entirely. What was he to do?

Then, he hit on an idea.

By British law, all printed election material has to carry an imprint stating that it is published by the agent of the relevant candidate. The distribution of the Hetherington leaflets would, without doubt, be regarded as material intended to influence the outcome of the election, but they wouldn't carry a candidate's imprint. Once Hetherington was in Thorpe's constituency, all my father had to do was go to the local police and ask them to prevent him from carrying out his proposed action. Thorpe would be appalled, though, by the prospect of the local police getting wind of his indiscretions, so my father knew this could be only a last resort.

Hetherington called again a couple of days later and my father had a question. 'Where are you planning to get your leaflets photocopied?' His thinking was that if a large quantity would need to be copied, it would have to be done professionally. That would be dangerous if the operator realised what they were dealing with and decided to keep copies. Hetherington sounded uncertain.

'I, er, I'll find somewhere when I get to Devon,' he said.

'That's what I was afraid of,' said my father, 'I have a better plan. Meet me in Saltash at midnight on the Monday. From there, we can drive to the Liberal Party office in Liskeard, where there is a photocopying machine. We can copy as many as you like there.'

'Won't there be someone there?' asked Hetherington, suspiciously.

'Not at that time of night. And I have a key. I've given a lot of thought to what you've said and I'm willing to do what I can to help you.' He had expected an enthusiastic response, but Hetherington sounded a bit flat.

'Oh, I'm glad,' he said. 'I'll meet you on Monday night as you suggest, then.'

My father still wasn't quite sure what he would do, but he thought his plan would at least give him an opportunity to see what the letters contained and, maybe, persuade Hetherington to leave the copies with him to photocopy. He could then destroy them. The following day, Tuesday, he would phone Hetherington and admit his deception.

A couple of days later, my mother returned to Cornwall for the last few days of the campaign. Thorpe and his wife, Caroline, arrived at Polraen, as arranged, on the Sunday. It was a warm afternoon, so the two men went into the garden alone to discuss 'business'. As they paced around the large lawn, my father outlined the arrangements he had made with Hetherington and his plan to obtain and destroy the documents.

Thorpe shook his head. 'He won't give them to you. He'd be a fool to trust you.'

'Yes, I know it's a long shot. But I think I have his trust.'

'I don't say you haven't persuaded him you intend to cooperate. If you hadn't, there's no reason why he'd be coming to see you. But the bastard isn't going to part with his evidence!' Thorpe's logic was sound. He continued, 'What do you intend to do if your plan fails?'

'I'll have to go to the police,' he said, in a resigned tone.

Thorpe stopped pacing and stared at him.

'What do you mean? Go to the Barnstaple police? Are you suggesting we go to them and say that that shit Scott has evidence? Oh, thank you very much!'

My father tried to console him. 'It doesn't matter,' he said, 'Homosexuality is not illegal any more, and–'

'I'm not talking about the law! The story would get out in no time and the gossip would emanate from the police station. Very nice!'

My father felt like giving up. He'd been protecting Thorpe for years. What was he *supposed* to do? 'Well, do you have any suggestions?' he asked.

'Yes,' came the prompt response. 'There's only one way you'll get those papers. Meet him off the ferry, get him in your car and, instead of going to Liskeard, go to the moor somewhere and kill him!'

My father was speechless. Was Thorpe serious? Had he, just as with Scott, entered some kind of fantasy world? My father was beginning to believe he had a homicidal maniac on his hands. Yes, Hetherington was threatening to be a problem, but to murder him? My father realised Thorpe was close to panic, and it was his responsibility to calm him down and restore some sanity to the conversation. For a moment, though, he couldn't think what to say. Thorpe broke the silence.

'You agree, don't you?'

'No. There are other ways.'

Thorpe started to plead. 'Peter, you've got to do this. It's not only about North Devon, it's the entire party.'

My father's mind raced as he thought about how to calm Thorpe's panic. 'Jeremy, I give you my word that I'll find a way of removing the danger.'

'You realise this means killing him?' he said.

'No, I don't accept that at all. But if you're saying… if all else fails… well, that's another matter.'

Thorpe took this to mean my father had promised to murder the man. 'How will you kill him?'

Realising he'd allowed himself to give the wrong impression, the question caught him by surprise.

'I'd rather not discuss it,' was the only response he could think of.

'Have you got a gun?' The conversation was becoming ridiculous.

'I have nothing except an unproved antique sporting rifle.' It was a double-barrelled 12-bore, which used to hang in the hallway at Polraen. Both barrels had rust spots, rendering it completely unusable.

'How about poison? Do you have any?'

My father was getting irritated, but he did his best to hide it. 'No, of course not.' He paused, then added, 'I've got some trichloroethylene. It's a dry-cleaning fluid, like ether–'

'Ether! Couldn't be better! You can soak a handkerchief in it, hold it over his face and it'll knock him out.'

He had interrupted my father, who had been about to explain that this particular substance was only lethal if ingested – it wasn't ether. As he put it later:

> *The absurdity of the proposal did not occur to me. I was only aware of the extraordinary change in Jeremy's mood. The combination of fear and determination had been replaced by excitement. Fantasy had taken over from reality. Unable to find a rational solution, Jeremy had slipped into a world of dreams and pretence.*

My father tried to bring him down to earth. 'Jeremy, it's murder,' he said firmly.

Thorpe turned cold, using an analogy he also famously applied to Scott. 'Peter, it's the same thing as killing a sick dog. Once he's out cold it'll be easy. Hit him on the head with something heavy. You know how to get rid of the body – down a tin mine.'

He was, of course, ignoring the fact that my father was a slight man and Hetherington was unlikely to sit calmly with a handkerchief soaked in ether being held over his face. Even worse was the probability that the police would eventually discover the body and the culprits, leaving Thorpe in a far worse position than if his gay affair was merely exposed. Hetherington did need to be dealt with, though; the risk, rather than the person, did have to be eliminated.

'I don't want to talk about it,' said my father.

Thorpe didn't take this as a declaration of my father's intention not to attempt murder. Instead, he took it as more of a nod and a wink. 'Ah, very well, Peter, I shall ask no questions. Better that I know nothing. I trust you completely. How will you let me know the outcome?'

'I'll phone you on Tuesday morning at eight.'

Later in the day, my parents drove Thorpe and his wife to their hotel. During the journey Thorpe turned to my mother and said, 'How would you like to be the Lady Bessell?'

My mother was too surprised and embarrassed to answer. Thorpe was suggesting he was intending to nominate my father to the House of Lords after his retirement as an MP, which was just days away.

Thorpe continued, 'I think old Bessell would look good in ermine. I mean it. Peter shall be the next Liberal life peer.'

My mother answered quietly, 'Yes, I think you need him, Jeremy.'

'We'll talk about it another time,' my father answered abruptly. Was this the reward for murder?

The following evening, my father told my mother he was going out on patrol around the constituency to check on the Liberal posters, which were often vandalised by the opposition. He was scared. He knew the only plan with potential was to somehow get the documents off Hetherington and destroy them. But what if that failed? As he drove along the quiet Cornish roads in the dark, he wondered if Hetherington might listen to reason. As he got closer to the meeting place in Saltash, he had made up his mind to try.

The town was deserted. As he turned into the car park, he saw a tall, overweight man on the pavement outside the Town Hall. He was walking in the opposite direction, but, when he heard the car pull up, he turned. My father pulled over and lowered his window.

'Mr Hetherington?'

'Are you Mr Bessell?'

'Yes. Get in.' My father was taking a risk. He was well-known in the area and might be recognised. Hetherington squeezed into the Triumph 2000. He wore a tweed suit and was carrying a briefcase, which he rested on his knees. He seemed too big for the car. His face was flabby, and his hair was almost white. My father placed him in his mid-50s.

'I propose we go straight to Liskeard,' my father said.

'How long will it take to get there?' asked Hetherington. His breath smelled strongly of alcohol.

'About 20 minutes.' My father looked at his watch. 'Oh, actually, it's a little early to go to Liskeard at the moment. Anyway, perhaps we should stop on the way and talk first.'

'Yes, I agree,' said Hetherington. He appeared nervous.

On the way, they found a lay-by and parked. He switched off the engine and headlights and turned on the interior light.

'I expect you would like to see the letters,' said Hetherington. He undid his briefcase, pulled out three letters along with a typed sheet of foolscap paper and handed them to my father.

My father looked at the first letter and knew, instantly, that something was wrong. Thorpe always wrote on House of Commons stationery or blue paper with a crest. This was plain paper and, more significantly, of poor quality. Thorpe might have used unheaded paper for a very personal letter, but cheap stationery was anathema to him. There was no doubt, though, that it was Thorpe's handwriting. The letter started 'Dear Norman' and was signed 'With love, Jeremy', but the contents were pretty harmless. My father looked at the next letter.

This made him even more suspicious. Thorpe had a curious habit of starting his letters well to the left of the paper and, as he wrote, the left margin gradually widened until, by the bottom of the page, the margin sometimes occupied almost a third of the sheet. The writing on this letter filled almost the entire width of the paper. And there was another flaw. Thorpe always abbreviated certain words – 'would' and 'should', for example, would be reduced to 'wd' and 'shd'.

Hetherington had picked on the wrong man in my father to try to dupe. My father's brain began to clear. When he spoke to Hetherington on the phone, he hadn't doubted for one second that he was hell-bent on destroying Thorpe's reputation. But, as he looked at the second letter, which was clearly a poor forgery, he realised Hetherington was not a character assassin – he was a blackmailer. His immediate reaction was one of immense relief, but it also occurred to him that he was on a deserted country lane late at night with a large man who might be capable of any number of things.

For a moment he looked at Hetherington and laughed to himself about the idea of covering such a huge man's face with an ether-soaked cloth. But he was in a dangerous situation, and he had to decide quickly what to do. Presumably, the man was here to get money, and he was starting to get restless as my father perused the documents, giving himself time to think.

'Well, they look genuine enough to me,' he said. 'Where did you get them?'

'A friend of Scott's wife.'

'Oh. I thought Susan Scott was related to you.'

'Well, er, yes. We are connected through marriage.' He continued to fidget nervously.

My father took the initiative. 'What do you suppose a set of documents like this is worth?'

Hetherington answered in a flash. '£5,000.'

That settled any lingering doubts my father might have had. He chuckled.

'That's out of the question. The Liberal Party doesn't have that kind of money.'

'Really?' said Hetherington, surprised. 'I thought there were many wealthy Liberals.'

'That might be true. But the party itself is always short of funds.

We need to be on our way.' He started the car and set off, handing the papers back to Hetherington, who sat with them on his briefcase. My father was still uneasy about being alone with this man. He sped up. Hetherington became more fidgety and, after a while, asked if my father still thought distributing the leaflets was a good idea.

'Well, it's a serious matter to wreck anyone's career,' said my father, still wondering what to do. But, for the moment, he wanted Hetherington to believe they were heading to Liskeard to copy the documents as originally planned. The pressure was now on Hetherington and, for a while, he remained silent, if nervy. Then, as they drove through a town which he evidently believed to be their destination, he blurted out, 'Alright, Mr Bessell, I'll take £2,000.'

My father relaxed and responded impetuously, 'Mr Hetherington, you have a deal!'

'When can I have it?'

'Do you have any other documents or copies of those?' asked father, pointing at the papers on Hetherington's lap.

'I can assure you I have neither.'

There was no way to check his word, but, for the moment, that didn't bother my father.

'When can I have the money?' Hetherington repeated.

'You can have it tonight. I have an office in Plymouth and there happens to be a fairly large amount of cash in the safe.'

None of that was true, but he wanted to get away from the deserted Cornish roads and into a large city. The journey took about 20 minutes and, as they drove in silence, my father wondered if, when they arrived in Plymouth, he should drive straight to a police station and hand him over. But the risk of the story getting out and affecting Thorpe was too great. He had to come up with an alternative by the time they got into town. He decided to try to find out how much Hetherington knew about Scott.

'How well do you know him?' he asked.

'Oh, I know him alright.'

'I don't like him. I never trust fair-haired men,' said my father, in the hope of tapping into what he considered Hetherington's genuine dislike of gay men.

Hetherington gave a half-laugh, putting his hand to his thick, grey hair. 'I used to be fair myself!'

'As blond as Scott?'

'Oh no! Not that fair.'

That was all the confirmation my father needed. Scott's hair was as black as coal. He wondered if he should admit he knew the letters were forgeries and ask where he had obtained a copy of Thorpe's handwriting. But that might have provoked an argument.

Then Hetherington asked, 'Do you know the times of the trains from Plymouth at this time of night?'

This gave my father an idea. 'I don't, but the station is on the way to my office, so we can go in and take a look at the timetable.'

'Will there be somewhere to eat there?' asked Hetherington.

'It's the middle of the night, so that's unlikely. But I have a flask and sandwiches in the boot. When we stop, I'll give them to you.'

There was a small car park beyond the station entrance, which, it being late, was empty. As they drove past the entrance, my father could see a policeman standing in the foyer. Never had he been more grateful to see one.

As part of the station building jutted into the street, the parking area was not visible from the station entrance. My father pulled up and said he would get the non-existent sandwiches. He unlocked the boot, took out his briefcase, and got back into the car. He always kept about £200 in cash in an envelope in his briefcase in case of emergencies. He thought he had about £170 left. He took out the envelope and held it up.

'Mr Hetherington, you see this?'

Without waiting for a reply, he dropped the envelope between his seat and the car door, and grasped the door handle.

'It contains £200. If you get out of the car, come round to my side and hand me the letters through the window, I will give you the envelope. If you don't accept my offer, I'm going to drive to the station entrance and inform the police officer on duty that I'm charging you with forgery and attempted blackmail.'

Hetherington laughed, but it was more nervous than genuine.

'You're not getting away with that. You made a deal. £2,000.'

With the police officer nearby, my father felt sure Hetherington was not going to attack him physically. He released the door handle and, with his briefcase still on his lap, started the engine.

'Wait a minute,' shouted Hetherington. 'What are you up to?!'

'Exactly what I said.'

Hetherington appeared genuinely surprised. 'You bastard!' he said, 'Think of the publicity if I'm charged!'

'There will be no publicity in a case of blackmail,' my father said.

'Fuck you!' said Hetherington, 'Fuck you!' Though more in disappointment than in anger.

'Get out of the car,' said my father.

Hetherington fumbled for the handle, opened the door, heaved himself out and almost ran round to my father's window, throwing the documents in. 'Bugger you! I'll get you all one day. Queers, that's what you are, all of you. Fucking queers!' He grabbed at the envelope, but my father held onto it for a moment and looked Hetherington straight in the eye.

'Remember, I now have the letters. If you try anything in future, I have the evidence of your attempt at forgery and blackmail.'

He released the envelope and Hetherington scurried off into the station. My father drove away, and, on the way back to Polraen, stopped at a lay-by and set fire to the documents with his cigarette lighter. It was 3am before he got home.

Just before 8am the next morning he got up and phoned Thorpe, as promised. His voice sounded strained.

'Well?' he said.

'We shan't be bothered by Hetherington again,' said my father, truthfully, 'Forget about it. I'll see you next Sunday.'

'Marvellous!'

CHAPTER TEN

THE END OF THE ROAD

TODAY, MENTAL ILLNESS among men is recognised as a major issue. In the 1960s, it wasn't. The stiff upper lip prevailed; a man was expected to be a man. Depression, whilst acknowledged to some extent among teenagers, was most certainly not admitted by middle-aged men. My father suffered from it – terribly – as a result of which he was prescribed the drug Mandrax.

In 1965, methaqualone, a sedative-hypnotic drug, was combined with an antihistamine, diphenhydramine, to produce a more potent sedative-hypnotic under the brand name of Mandrax. Within weeks of its release, there were signs Mandrax was being used as a recreational drug. It offered the user a heightened sense of well-being and had aphrodisiac properties – not what my father needed.

Mandrax pills became colloquially known as Mandies. My father was initially prescribed them to help him sleep. Unfortunately, they were highly addictive, and it didn't take long for my father to become dependent. As well as using it to sleep, he used Mandrax to escape reality, perhaps hardly surprising given everything going on in his life. Obtaining large quantities of Mandrax was no problem – many MPs were doctors, and my father could simply stop one of them in the corridor and ask for a prescription. They were generally only too happy to oblige.

He wasn't the only MP of that era to be affected by Mandrax. John Stonehouse, the Labour Minister who faked his disappearance off a beach in Miami in 1974, was another whose family claim had his life turned upside down by the drug.

By the late 1960s, my father's life was running off the rails, though even those who knew and loved him were quite unaware of this. His expenses continued to grow and, as he had so little time to concentrate on his business, he started to borrow from friends and institutions to make ends meet. Many of those friends were Liberals, who didn't want to see one of their MPs go bankrupt for fear of the detrimental effect it would have on the party.

Others were friends, who were simply impressed by his apparent success, and considered him to be a good business bet. But then, in 1969, just as things were beginning to look really desperate, he received a call from Norman Graham, in the US. He was someone my father knew well, and with whom he had done excellent business in the 1950s.

Graham had launched the Plastic Carton Corporation of America to produce a new and profitable line of egg cartons. These were a much cheaper and apparently healthier option than the old cardboard egg cartons. At the time, having a patent on a form of plastic production appeared to be a licence to print money. My father arranged a credit check of the corporation, discovering that it had gone public, with very strong financial backing.

So, during one of his visits to New York, in August 1969, Graham and my father completed plans for a British subsidiary. Much was made about this in Cornwall, where it would be established in my father's constituency, and provide badly needed jobs. The shares in the British company would be held 80 per cent by the US company and 20 per cent by my father's London company, Peter Bessell Ltd. and my father was appointed deputy chairman.

As he wrote: 'Plastic Carton Corporation of America was a mundane but practical solution to my financial difficulties. Moreover, before retiring from politics, I would be giving practical help to my constituents. I returned to London flushed with triumph.' In fact, the company was anything but mundane; it was a very big deal. The factory was to be built near Liskeard in his constituency at a cost of about £6 million, almost £83 million in today's money. Most importantly, it would provide about 800 jobs in a community where unemployment was high. The local council was closely involved in the project, setting up a dedicated subcommittee to handle the development. They also began the construction of a substantial number of new homes in the area, simply to house the employees. For many people in the area, the factory offered potential salvation. My father was lauded for putting the whole project together. It was to be his swansong as an MP before retiring from politics in 1970. It was a win-win.

Not everyone was pleased and some complained about an American company moving into the area but, after they sent a senior executive to assess the mood in Cornwall, it was full steam ahead again.

In April 1970, Norman Graham and his wife came to London to oversee the planning of the factory. Graham had suffered from heart problems since a coronary in the 1960s and, by 1970, he was having to take nitroglycerine tablets regularly. Nevertheless, he was determined to see the project through. But, in July, whilst planning for the project was still in full swing, with no warning to my father, Norman and his wife suddenly returned to the US. A few weeks later my father followed. When he arrived in New York, he discovered the American corporation had run into financial difficulties and immediately urged the separation of the British subsidiary from the American parent corporation. Graham agreed, not least because the British company was inundated with requests for its products. In October, however, Graham died, and sudden pressure from the creditors caused the American company to collapse.

As construction had already started in Liskeard, my father entered into personal guarantees with the builders and other parties to keep the project going. The European patents were secure, but he didn't have the financial means to complete the building and purchase of manufacturing equipment on his own, so he desperately sought another investor. However, this would take many months – time he did not have. His guarantees meant his personal debt as a result of the factory project alone was about £500,000 (£6.5 million today). This, along with debts he accrued whilst working as an MP, was ruining him. He quickly realised he was facing disaster and very public humiliation – disgrace he felt unable to bear. It was in this frame of mind he visited New York in January 1971 in a last-ditch attempt to persuade the American banks to continue to support the British company. He failed.

But he did find a way out. Every evening, he lay on his bed and took a couple of Mandrax. For a while at least, this would take him to another world, which was gentle, and made him feel he could face literally anything. But he would wake again each morning feeling even more desperate. And the more desperate he became, the more he came to rely on his nightly escape. Ironically, the more he relied on this escape, the more desperate he acted when it eventually wore off – to the point where taking his life seemed the only solution. He began formulating plans. It was at this moment, when my father could barely cope with his own problems, that Jeremy Thorpe's issues made themselves felt once more.

Since his trip to Ireland to warn off Scott, my father kept in regular contact with him, offering him occasional jobs around the office and paying him a small 'retainer' of about £5 per week to help him live. There is no doubt he felt genuinely sorry for Scott, but he was also very keen to keep him quiet and out of Thorpe's mind. According to my father's memoir, this plan wasn't always successful and, from time to time, Thorpe would concoct wild plans to have Scott murdered. Bizarrely, Thorpe felt this was the only way he could get peace of mind as, to him, Scott was a constantly ticking time bomb. Every morning, Thorpe would wake, sick to the stomach with the fear his career could be destroyed at a stroke.

Thorpe's frame of mind wasn't helped by his decision, possibly for the sake of his image, to get married in 1968. This was an unlikely liaison and it worried him. For one thing, he didn't know how to have sex with a woman. No doubt he considered my father an expert on heterosexual relationships. On a taxi ride back to the House of Commons following a lunch, he brought the matter up.

Having leant over to close the window between the passengers and the driver, he blurted out, 'Pedro, how the hell do you fuck girls?'

Before my father could answer, Thorpe explained that he had taken a girl back to his flat a few nights previously and, when he saw her naked on his bed, all he could do was laugh. He pretended he'd had too much to drink. She was understanding, and he sent her home in a cab. My father thought this experience was a good thing, for the simple reason he couldn't see a marriage working. But Thorpe continued, 'I'm taking a rather nice lady to the theatre on Thursday and I'm hoping for an invitation to her flat afterwards.' He paused for a moment, then said, 'Think how ghastly it would have been the other night if she hadn't left. Christ!'

My father thought it best to humour Thorpe. 'Go slowly,' he said, 'and don't appear too anxious to make love – it makes women feel uncomfortable with someone they're with for the first time.'

Thorpe was impatient. 'But how do you do it?'

'I told you, take it slowly – initial love play is important to women.'

Thorpe grunted, and looked out of the window.

'Is there anything at all about a woman's body that arouses you?' my father asked.

'No. What is it that sets the old Bessell blood coursing?'

My father sighed. 'I'm really not sure you'd understand.'

'Oh, come on!'

My father was embarrassed, even with a close friend. 'Well, let's see, er, well, men usually focus on a particular part of a woman's body and, er, for me, for example, well-shaped legs have always been attractive … and …' He was getting nowhere.

'And? And?'

'Nylon-covered pillars leading to paradise,' was the best my father could come out with.

'Oh, for goodness' sake, what on earth is that supposed to mean?'

My father tried another tack. 'Have you ever heard of the Havelock Ellis theory about Beethoven's fascination with water tumbling over rocks, that it was this that inspired part of his Sixth Symphony and was conveyed in some of his other works by muted violins?' He was not entirely accurate, but it made the point.

Thorpe looked incredulous. 'No. I have not.'

My father then explained one of his earliest fantasies, which he had never divulged to his son I'm relieved to say, and how, for him, it often formed part of initial love play.

'Oh, God! Why is it all so complicated?' Thorpe said, sadly.

'I don't think it is,' my father said. 'It's just that people make it so by their inhibitions.'

'But you can't ask a girl over coffee and brandy whether she'll oblige with a private performance, can you?'

'I don't wait that long,' said my father, laughing. 'I ask over soup.'

But however limited the impact my father felt he'd had, clearly his advice helped. Thorpe was soon married to Caroline Allpass, and happily so. Ironically, though, this only increased his fear of Scott, particularly after Caroline had a son, Rupert. After all, exposure of his affair with Scott would now not only ruin his career; it would ruin his marriage, too, and he had grown to genuinely love Caroline. Tragically, in 1970, Caroline was killed in a car crash.

This was the backdrop to my father's final, disastrous meeting in New York, which confirmed the Plastic Carton Corporation was a dead duck. At that moment, when my father was at his lowest ebb, one of Thorpe's closest friends, David Holmes, turned up.

My father had first met Holmes in Greece in 1965 whilst on a trip to raise money for my father's business – a quest with which Thorpe was helping. Holmes and Thorpe were on holiday and the three dined. It was obvious to my father Thorpe and Holmes were close and, over the coming years, Holmes was integral in the efforts to keep Thorpe out of trouble, often present when my father and Thorpe discussed the Scott issue. My father liked him and trusted him.

But the timing of his arrival in New York couldn't have been much worse. As my father wrote, 'It took a supreme effort to switch from my problems to Jeremy's. Nevertheless, I met David for lunch at the Algonquin Hotel.'

The two men discussed Thorpe's state of mind. He was, understandably, struggling with Caroline's death, and his behaviour, according to Holmes, was becoming increasingly erratic.

'Is he on the verge of a breakdown?' my father asked.

'I don't think so,' said Holmes. 'His mind, his wit are as sharp as ever. His concentration's unimpaired. He's always like a racing car in top gear. It's just that he–'

'Doesn't pull into the pit stop for running repairs?' interjected my father.

'Yes, exactly,' said Holmes.

Thorpe apparently hadn't forgotten about the idea of having Scott murdered. In fact, my father was convinced that he genuinely wanted Scott killed and, considering Thorpe had asked Holmes to buy a revolver and do it himself, so was Holmes. Over lunch, my father and Holmes tried to formulate a plan to finally convince Thorpe that murder was a ridiculously impractical idea. Holmes was fed up with having to try to dissuade Thorpe on an almost daily basis, and my father was in no fit state to be making decisions about anything, particularly when he was being spirited away nightly by Mandrax. At that moment, he was ready to grab at any chance to end Thorpe's homicidal plans, so that, if my father took his own life, Holmes would not be left as the only person trying to dissuade Thorpe. At least, that's how my father justified his actions to himself.

The two men decided to build Thorpe's expectations to fever pitch so that, when the plan failed, he would be so deflated he would finally give up on the idea. They planned to persuade him that my father had obtained a US work permit for Scott and would be shipping him off to America to live. They would tell him that Scott was due to arrive in Miami shortly where Holmes would murder him. When the 'murder' failed, they would break the news to Thorpe, who would then give up on the whole idea. This was all very well, but Thorpe would be inquisitive, of course, and ask searching questions.

'He'll want to know where I bought a gun,' said Holmes.

'Damn it! Yes, he will,' said my father. 'Perhaps a trip to Chicago would be in order. Let's face it, in the mind of the average Englishman, Chicago is riddled with gangsters peddling guns on every street corner.'

'Seems a long way to go,' said Holmes, 'Isn't there somewhere closer?'

My father knew the area quite well. 'Well, you could take a drive to Newark or Patterson and find a couple of run-down bars for a drink in the middle of the day. That should arm you with a nice descriptive atmosphere to prove to Jeremy you've been where you said you've been to buy a weapon.'

And so, it was agreed.

My father was due to fly to Palm Beach a few days later. He and Holmes agreed to meet in Fort Lauderdale, where they would finalise the setting for the fake murder attempt. Meanwhile, Holmes would undertake his trip 'to buy a gun' and build the tension to fever pitch, so that Thorpe would be convinced the deed was about to be done. Then, at the last moment, Holmes and my father would burst the bubble by letting Thorpe know that Scott had failed to arrive. It was an absurd plan; but, in one sense, it was also very real.

My father spent that weekend with Diane, in New York, then flew to Palm Beach. Holmes arrived at Fort Lauderdale, about 30 miles to the south, the following day. The purpose of my father's visit had been to find a place and make a plan to kill himself:

> *[I]f I killed myself I wanted to do so in a climate where I could feel the warmth of the sun, listen to the sound of the ocean and see a velvet night sky above me. Throughout my life I had dreaded winter. Autumnal colours merely depressed me. Snow and chill winds caused more than physical discomfort; they produced a sense of despair.*

My poor father suffered these feelings completely on his own, despite being surrounded by many people who loved him. Of course, no one had any idea of his intentions on this trip. I have no doubt he'd told everyone it was a business trip, or that he was going away to do secret work.

As he stepped off the plane in West Palm Beach airport, the midday sun and the sight of palm trees immediately revived my father. Within an hour of arriving at his hotel, he answered the phone to Holmes. They arranged to meet the next day at a Howard

Johnson Motel in Fort Lauderdale. When he drove into the parking lot, my father saw Holmes already waiting for him. Before they went into the coffee bar, Holmes asked him to look at something on the back seat of his car.

'What on earth?' my father gasped.

'I kept my word to Jeremy. I got a gun. It's a most suitable weapon.'

As he stared at the gun in bewilderment, my father's first thought was that if a police officer spotted it, Holmes might end up in jail.

'But, David, why?' he asked.

The car was a two-door coupé. Holmes opened the driver's door and pulled back the seat.

'Take a closer look,' he said, almost coldly.

Perhaps Holmes's voice gave him away, but something about the gun's appearance made my father suspicious. He picked it up and at once they both dissolved in laughter.

It was little more than a toy, made mainly of plastic.

'Oh, my goodness, you had me worried! I should have known your sense of humour, but you had me completely fooled!'

'I've been taking target practice,' Holmes said, grinning, 'at rather short range. It's not very powerful!'

Once in the coffee bar, they laid out a map on the table to plan the fake murder. Fort Lauderdale is close to the Everglades, an area of largely uninhabited swamp and wetlands, and backs onto an area aptly named the Big Cypress Swamp. This looked like an ideal place to murder someone, then dispose of the body, which would decompose rapidly in the heat or be eaten by predators. DNA identification was, of course, unknown back then.

Holmes suggested he take a trip into the swamp that evening to reconnoitre, so he could give a description to Thorpe. My father agreed and set out back to his hotel in Palm Beach. But, as he drove, he wondered if he could trust Holmes to do a decent job. It would be important to give a detailed description so Thorpe didn't become suspicious. So, he took a drive out there himself. He was surprised to find many small roads, not marked on the map, with deep ditches on either side, ideal for rolling a body into, so it wouldn't be discovered for some time. The horror of this image didn't escape him. He imagined how it would be to go through with the murder. Thorpe, if he truly thought through the consequences of his wish, couldn't possibly sanction such an idea, could he?

My father drove back to his hotel, where he ate alone, a feeling of detachment overwhelming him. As he watched couples dance, his thoughts of lonely roads and murder were gradually replaced by equally unwelcome ones. He had not come here to help Holmes pretend to murder Scott; he had come here to kill himself. By forcing himself to think of his own plight, he seemed to separate himself from the people in the dining room. They were part of a world he could no longer share. He signed the check and went back to his room to take a Mandrax..

The next morning was clear and warm. But my father woke with a feeling of hopelessness, to which he had grown accustomed. As he put it:

> *I could take no more of the disappointments and frustrat ed hopes of the wheeling and dealing that were essential for survival. Just as the body demands rest, so my mind demanded peace, and if the price was permanent oblivion, then that was better than returning to the struggle, running the extra yard, lifting the additional ounce.*

That evening, he dined with Holmes and said the the horror of the situation had dawned on him. Holmes, having driven deep into the night himself, said he felt the same way. They agreed it was imperative to convince Thorpe that his proposed 'solution' was impossible. Meanwhile, a strike in the UK was making phone calls to

London difficult and Holmes had been out of touch with Thorpe for a few days. They hoped that Thorpe's vivid imagination had conjured up all manner of thoughts over that time, such as that Holmes or my father had been caught, or forced to go into hiding, or Scott had escaped to tell the police of the attempt on his life. Their hope was that when Holmes finally told Thorpe that Scott hadn't shown up, he would be so relieved, after days of fevered speculation, the subject would never be broached again. David agreed that, on his return to the UK, he would do his best to convince Thorpe, finally, that the plan was impossible. As later events would prove, evidently he failed.

With that plan in place, the two men went their separate ways and my father returned to reality and his plans to end his life.

That evening he dined with Harold Sweatt, a close friend and very wealthy fellow businessman. My father outlined his problems to Sweatt who was sympathetic and even offered to invest a little to help things out. But, grateful though he was, my father was beyond all that – it just meant more of the same.

Now, prior to his final moment, there was one more task to undertake for Thorpe, which was to meet Liberal benefactor Jack Hayward in The Bahamas. Hayward was a slightly eccentric millionaire philanthropist and businessman, with a passionate devotion to Britain. Despite his vast wealth, he lived unostentatiously in The Bahamas, just a short plane ride from Miami. Hayward enjoyed sports, particularly cricket and football; he later became the owner of Wolverhampton Wanderers Football Club. He and his business partners owned large swathes of The Bahamas. When he met Thorpe, he was impressed by what he saw as his political integrity, and became an important donor to the Liberal Party.

My father flew out to Freeport in Grand Bahama. Hayward was at the airport to meet him and greeted him warmly, before driving him to his home in his Rolls-Royce, with a Union Jack fluttering on its bonnet. He was known on the island as 'Union Jack Hayward'. They sat on the terrace to talk. In a remarkably matter of fact way, my father explained his problems and his intention to take his own life. Hayward was shocked and asked the full extent of his liabilities, but my father believed, given the type of man he was, Hayward might have considered suicide an honourable way out for a former MP. It remains a mystery to me not only that my father was able to discuss such a personal matter with someone he hardly knew, but that Hayward, with his vast resources, didn't immediately seek help for him. But things were different in those days. However, he did offer to help financially, an offer my father refused at the time, writing in his memoir, "It was a typical reaction of an extraordinarily kind man." Hayward read the memoir and, as far as I am aware, didn't deny the event.

My father swiftly steered the conversation to the reason he had travelled to meet him – Thorpe and Scott. He outlined Thorpe's difficulties with Scott, though obviously leaving out Thorpe's intention to have Scott murdered. Hayward appeared neither shocked nor surprised; he was almost certainly fully aware of Thorpe's private leanings. He asked what he could do.

'The thing is this,' my father continued, 'Scott recently married, but, for obvious reasons, the marriage failed, and a divorce is pending. It's quite possible Scott will use his court appearance to blurt something out about his relationship with Jeremy.'

'I see,' said Hayward.

My father continued. 'Of course, if he does, court privilege means it would be a free-for-all for the media. It could be pretty disastrous for Jeremy.'

'And?'

'For years I've been supporting Scott with regular small payments to help him out and, of course, encourage him to keep quiet. I think it might be a good idea to help Scott with the legal fees for his divorce. That way he may be less likely to be indiscreet. It would also be incredibly helpful to provide the occasional help for him as I used to. I simply can't afford to do that any more, Jack.'

'I have no problem with that,' responded Hayward immediately. 'Happy to help out. You can count on me. But there is one condition.

'What's that?'

'Scott must never know where the money is coming from. If he should find out, he might think he's struck a bottomless well of money!'

My father laughed. 'No, that's fine! The money can be filtered through my solicitor in London. Jack, it's important Jeremy doesn't know about this, otherwise the funds could be traced back to him.'

Hayward drove my father back to the airport and warmly shook his hand farewell. He even stood on the tarmac waving until the plane was on the runway.

My father still intended that the following day would be his last.

CHAPTER ELEVEN

DESPERATION

BY THE LATE 60S AND early 70s, my father's life was a mess: problems with the Plastic Carton Corporation; Scott; Holmes; Thorpe; three lovers, whose existence he had to keep secret from one another; and his secret work, of course. It's no wonder he needed Mandrax to sleep.

My sister, my mother and I weren't aware he was suffering from bouts of depression. When he was around us, he was always joking and talking optimistically. He had many interests outside of business and politics – music, cars, DIY, writing and tropical fish. One tends to think of a depressive as someone who retreats into a corner, but that was far from the case with my father.

By the time the Plastic Carton Corporation was falling, I had left school to take up a position as a left-wing hippy. Work was alien to me. My father had bought me a car and was giving me a monthly allowance. I was living with my sister and brother-in-law in their flat in Holland Park, London. I did literally nothing. I would wake in the afternoon and perhaps go out for a stroll before returning home to watch television or sit in my bedroom playing my guitar. I'd go to bed in the early hours of the morning. My brother-in-law, Tony, was a professional songwriter and we tended to keep the same hours. Having me around in such a small flat must have been annoying to say the least, but he was a kind and gentle man, and I learned a great deal about the music industry from him. My sister was working as the personal assistant to John Junor, the editor of the *Sunday Express*. She was effectively supporting Tony and me, with the help of my father.

My mother was using her time, and my father's money, wisely. Through him, she made contacts at the United Nations, and was travelling the world on a voluntary basis, working as an assistant for UNICEF. Eventually, she took an apartment in expensive Midtown Manhattan, on 54th Street, to be close to the United Nations building. The house in Cornwall was looked after by the household staff. It was a most satisfactory existence for all of us – except my father. His situation had become so desperate and his despair so great, that he had written a letter to my mother to be opened only upon his death, perhaps preparing for suicide. The envelope was addressed to 'PAULINE BESSELL', with the following instruction on the next line: 'TO BE GIVEN TO HER UPON MY DEATH OR AT MY INSTRUCTION ONLY'. Written on House of Commons paper, it was dated 'Saturday on train' and read:

My dearest darling love,

Just in case anything should happen to me, this is to say that I am sorry if I have left you with awful problems. For the last two years I have had to beg and borrow money where I could. My accident policy of £25,000 and life policies of £3,000 will be absorbed in my debts – but I believe that some of the people will be merciful, and as it cost me so much to become an MP if they are real Liberals they will let you off most of it – they are all very rich men – [illegible], Beaumont, and a little from Robert. It will all be so horrible for you, but darling I had no choice.

There is one big hope. The case I have against Capital and Counties. I am sure that if the lawyers are firm, it will be settled out of court. You will get at least £10,000 from this and it could be much more.

Darling, do not let anything else worry you. There is no need, for I have only loved you – ever. You were, and are, my whole world. I swear this before God, knowing that if you ever read this, I shall be no longer alive. It is my last word to you – I love you alone.

Your own,
Peter

He was expecting to die, at his own hand. But the thought of doing so offered no release because, of course, he was aware of the desperate situation into which his wife would be thrown. His idea that she would get £10,000 from a court case was a fantasy. The truth was that she would be left homeless and destitute.

His absolute belief in God and that, when he died, he would be going to a better place must have been very reassuring.

It could be argued that all his problems were self-inflicted, so sympathy would be misplaced. He could simply have got himself a steady job when he retired as an MP. But my father could never have done that. He was fiercely independent and couldn't have answered to anyone other than himself. He had no qualifications other than his experience as an MP, so what would he have done? And he wouldn't have been able to explain his whereabouts when with his women or doing secret work. It wouldn't have been long before the truth came out and his life ended in tatters.

His greatest weakness was a complete inability to say no to anyone. My family had never wanted for anything, whether he could afford it or not.

As I've mentioned, my father adored American cars of the 1950s and 1960s and, on one of his trips to New York to negotiate the Plastic

Cartons Corporation deal, he told Norman Graham how much he admired his Buick Riviera. It was an unusual and eye-catching car, jet black with wire wheels and white upholstery, also very fast.

Norman generously gave the car to my father, arranging for it to be shipped to the UK. I loved that car, as did all my friends, and for my 21st birthday my father announced he was going to give it to me. I should have been grateful, but was I?

The next day I went to see *Live and Let Die*, the latest James Bond movie, which includes an extended, thrilling speed-boat chase. I came out of the cinema wanting a speedboat just like James Bond's and immediately drove to the London Boat Showroom in Kensington to ask what kind of speedboat James Bond had used. They told me it was a Glastron, an example of which they had in the showroom. It looked great!

'How much is it?' I asked.

'£2,500.' (£26,000 today.)

I was genuinely surprised. 'That cheap?' I said.

The salesman looked like he'd died and gone to heaven and moved in for the kill.

'Where will you be using the boat?'

'Off the coast of Cornwall,' I replied, thinking I would keep it at Polraen and use it in the summer.

'In the sea, you mean?'

'Yes.'

'Then a Glastron isn't for you. It has a shallow hull, only really suitable for inland use on calm water. What you need is a speedboat with a deep V hull designed to tackle waves such as you get off the coast in Cornwall. This Fletcher Arrowsport over here is the boat for you.'

He led me over to the other side of the showroom, where he showed me a gleaming red, Fletcher Arrowsport. I fell in love with it on the spot.

'Not only does it have a deep V hull, it has a Ford two-litre inboard engine. It's *very* fast.'

I had to have that boat. The next morning, I met my father at his office and told him I didn't want the Buick, I wanted a speed-boat. His face dropped – now I know of course he couldn't afford the speed-boat. He was giving me the car because he couldn't afford to actually buy anything, but wanted to give me something special. But he put a deposit on the boat and took out a loan to cover the rest of the cost. He also gave me the Buick, which the London Boat Showroom had a towbar attached to, at another considerable cost.

A few weeks later, I returned to the showroom. Waiting outside was my beautiful red boat attached to my beautiful black car. I couldn't have been happier, or more eager to show them both off.

For my birthday party, my father reserved a table for 14 at Small's Restaurant in Knightsbridge. I have no idea how much that cost. At the time, he could barely afford to eat, and was being fed marmite sandwiches each evening by Sally.

X

By late 1970, just after his meeting with Hayward and hoping he'd tidied up any loose ends with regard to Scott and Thorpe, my father turned his mind to his method of suicide. Life insurance companies do not pay out for suicide, so his chosen method was a carefully staged car crash in which death would be instantaneous. He didn't think he had the courage to kill himself in any other way.

The evening after he saw Jack Hayward in Grand Bahama, my father set out on another journey into the Everglades, this time to find a suitable spot to crash his car at high speed. As Mandrax gave him such a powerful sense of well-being it almost obliterated any fear of death, he decided he would take a pill about 15 minutes before committing suicide. A post-mortem would presumably have found the drug in his system, but it was the only way in which he could face what he felt he had to do. He drove for an hour, looking for somewhere he could crash his car without endangering others. He didn't find a suitable spot, so he stopped at a café for a cup of tea.

When he returned to his car, a new emotion overwhelmed him:

> *Above everything, I wanted to see Diane again. As I continued driving, looking still for suicidal objects, she dominated my consciousness. Gradually my concentration on finding a means of death turned to devising some means of seeing Diane once more. To touch her, feel her beside me, look into her beautiful eyes and to know the eager warmth of her arms around me – if only I could snatch from life one last weekend alone with her, death would be so much easier.*

It's a good thing my mother never read my father's memoir. While all this was going on, he was writing love letters to her. She would have given him all the support and love he could possibly have needed. To have learned he was yearning for Diane would have been devastating to her, as it would have been to Sally, too. It's possible he wrote this because it was Diane who typed up his memoir for him. Probably, over his cup of tea, he realised he would be unable to go through with the suicide for a combination of reasons, Diane being one of them.

He left the café and drove back to the Holiday Inn. He needed an alternative plan. He wondered if there wasn't something after all in previous offers of financial help from Hayward and Sweatt.

He decided to speak to Hayward first, as he felt they had more in common, so he flew out to The Bahamas again. Hayward readily made a firm promise to help. That same evening, my father went to see Sweatt, who started to back off. He knew just how extensive

Hayward's resources were, so he urged my father to return to The Bahamas to see if he could persuade Hayward to offer more money. He did as suggested and told Hayward of Sweatt's response. Hayward told him to keep trying and said that he would be in New York the following week, when they could meet again. In part because of all the travelling he was doing, my father's already meagre resources were fast dwindling. He was living off credit cards and overdrafts, which would soon be called in.

Back in New York, he threw himself into Diane's arms at the airport. Diane took control of the situation. She saw Hayward on her own when he visited New York, then flew to Palm Beach to talk to Harold Sweatt. Back in New York, she spoke to her wealthy father, Fred Miller, who owed my father a debt of gratitude for a previous favour.

Somehow she persuaded Hayward and Sweatt to invest in my father's business and my understanding is that they offered a combination of loans and loan guarantees. Her father, however, invested directly in the business. He agreed to finance the setting up of a US corporate subsidiary of my father's London investment brokerage, on condition that he was made the financial consultant.

An extension of my father's business would be critical to the success of any plan to satisfy his creditors, to reassure them there would be future income with which to repay them. The creditors of the Plastic Carton Corporation accepted that my father had taken a considerable risk in offering personal guarantees for the funding of the project, so they allowed small down payments and a long-term settlement. One personal creditor even wiped out my father's debt on receipt of the down payment. Two or three other small projects my father was working on also brought in fees earlier than he expected, providing funds to reduce his overdrafts.

While he was in London, he called me into his Pall Mall office for a chat. No doubt my sister was sick of me living with her, and he was equally sick of paying for a son who didn't appear to have any other ambition than to play the guitar. He told me he was opening an office in New York, and he wanted me to move there and work for him as a director of both his British and American companies. It was evidently an offer I couldn't refuse.

The worst part of the deal was that I had to get my hair cut and wear suits he had tailor-made for me in Savile Row. As soon as the New York office opened, I would move to a small apartment of my own at the Beaux Arts Apartment Hotel on East 44th Street in Midtown Manhattan, opposite the United Nations building. My job would be to support my father in his business dealings, learn the trade of being an investment broker and take care of the office when he was absent, which would be quite often.

Within weeks, my father had a small but highly desirable office on the corner of 54th Street and 5th Avenue, one of the most exclusive areas in New York, and I was on a Boeing 747, crossing the Atlantic to my new home. At the time, I had no idea of the desperation which had led him to open an office in the US. As far as I was concerned, my rich father, having retired as an MP, was simply choosing to expand his business, and bring his son on board.

I told my father I couldn't live in New York without a car, so he duly bought me a Volkswagen Kombi 'Microbus', the type that hippies drove, which I felt would be most suitable for driving around New England with my new-found American friends. Just the cost of parking it in a multi-storey car park in Midtown Manhattan was more than the average rented apartment in a normal town. It was a ludicrously unnecessary expense for someone in my father's financial position, of which I was blissfully unaware. Once again, he was simply unable to say no.

My mother had moved to an apartment close by so she could be near her voluntary work at UNICEF in the United Nations building. A brief stocktake of my father's monthly outgoings at this time, excluding essentials such as eating, included: a large, staffed house in Cornwall; four cars, one of which was a Bentley; an office suite in Pall Mall near St James's Palace; parking for his car at the Ritz Hotel; the apartment in London for himself and Sally; international travel for him and his family; an office on 5th Avenue in New York; an apartment for my mother in New York; an apartment for me in New York; my salary; my sister's salary, when she, too, joined the company; a secretary in London; the salary of a close friend of his from Cornwall, Dr Mervyn Cooper, who gave up his practice to emigrate to New York and join my father's business; and other perks, such as a limousine to meet me and other family members, when we travelled to JFK.

Where on earth was all the money coming from? Not only were his basic monthly outgoings extraordinarily large, but his general standard of living was also extravagant. A few months beforehand, he had been on the verge of suicide as a result of financial troubles; now there appeared to be no limit to his spending. Either he had a secret source of income, or he was simply allowing debt to accrue at an incredible rate. Our lifestyle was extraordinary; only my father knew how borderline it all was.

My mother had a beautiful apartment in one of the most sought-after parts of New York, but my father never spent the night there. Every evening, he would head off to undertake his secret work, where he said he was fed and given a bed for the night, as it was impossible to know when negotiations – the Vietnam peace talks – would end for the day. This could, of course, simply have been an excuse for him to spend his free time with Diane in their apartment and, no doubt, he often did. It was also quite likely that on many occasions when he was away from Diane, he would be feeding *her* the same line. But Diane told me that he often discussed with her what was happening in the talks, which were, apparently, a cover for the Paris peace talks (seeking a settlement to the war in

Vietnam) – the real negotiations took place in secret, then, the following day, the public talks in Paris replicated what had already been discussed, leaving out the more contentious issues. These secret talks culminated in the Paris Peace Accords of 1973.

Diane said to me he mentioned things that were indeed discussed in public days later. My sister confirmed this. One event, which they told me about independently, was the introduction of the round table at the peace talks in Paris. The North Vietnamese favoured a circular table, giving equal importance to all parties, while the South Vietnamese representatives preferred a rectangular table, to show there were two distinct sides to the conflict. Eventually, a compromise was reached whereby the North and South Vietnamese sat at the round table, while other parties sat at rectangular tables apart from the main table. My father told Diane all about this long before it became public, one of many examples which convinced her that he was some kind of confidential adviser. Despite his no longer being an MP, it's not unreasonable to suppose the Americans would seek his advice, particularly as he had visited Vietnam in support of the US position as an MP, and I have communications between him and the US Embassy in London supporting a friendly familiarity between them on the subject.

There was seldom anything in writing, but small examples of how he explained his work at that time are contained in two letters he wrote to my mother. The first outlines how he would discuss his work when on the phone to her: 'In all our conversations on the telephone I shall refer to "my company", which means my friends, and to "the other company", which means the other side. I shall talk as though it was all a business deal between companies and refer to "the Directors" etc. I think this is the most sensible way.'

In another letter, he employs the method outlined above:

I have made good progress and did not encounter as many

difficulties as I feared. Now the other company has agreed to send its principals to see me. Alas they cannot come to the United States and today (Saturday) we are trying to agree on a suitable country – Canada is my choice; theirs is South America – Mexico or Cuba. My company suggests the Bahama Islands. No doubt we shall find a compromise. Which means I shall not be in New York all the time, but I should be able to tell you where I am going by the time we speak on the phone tomorrow. Everyone knows my latest possible date of return is January 15th. So, there is no possibility of delay after that.

This was typical of how he explained things to all of us. But it was his constant disappearances that caused my mother to open his briefcase when he left it behind that fateful evening. When she told me the story, I suspect we both thought it might be Diane. But things I discovered later cast some doubt on that.

It's quite possible that the phone number my mother used to contact my father was for Diane's apartment. He used to have a second telephone installed wherever he lived for his use only, for contact with his secret government organisation. Secret work allowed him to cover almost every eventuality.

My father flitted between London and New York almost weekly, hence the need to have me look after the office in New York while he was in London. When he was in neither city, he could have been almost anywhere in the world on business, or secret work, although some of those business trips were certain to have been romantic getaways with one of his women, most likely Diane, whom he would often take to The Bahamas. I wonder how often she thought 'you do realise this is my father's money you're spending?!' But maybe it wasn't – at least not all of it.

On my first flight to New York, I was so excited. All I knew about America was what my parents had told me and what I had seen in the movies. It sounded a wondrous place and, as I stepped off the plane and got into my chauffeur-driven limousine, I honestly felt as though I was meeting a movie star for the first time. I was completely in awe, though that was shattered within minutes. The drive from JFK to Manhattan takes you through Brooklyn and I'd never seen such dirt and dilapidation.

For the first couple of weeks, I didn't like New York. But as I got under the skin of the city, I fell in love with it. The town was packed with energy day and night, and my apartment was ideally situated, within walking distance of, or just a short bus ride away from, almost any part of Midtown Manhattan. Wherever I went, people would pick up on my English accent. In those days before budget air travel, English people were rare in the US, even in New York. Americans would often ask me to talk just to hear my accent, making me feel like a performing seal. But my curious accent had its advantages.

Not far from my flat, on the corner of 1st Avenue and 63rd Street, was the first incarnation of TGI Fridays, not the chain restaurant we know today, but the original Fridays Bar. Opened in 1965, it was marketed with the timeless promise of 'In here, it's always Friday'. As Fridays themselves put it, 'a red and white phenomenon was born', bang in the middle of 'air crew land', where overnighting crew would socialise. Cocktails, served by charismatic bartenders, flowed freely. TGI Fridays quickly became *the* singles bar in New York. It was so popular that barriers were needed to handle the huge numbers of people trying to get in almost every night of the week, except perhaps on a Sunday.

Fridays became my haunt and, before long, I befriended one of the bartenders, Paddy, who had a fantastic voice and would regularly stand on the bar and sing to the packed crowd. Everyone loved Paddy. I never had to stand in line outside and, if there were no seats at the bar, Paddy would arrange one for me. I never paid for a drink. And all I had to do was start to speak and with my English accent I quickly became the centre of attention. In no time, I had made many friends, both male and female. I spent almost every evening there.

I was not fast and loose with the women at Fridays. That was a characteristic I didn't inherit from my father, and I knew that for most of them my accent made me simply a novelty they could show off to their friends. But my social life was second to none. I realised why my father spent so much time in New York. Many nights I would stay out late, go to bed in the early hours of the morning, wake up early and trudge to the office where, if I was the only one there, would mind the phones while catching up on my sleep lying on the floor. I really wasn't much help to my father, but, on the other hand, he didn't give me that much to do, and I wasn't skilled enough to raise investment on my own. When I first arrived, I was only 19 and investors such as multinational banks were wary of a teenager seeking millions of dollars for some obscure investment in the UK.

When, sometimes, I was asked to return to London to take care of the office there, my business life would be overwhelmed by my social life. I had my apartment in Chelsea, funded by my father of course, and my Buick and speedboat. Summer holidays were spent at the family home in Cornwall and weekends would always find me in Saffron Walden. Just months after my father was facing potential humiliation and contemplating suicide as a result of financial problems, such was my life. I was a spoiled rich boy. But everything rested on the shallowest of foundations.

CHAPTER TWELVE

RUSSIAN ROULETTE

SEVERAL VISITORS TO the New York office were a bit mysterious, but none more so than 'Chips' Nura. He regularly showed up in a black limousine, driven by a chauffeur, who had no compunction about parking in a no-parking zone. As soon as Chips appeared, he and my father disappeared into my father's office for about five minutes, following which he departed as swiftly as he arrived. I was never allowed to be a part of these meetings, though my father did introduce me to Chips.

Chips was probably in his mid to late-30s, olive-skinned, dark-haired and always impeccably dressed. Whenever my father said the name Chips, he said it with a knowing smile. 'Chips' does have a gangster ring to it, like 'Fingers' or 'Spats'. I concluded he was with the Mob, and the meetings were for my father to pay protection money. Recently, I asked a friend who knew a New York Mafia historian about 'Chips Nura'. He'd never heard a name like that, but he *had* heard of Bessell!

Another visitor to our New York office was the author, Guy Richards. He and my father became friends after my father read Guy's book, *Hunt for the Czar*, published in 1970. The book maintains Czar Nicolas II of Russia and his family weren't assassinated during the Russian Revolution, but escaped, with the help of the British Royal Family and the US Government.

My father was sufficiently intrigued by the story to raise the matter in the House of Commons, not long before he retired as an MP. He later extended his enquiries to Washington, where he had contacts. Through Dr Robert Miller, who might have been a researcher attached to Henry Kissinger's staff, he was shown a set of documents that purported to disclose how the Czar and his family had escaped. My father had an affidavit typed up in which he describes Dr Miller and the documents themselves. Following my father's death and the introduction of DNA evidence, the escape theory has been fairly comprehensively debunked, but the saga's relevance to our lives was substantial. The papers my father claimed to have seen in Washington subsequently became known as the Chivers Papers. The name came about as a result of Dr Miller using a State Department coding booklet to disguise the name Romanov as Chivers, as described in my father's affidavit. The existence of these papers has been vehemently denied by the governments of both the UK and the US, and Kissinger referred to my father as a fraud. This suggests my father's extensive, detailed, 35-page affidavit is no more than a figment of his fertile imagination. That's possible, of course, but why would he have gone to the trouble of drawing up the affidavit. Journalists have often asked me if I found copies of the Chivers Papers in my father's archive, but I didn't. If I could confirm their existence, it might once and for all show my father to have been honest and Kissinger to be a liar. If they could be proved never to have existed – not easy – it would cast doubt on everything my father ever said. The Chivers Papers are central to understanding my father, but no government will ever admit to their existence.

I have the affidavit, though –a written statement, confirmed under oath, which can be used as evidence in court. It's a strong affirmation of my father's version of events in which he offered to appear before a Congressional committee if requested. I have confirmed that there was a Dr Robert Miller attached to the White House staff at that time and Sally has said that she saw my father's transcriptions of the Chivers Papers, which she typed out. She even wrote a book based on them. I think the papers do exist and my father did see them, but I believe they might show a potential escape route, rather than one actually used to escape. The Romanovs were murdered before they had a chance to get away. The Portuguese royal family, led by King Manuel II, escaped Portugal in 1910 during the October 5th revolution with the help of the British Navy. There is absolutely no reason not to assume such plans would have been in place for the Russian royal family – in fact it would have been far more surprising if there weren't.

Guy Richards visited the office regularly. He was also, according to my father, involved in his secret work. I had no idea at the time that he was also an investor in my father's company, and was key, along with Sweatt, Hayward and Diane's father, in keeping him in business.

After I'd been working for my father for about a year, it began to dawn on me that I hadn't seen a single deal completed. I became concerned that we needed to earn something from somewhere. I wrote a pompous letter to my father, pointing this out and saying that, as a company director, I had a right to know the financial position of the company. I didn't receive a reply.

Richards introduced my father to William 'Bill' Lawrence, a billionaire whose family owned the New York suburb of Bronxville. Bronxville is just a square mile of Westchester County, 16 miles from Midtown Manhattan. In 2016, it was rated by CNBC as the most expensive suburb of any of the 10 largest cities in the US. In 1972, when Richards introduced Bill Lawrence to my father, the Lawrence family was anxious to dispose of many of their Bronxville properties, provided they could be certain any redevelopment would be in keeping with the standards they had maintained up until then.

Lawrence and my father got on well. My father would usually have acted simply as a broker for the sale and collected a healthy commission if he found the right buyer, but on this occasion the arrangement went further. Lawrence sought an arrangement whereby, instead of receiving a brokerage fee, my father had an equity interest in the properties and oversaw the development, thus ensuring standards were maintained. My father formed another US Corporation, Twentieth Century Securities Inc., in which he and Lawrence had a controlling interest. The remaining shares went to an outside investor who provided a mortgage to enable Twentieth Century Securities to purchase the properties from Lawrence and undertake the development. It was a fantastic package from everyone's point of view. Although my father's companies would have to deal with all the complexities of zoning and planning, he and the rest of his family could look forward to permanent financial security – indeed, great wealth.

With this huge undertaking in mind, he looked for a suitable UK investor – required by the Lawrences and staff with the skills to deal with every aspect of such a development. Dr Cooper and I had already joined the company, my sister was shortly to follow, and my father promised to involve Michael Decent, my mother's brother-in-law, who gave up his architecture practice to allow him to spend time on Bronxville, and Leonard Ross, the company solicitor who was fed up with the law and wanted to enter commerce. My father offered him the opportunity to run the London office, as the rest of us would have our time taken up in New York with Bronxville. Everyone involved was going to be rich and there was no shortage of potential investors to provide the necessary mortgages on the Bronxville properties. What could possibly go wrong?

Under UK currency regulations at the time, it was necessary to obtain Bank of England exchange-control permission for the London company, Peter Bessell Ltd, to become a shareholder in the new US corporation, Peter Bessell Inc., and for a British investor to provide the mortgages. I was a director of both Peter Bessell Ltd, the UK company, and Peter Bessell Inc., his US company.

Crucial months passed before that permission was given. When, eventually, it was received, a credit squeeze (when banks suddenly reduce the general availability of loans and mortgages, usually due to a sudden rise in interest rates) in both the US and the UK compelled most of the largest investors to back off and the remainder to dawdle. As reported in the *New York Times* in August 1972, Wall Street was nervous and full of gloomy talk that a squeeze would be introduced in 1973. With everyone involved eagerly anticipating imminent wealth – I was planning on ordering a brand-new Aston Martin – the Bronxville deal stalled. The Lawrences were under pressure from minority stockholders as a result of which my father was compelled to pay $25,000 ($183,000 today) to extend his option to avoid the Lawrences pulling out. By 1973, his total expenses on the Bronxville deal alone, excluding all his other mounting debts, exceeded $100,000 ($750,000 today). In total, his overall indebtedness amounted to well over $3 million in today's money. As all his business attention had been focused on Bronxville, there was no other income to help reduce the debt. In fact, his debt was growing month by month at a staggering rate. In order to keep his creditors and the people who were expecting to work on the Bronxville project on-side and optimistic, he had to spin a web of lies. It was a gigantic gamble, which failed. It seemed he had no option but to declare bankruptcy. He was right back where he had been three years previously, with Mandrax as his only salvation.

Eventually, my father's conscience got the better of him and he told Diane's father, Fred Miller, who was funding much of his debt in the US, the truth. Remarkably, Miller accepted my father's explanation and decided the best way out was to lend him more to see him through to the completion of the Bronxville deal, which he did. But my father couldn't keep accepting money from Miller without giving some security in return, particularly in the event of my father's death. A coded document I found in his papers showed he had given a first charge on the family home in Cornwall to Miller, meaning the money he was owed would be first to be paid off from the property's value. He also made him the beneficiary of an accident policy and took out an additional life insurance policy, ensuring that, if everything else failed, he could take his own life – while making it look like an accident – just as he had considered doing in Florida a few years previously. Everybody else, including my mother, my sister and I would be totally destitute, but Miller would recover some of his investment.

My father wrote that all these actions and lies resulted from his 'sick desperation'. He referred to taking his life as the 'ultimate solution'. There were other, smaller creditors, who also had various forms of essentially meaningless security. One was an old friend from Cornwall, Gerald Whitmarsh, who had a charge on Polraen. He was unaware that my father had given a first charge to Miller. If my father committed suicide or was declared bankrupt, Whitmarsh would get nothing. A couple of UK banks, most notably National Westminster Bank, also had personal guarantees from friends of my father, mainly Hayward.

When things were becoming quite desperate, and Bronxville was still delayed, he asked Whitmarsh for a further advance. Whitmarsh agreed and said he would ask his lawyer to make up a promissory note, effectively a personal guarantee. A few days later, my father went to the lawyer's office to sign the documents and was shocked to realise the note was another charge against Polraen. He sat there, not knowing what to do. If he disclosed that Polraen was no longer his, there were obviously several dangers. The greatest was that the loan might be cancelled. He had already sent off several cheques, which would bounce, bringing immediate disaster. Or, if he heard about Miller's first charge on Polraen, Whitmarsh might be furious enough to demand the original loan against Polraen be paid off immediately. My father had no time to think. He decided that by permitting the second charge, at least he was not endangering Miller, because Whitmarsh's charge would have no validity in law, having been granted fraudulently. He duly signed the document and left. One can only wonder how he felt at the time. He may have been simply beyond caring.

There was one final chance of salvaging things. Some months previously, Thorpe had told my father that Hayward and his partners were considering selling their substantial interests in The Bahamas. Thorpe suggested to Hayward that my father might find an American buyer, and, if necessary, help that buyer to get the necessary US Government licences for the deal. Bronxville was keeping my father far too busy for him to take the suggestion seriously, but one day he mentioned it in passing to Bill Lawrence's son, George, who was very well connected. He knew two senior executives at Mobil Oil and offered to introduce my father to them.

George was also a special assistant to New York Senator James Buckley and was able to offer an introduction to the Secretary of Commerce, Maurice Stans, to discuss the government licences needed. They recognised there were political considerations outside the jurisdiction of the Department of Commerce and decided also to arrange, if possible, to meet with the Secretary of State, Henry Kissinger.

Thorpe had married again by this time and he and his new wife, Marion, Countess of Harewood, previously married to the Queen's first cousin, the Seventh Earl of Harewood, visited New York on their honeymoon. My parents were happy to show them around the city, and they all had a wonderful time for a few days. One evening, they dined at the Rainbow Room at the top of the RCA building, now the Rockefeller Plaza and, for a moment, Thorpe and my father found themselves alone. Given their wives would shortly rejoin them, Thorpe was blunt and to the point: 'How's your marriage? You and Pauline are obviously not living together.'

In the short time available, my father told him about Diane and his feelings for her. The next day my father and Thorpe flew to Washington to meet an aide of Kissinger and to introduce Thorpe to George Lawrence, to set up the Bahamas deal. The flight provided an opportunity for another personal conversation. Thorpe talked of his marriage to Marion and the dramatic rise of the Liberal Party, which had made him a national figure.

'I have to be discreet, of course,' he said, 'but I can't deny continuing to have gay relationships whenever possible.'

'Does Marion know?' asked my father.

'No!' came the quick response, 'And it's a problem. I raised the subject with her in casual conversation, much as I did with Caroline, but Marion reacted more strongly.'

'She was shocked?'

'Worse. She was disgusted. Of course, I only spoke in general terms. She hasn't the slightest idea about me.'

The conversation moved on and they prepared for their meetings in Washington. It was agreed that Thorpe would report to Hayward while George Lawrence and my father opened negotiations with Mobil. But the deal wasn't at the forefront of my father's mind; Bronxville was, and keeping the Lawrence family happy while the delays were handled.

Following two meetings with senior executives of their real-estate company, Mobil said they were seriously interested and were initiating a full investigation into the proposal. George Lawrence had provided invaluable help, for which he expected a brokerage fee.

After a few delays, one of Hayward's associates gave my father the price of the properties which enabled Lawrence, my father and Thorpe to make a rough calculation of commissions. Thorpe and my father would split $1.2 million and $1.4 million between them (just under $10 million today) and Lawrence would receive about $700,000 (almost $5 million today).

'It should be at least that amount,' Lawrence said, 'and it will have to be paid in the United States.'

His tone suggested to my father that George was not happy with the terms. He was, after all, a very rich man, and sums like that were piffling to him.

'Well, I'm happy to put any proposition you suggest to Hayward.'

'There will be heavy expenses,' Lawrence said, 'They might come close to that figure.'

Mistakenly, my father interpreted 'expenses' to mean, as he put it, 'off the record political contributions to smooth the way for Government licences that would be separate from George Lawrence's fee'. In other words, bribes. Subsequently, he arranged a private meeting with Hayward in his London office a few weeks later, and asked me to be present throughout the meeting.

It was a friendly meeting at which my father was able to outline the status of the deal before raising the matter of commissions. He explained that George Lawrence was involved and said, 'He's told me there may be expenses amounting to as much as $700,000.'

Surprisingly, Hayward didn't balk, which I think bothered my father slightly. He clearly felt he needed to push the point a little further, to ensure that everyone understood.

'It's possible,' he said, 'that a substantial payment may be required at the contract stage, rather than on completion.'

Hayward was sitting in an armchair in front of my father's desk, facing me, as my desk was at right angles to my father's. He looked directly at me and smiled.

'You produce the contract, Peter. If you can do that, I don't think your father ought to be worried about expenses, do you, Paul?'

I laughed and shook my head. I knew exactly what my father was referring to, but did Hayward?

My father decided to get clarification from Lawrence on his return to the US. Having told George about the meeting with Hayward, he told him they had also discussed the matter of fees.

'I said that as far as you were concerned, George, there might be as much as $700,000 in expenses.'

Lawrence stared at him, bewildered. 'I didn't say that. I only wanted it understood that my expenses must be separate from my commission – but the total for me will be $700,000.'

My father always blamed himself for making a monumental error. The bottom line was he thought palms needed to be greased in Washington, and he was wrong.

A few days later, he made another trip to London in connection with Bronxville and spoke to Thorpe. He explained his error and Thorpe said he was seeing Hayward shortly and would explain the situation to him.

'Thanks,' said my father, 'that'll save me a letter.'

'I'll be glad to tell him.' Thorpe responded. 'I always like giving good news to rich men!'

My father had arranged a meeting with Grosvenor Estates in London. The company owned great swathes of London's most desirable properties in the West End. It had expressed an interest in the Bronxville properties and sent a representative to inspect them. Because of the size of the project, Grosvenor brought in another major property company, Capital and Counties. At this point my father's back was well and truly against the wall; he desperately needed money from somewhere. If this meeting with Grosvenor and Capital wasn't decisive, it would be the final end of his struggle in every sense of the word.

The meeting, held by candlelight because strikes were causing regular power cuts, went well. The candlelight and the general gloom and drizzle of a London winter's day, added to my father's sense of despair, to which he had always been prey during the winter months. Normally, he would have been delighted with the outcome of the meeting. There was no doubt that both property companies were extremely enthusiastic, but my father desperately needed more than enthusiasm. He needed a firm commitment, but, given the need for due diligence, he was never going to get that in the course of a single day. When the meeting ended, he believed that nothing could be achieved in time to help him and reassure everyone to whom he had given irresponsibly optimistic promises before his departure from New York.

My memory of this meeting is that I drove him to Grosvenor Estates' offices and waited for him in the car, simply because parking in Mayfair was difficult and he didn't want to risk being late. I clearly remember his mood on the day. His usual sense of humour was absent to the extent that it had a real effect on me. At the time, I put it down to his being distracted by such a complex deal.

My father's memory is that he hired a car during his short stay in London. He didn't stay with Sally, as he would normally have done. Instead, he stayed at the Excelsior Hotel, next to Heathrow airport, and drove himself to and from the meeting. It's quite possible he hired a car and I drove it. I don't remember the car we were driving – we often hired cars – but I do know that I was driving.

When he came out of the meeting, I asked him how it had gone.

'Very well,' he said. That was all. I then drove him in silence to the Excelsior.

At the hotel, my father threw himself onto the bed and stared at the ceiling, trying to think what he could do. He decided he had no choice but to play for time. He started phoning everyone to tell them the great news that the agreement had been finalised with the purchasers, but it would be a month before any money would be received. Nothing would be achieved in that short amount of time, particularly as it was Christmas. According to his memoir, he called me first, though I don't remember the call, then everyone else in New York.

He later claimed that, at first, he had decided to tell me the truth, but to have done so would have been to invite me to join him in the deception. I'm glad he didn't, because if he had done, there would have been significant consequences for me in the months to come. Instead, he had to accept the congratulations of everyone involved in the full knowledge that none of what he had told them was true.

CHAPTER THIRTEEN

BREAKING DOWN

IN THE AUTUMN of 1973, my parents had dinner together at my mother's New York apartment. This was an almost nightly occurrence when he was in New York during the early 1970s. After dinner, he headed off to do his secret work, which, according to him, he often did at the Stanhope Hotel, where he then spent the night.

On this particular evening, he arrived at about 6.30pm. My mother was due to fly back to England the next morning to prepare Polraen for what she thought would be their permanent return as a couple to a life in England as a result of the Bronxville deal. On arrival, he kissed her on the cheek as usual – she only ever allowed him to kiss her on the cheek – and, rather than having their usual vibrant exchange about work or Beethoven or politics, he sat quietly on the sofa while she cooked. She noticed he appeared a little down, but let it go as, while male depression wasn't generally acknowledged in those days, she was keenly aware of his moods. They ate supper almost in silence, with their plates resting slightly awkwardly on their laps. Eventually, my mother spoke.

'What's the matter?' she said.

'Nothing. I'm just tired and I've got a steaming headache.'

'Have you taken anything for it?'

'No. I haven't had a chance,' he said.

'I'll get some aspirin.' She went to the kitchen to get two aspirin and a glass of water and carried them in to him. To her astonishment, she saw something she hadn't seen for at least 20 years. My father was sobbing over his food. Shocked and not knowing how to respond, she sat down next to him.

'Peter? Peter! What on earth is it?'

He fought back the tears. 'Don't worry, I'll be okay. It's just been a tough day.'

My mother was irritated at being kept out. 'No, I'm not letting it go at that. Please tell me.'

He looked at her a little desperately. 'All I want is to live here quietly with you.'

'You can.'

'No. No, I can't. Not yet.' He paused and pulled himself together. 'But I'm sure my masters will soon let me go.'

My mother took this to be a reference to his secret work. This was something she wasn't allowed to interfere in, so she did let it go. The next morning, my father arrived in a limousine to take her to the airport. They barely spoke on the way, but, 20 years later, she wrote: 'I squeezed his hand in the car which took us both to the airport to take me on my last visit to my home. He responded and I can still feel the warmth.' Even two decades later, despite everything that would happen, she was still clinging to any suggestion of his love for her.

The weeks she spent in Polraen were happy. Her 'odd' life, as she referred to it, would soon come to an end. Bronxville would be completed; my father would be able to spend more time at the home he loved; and they would be able to live together as a couple again. My father had promised to follow her there. When she arrived, there was a telegram waiting for her: 'Welcome to our world. All the world, P'

She spent the next few weeks decorating, buying new domestic appliances and organising the staff. Her hope was that my father would take up local politics. The plan was to keep Polraen and to have small homes in New York, Vienna and California. At the time, these dreams seemed realistic.

Over Christmas, while my father struggled with the Bronxville deal, he was constantly phoning my mother with excuses as to where he was and what he was doing, saying there were some difficulties with the deal. She returned to New York via Miami, where she briefly met my sister, who subsequently went on to Jamaica for my father on business.

When my mother arrived in New York, my father appeared distant. He explained he was having visa problems, so would have to return to the UK and to Polraen before Christmas. My mother did not know this, but these were my father's last desperate bids to save Bronxville and the Bahamas deal. His fateful stay at the airport hotel in London while his world collapsed around him was explained away as the visa issue and problems with plane schedules.

The day after the Grosvenor Estates meeting, my father drove to Polraen. My mother and sister were in New York and I was at my flat in Chelsea, so the large house was deserted. Polraen was the scene of the happiest moments of all our lives, so I understand why he went there to seek solace, despite it being potentially a lonely place, hidden away in the Cornish countryside. My father could be close to where he had been born, in familiar, comforting surroundings, filled with happy memories.

Many years later, he wrote a series of children's books about the adventures of Moon, a pixie-like alien who comes to Earth and accompanies my father, the narrator, on various adventures. At one point, they visit the home of the narrator, Camelot, which, of course, was Polraen. In his stories, he describes, through himself and animals, his memories of our life there – including me – and, most heart-breakingly, his departure. There is nothing that gives a clearer insight into everything he was at risk of losing – his compassion for animals, his love for his children, Cornwall, his constituency and his devastation at leaving Polraen.

And, when people ask me how I could love my father, I think how could I possibly *not* love a father with that kind of heart? Whatever his failings.

X

My father always spoke most highly of Fred Miller, Diane's father, largely to protect her. But, despite Fred lending my father large amounts of money, through apparent goodwill to my father and his daughter, Fred was no more an angel than most businessmen of the time.

Although the details are sketchy, some years before the Bronxville project, Miller made a number of business and tax paperwork errors which could have had serious legal consequences for Miller and his family.

By that time, my father, seemingly through his secret work, knew many people in high places who were very keen to retain his services for as long as possible. My father tended to write in code about this secret work, as he did in the document relating to this. He wrote that he went to see one of these people about Miller's problem, eventually talking to, as he put it, the 'Vice-Chairman'. The people he spoke to agreed to try to help. When the time came for Miller to give an account of himself the problem had miraculously been resolved. According to Diane, it was in return for this favour that my father was compelled to continue his secret work – whoever it may have been for, otherwise the problem would be raised again. Whoever resolved the problem would have been extremely influential. This was to have a significant impact further down the line.

While my father was at Polraen in late 1973, he saw a psychiatrist friend, Jim Pencheon, and spilled his financial difficulties to him. Pencheon suggested my father must have a friend who might be prepared to try to raise money on his behalf, enough to give him time to complete the Bronxville deal. My father was not a particularly sociable man, and had very few close friends. But there was one person he was close to, who owed him many favours – Jeremy Thorpe.

Pencheon pressed my father to talk to him. Evidently, he didn't realise Thorpe was a disaster in waiting. While his idea of seeking help was sound, his choice of suggested helper could not have been worse. My father resisted. There would soon be an election, and he thought Thorpe would be far too busy to deal with an additional problem. But, sensing my father's desperation, Pencheon pressed the issue.

'Jeremy owes you a great deal. If you're going to get anywhere, you must go to someone who owes you a favour,' he said.

He was right, but my father was still reluctant. Growing impatient, Pencheon said if my father wouldn't call Thorpe, he would. My father left and returned to Polraen where, about an hour after his return, the phone rang. It was Thorpe.

'Peter, I've just spoken to Jim Pencheon. Now listen. We're going to find a way out of this one. How soon can you get back to London?' My father tried to resist.

'It's wonderful of you, but–'

'Now don't give me any old crap! I said we're going to find a way out of this. Can I see you tomorrow night?'

'Well–'

Thorpe interrupted again. 'Good. Here at Orme Square. What time?'

'8pm?'

'Couldn't be better. Now, go to bed and forget about it. Remember, we've never been beaten yet. And we're not going to be beaten now.'

On the Monday morning, my father left Polraen for what he thought might be the last time.

In the evening, he joined Thorpe at his opulent London residence and poured out his story. He also put it to him that Thorpe might know someone who could move more quickly on Bronxville than Grosvenor Estates and Capital and Counties. Thorpe promised to work on it and arranged a meeting for the following evening with his business adviser, Robin Salinger. None of them doubted that Bronxville was eminently marketable, but Salinger saw no possibility of completing a deal in the time frame my father needed – within three weeks by now, and over Christmas and New Year. When Salinger left, my father suggested one person who might be able to help – Hayward. Thorpe agreed and asked about the status of the negotiations with Mobil for the Bahamas properties. My father was not expecting a report from them until the New Year, but told Thorpe, truthfully, that there had been no weakening of enthusiasm on the part of Mobil or, as far as he was aware, of the interest that had been expressed in political circles in Washington.

'If it goes ahead, how long will it take?' asked Thorpe.

'We might get to the contract stage in six months,' said my father. 'But, anyway, how would you feel about asking Jack to help me? He would respond much better to you – after all, I still owe him money.'

Thorpe considered it for a moment. 'I'm willing to try anything. But I don't want to go to Jack except as a last resort. I need his help with election funds.'

The next morning Thorpe phoned to say that another prospect he hoped might come through had shown no interest.

'But don't worry. We'll find a way.'

My father wasn't convinced. 'Jeremy, we've never fooled each other. I've got to face it, haven't I? This is an impossible nut to crack.'

Thorpe paused. 'It doesn't look hopeful,' he said.

'What about Jack?' my father asked.

There was a resigned tone to the whole conversation. Thorpe said if my father was certain of Mobil going through with the deal, he could ask Hayward for an advance of my father's share of the commission. But my father was in no position to speak on behalf of Mobil. Thorpe went on.

'Is there anyone who can independently vouch for Mobil's enthusiasm other than Mobil themselves? Hayward might ask.'

'The only other person I know would be Diane. Hayward has met her. She's a mortgage analyst with a major insurance company and knows a great deal about The Bahamas. She probably has the kind of expertise which would be acceptable to Hayward. But that's it,' said my father.

'Okay,' said Thorpe, 'Ask her to call me tomorrow evening. I think I have an idea of how to approach Jack. I'll tell you about it when we meet.' My father contacted Diane to ask her to call Thorpe the next evening.

Thorpe's unexpected enthusiasm buoyed my father, at least for the following day. In the evening, he went to Thorpe's to be with him when Diane called. Thorpe answered the door with a huge grin.

'Come on in! I've got it!'

He marched my father down the long corridor into the drawing room and closed the door. My father sat down. Thorpe perched himself on a nearby table.

'Now, listen. First, I don't want to know that it's Diane who's telephoning me.'

'But–'

'No buts. You'll understand later. Next, and this is very important, who knows about the commission on the Bahamas deal that was to be paid in advance?'

'You mean the expenses? I told you a couple of months ago, it was a misunderstanding.'

'Right,' said Thorpe, excitedly, '*You* know that. And *I* know that. The question is, does Jack know that?'

'I asked you to tell him,' said my father.

'Yes, but I didn't. Did *you* tell him? Think carefully.'

It required no thought from my father at all. He hadn't seen or spoken to Hayward for at least three months. With that, Thorpe jumped from the table, grabbed my father by the shoulders and shook him.

'Ah ha! Then we've got it! Don't you see? We've got it!'

My father was bemused.

Thorpe took a deep breath and calmed down. 'All we've got to do is to tell Jack the time has come to cough up! You've come to London to report to me. I've spoken to Washington and confirmed that the deal's on, but before they will go any further, we've got to provide the advance commissions!'

This was why, of course, he had asked not to know it was Diane who was about to call him. If everything went pear-shaped, he would be able to claim he was misled into believing Diane's call was from a Washington official. But I don't think this occurred to my father in that moment. Suddenly, he saw what Thorpe was getting at. There were no expenses, but he could use the money to settle his debts, and Hayward would believe it had gone to smooth the way for the sale of the Bahamas properties. His reaction was instantaneous.

'The whole idea is far too dangerous. It's impossible.'

Thorpe was not pleased. 'Why?' he asked.

My father took a moment to gather his thoughts. He knew Thorpe was putting himself at enormous risk to help him. He felt he couldn't tell him it was out of the question simply because it was fraud. Thorpe appeared to be a man whose conscience was untroubled by fraud and murder. My father began to wonder if there wasn't something in the suggestion. He started to look for reasons to justify it to himself, in the same sort of way that a heroin addict justifies shoplifting. It's not something they *want* to do; it's something they *have* to do simply to stay alive.

'Of course, I can repay Jack when I complete Bronxville,' he muttered to himself.

'Or you can take it out of your commission on The Bahamas, if it comes off!'

My father agreed, but said he did not require such a large amount to pay off his debts. 'Doesn't matter,' said Thorpe, 'You don't have to use it all.'

My father said he was not prepared to take more than $450,000. In his memoir, he described this as 'a sudden flash of morality', as if taking $450,000 made the fraud more acceptable than taking $700,000, but he accepted that such justifications were utterly bizarre in the context of the conversation.

'Make it $500,000,' said Thorpe, 'I need at least £10,000 to settle the Scottish matter.'

This was a reference to Norman Scott, which baffled my father, but he said nothing. At that moment there were more important considerations than Scott.

'You can tell Jack,' Thorpe continued, 'that you've managed to knock down the price a bit. That should please him!'

My father was frightened, and it was obvious to Thorpe that he had doubts.

'Peter, Jack's expecting to pay it,' Jeremy responded impatiently. 'And if he gets $80 million for The Bahamas, it's bloody well worth it. If you go under, I've no time to deal with The Bahamas and Jack's worse off. Anyway, you don't have another option.'

The phone rang. Diane was calling. He asked her just two questions. The first was how she rated the chances of Mobil going ahead with the Bahamas purchase, the second was to ask her what she knew about the town of Freeport, where most of the properties were situated. She responded that she thought the project was very marketable. To Diane, the questions were so banal they only added to her uneasiness about my father's situation.

It appears Thorpe pretended he was talking to a Washington official. But, while she and Thorpe talked, my father tried to come to terms with Thorpe's proposal. There would be no difficulty in selling Bronxville. Even if Grosvenor Estates and Capital and Counties dropped out, there would be other interested parties. He started to think of returning to New York and Diane with all his difficulties solved.

I could live – and live without the shadow of disaster hovering over me. No more waking up in the morning, sitting on the edge of the bed, smoking cigarette after cigarette until I could force myself to face another day.

Thorpe finished the call and turned to my father. 'Well?'

CHAPTER FOURTEEN

LAMBS TO THE SLAUGHTER

ON THE MORNING of 14 December 1973, my father met Thorpe in his office at the House of Commons. Both men were nervous, but Thorpe picked up the phone and demanded a line. There was a delay, which made him even more jumpy. Eventually he got through to Hayward's number in The Bahamas. He was out, but whoever answered the phone said they would find a number where he could be reached. As they waited, Thorpe mumbled.

'I've baited my trap – and I can't find my fox.'

But a few minutes later, he tracked down Hayward, who happened to be in London. Thorpe got down to business.

'Anyway, Jack, I have a marvellous surprise. Peter has unexpectedly arrived in London and he's with me now with news about the interest in your properties. Everything is ready for the principal's proposal to be transmitted to Washington. In other words, all the government guarantees that are required will be forthcoming.' There was a pause while Hayward spoke.

Thorpe continued. 'Yes, it is good news, isn't it? What's more, I talked to a Washington official myself yesterday evening and was given an assurance that the formalities will be completed without a hitch.'

This, of course, had been his conversation with Diane. 'Now, Jack,' Thorpe continued, 'there's something you must do. You'll recall we discussed an advance commission that would have to be paid.' Presumably, Hayward confirmed that he did remember, as Thorpe went on: 'It has to be paid at once. That's why Peter's come over. He must return to New York in a couple of days, but if you arrange for the money to be paid into his bank here, he'll have it transferred to New York. You'll be glad to know it's less than we expected. It's only $500,000. Would you like to talk to Peter?'

This took my father by surprise, but he took the phone.

'Hello, Jack.'

'Peter! Congratulations on the deal. I'm returning to The Bahamas tomorrow and I'll tell my partners. They're going to be very happy!'

'Thank you, Jack. It hasn't been easy. I'm just sorry it has to be such a large sum of money.'

Hayward was clearly puzzled. 'Well, we expected it, didn't we?'

My father responded quickly. 'Oh, yes… yes, absolutely.'

'Very well,' responded Hayward. 'Tell me, Peter, will the money be required in dollars or sterling?'

Another question my father was unprepared for, despite it being an obvious one.

'Oh, it doesn't really make any difference, but it would probably be easier for it to be paid in sterling.'

There was no logic in that response, but Hayward agreed. 'Very well,' he said, 'I'll speak to my lawyer and make arrangements at once.'

Thorpe threw back his head, ecstatic. They both stood up, Thorpe grabbed him by the shoulders and waltzed him around the room shouting, 'We've done it, we've done it, we've done it!'

The $500,000 my father and Thorpe were requesting in 1973 would be the equivalent of more than $5 million today. And the

$80 million Hayward and his partners were due to receive from the sale of their properties, would equate to more than $800 million. It would not be surprising if Hayward was blinded by his desire to push the deal through. But had he been? He was getting his lawyer involved. How did he intend to explain that the funds were needed for an advance on commission with nothing to show for it. It's hard to imagine any lawyer supporting such an idea.

That evening, as my father dined with Thorpe at Orme Square, Hayward called. He said all the arrangements had been made and wished my father a pleasant journey back to New York. A few minutes later, Hayward's lawyer called to confirm the amount and which bank the funds should be paid into. My father said subsequently that he was ashamed he was elated, and supper with Thorpe and his wife turned into a celebration. The next morning, Friday, he woke in his hotel to a call from Thorpe. Despite the fact it was pouring with rain outside, he could think of nothing else to say except, 'Oh, what a beautiful morning!'

When my father put the phone down, he ordered breakfast, but pushed it aside, uneaten. His elation had vanished. As he drove to his London office, his unease increased. He wouldn't be able to relax until the money was transferred. Perhaps it was a sudden sense of panic that Hayward might have rumbled them. My father's bank, Chase Manhattan, suggested the funds be deposited into a different London branch to the one previously suggested, to facilitate faster clearing. So, my father phoned Hayward's lawyer to pass on the details. All seemed fine, and he made another few calls. When he replaced the receiver following the last call, his secretary buzzed through on the internal intercom.

'Jack Hayward called while you were on the phone,' she said. 'He says there's been a hitch in the arrangements and if you call his lawyer again, he'll explain it to you.'

The room swam before my father's eyes. For a moment, he

thought he might faint. But he pulled himself together and called the lawyer who was out, so he called Thorpe, who was equally alarmed, and said he would also try. In the end, it was my father who got hold of the lawyer first. He was hesitant, but said the funds would have to come from the Channel Islands, which might take several days. This is something they would have known the previous day, but hadn't mentioned. My father asked if he should wait in London, but the lawyer suggested it would be best for him to return to New York.

'Well?' said Thorpe, when my father called him.

'Disaster.' My father repeated what the lawyer had said.

'I'm not worried about this one,' Thorpe replied. 'I know Jack keeps most of his money in the Channel Islands for tax reasons.' But he sounded far from elated, as he had been the day before. They agreed that my father would phone Hayward when he was back in The Bahamas, so my father returned to the Excelsior Hotel to wait the agonising few hours until he could be sure that Hayward's flight had arrived. Eventually, he had a call put through, and spoke to Hayward.

Hayward wasn't unfriendly, but he was noticeably cooler than before. He soon got to the crux of the matter.

'Peter,' Hayward began, 'it's difficult for me to do as Jeremy has proposed on my own. I need to discuss the matter with my partners. In particular, I have an associate in New York I must talk to first.'

This was a completely different reason from the one given by his lawyer a few hours earlier. Hayward continued, 'I think it would be a very good idea for you to see him, too. When are you getting back to New York?'

'I'm booked on the Pan Am flight on Christmas Eve – next Monday.'

'Oh, that's no good,' said Hayward, 'Can't you get back sooner?' He sounded eager to be able to trust my father and Thorpe. After all, in his mind there was an $80 million deal at stake. But there was a fuel shortage at the time and flight schedules were unreliable.

'I'll do my best, Jack,' my father said. But he didn't do anything. He was sure a meeting in New York with the associate would be fruitless, as he would not be able to put the proposition to him in the same way Thorpe had been able to do with Hayward. To a stranger, it would sound preposterous. His will to fight had evaporated. He called Thorpe to tell him, but, alarmed at the prospect of being found out, Thorpe persuaded him to do all he could.

'You've got to pull it off, Peter, or we're both in the shit – and in a big way! Christ!'

Next, my father called my mother and told her that he couldn't be back in New York for Christmas, so she should spend the holiday period with friends in California. When my father left the UK on Christmas Eve, he did not expect to return. Either he would manage to persuade Hayward's associate that the idea of Hayward advancing half a million dollars to pay bribes in Washington was a reasonable one; or he would have to take his own life. My father accepted the latter was the most likely option, not least because it would protect Thorpe, who would be able to tell Hayward the whole idea was my father's. On the flight to New York, he chain smoked, feeling sick to his stomach.

When he arrived, there was a message waiting for him, to meet the associate, whose identity remains unknown, at his apartment about an hour later. My father was jet-lagged, but he went, knowing there would not be another opportunity until after Christmas and New Year. He rehearsed his story over and over on the flight. The associate listened politely, though with evident scepticism. When my father finished speaking, the associate said that under no circumstances could he recommend to Hayward and his colleagues the payment be made. 'I left him with a feeling close to relief,' my father later wrote, 'I no longer wanted this solution. I returned to my office. Fifth Avenue with its brightly lit stores and last-minute Christmas shoppers seemed to belong to a remote world from which I had become detached.'

These kinds of feelings are common to those on the point of suicide. Unlike today, when help is more readily available, my father was suffering alone. As soon as he got back to his office, he called Thorpe who, true to form, became frantic. 'For goodness' sake,' Thorpe said, 'We *have* to make this work! Please don't give up!' He paused while he thought for a moment. 'Look, what we have to do is drive a wedge between Hayward and his associates.'

'I can't do that alone, Jeremy. You know that. My meeting today proves it.'

'In that case,' said Thorpe, 'call Jack and tell him that you and I will come to The Bahamas to see him this weekend.'

My father said he would consider it, and put the phone down. He then went to the apartment he shared with Diane, who had gone to her parents' home in Pennsylvania for Christmas. Now he was as alone as he had been at Polraen and, just as he had done there, he tried to view the situation objectively. He realised that in the 10 days since Thorpe came up with his plan, every decision Thorpe made had worsened my father's position. It was absurd to allow Thorpe to fly with him to The Bahamas for what would doubtless be an abortive meeting. 'As I paced up and down the tiny apartment,' he later wrote, 'I believed that now was the time to end my life.'

X

Over the years, one Christmas has tended to blend into another in my memory. Polraen at Christmas was a magical place, filled with lights, Christmas trees and the most wonderful presents. My mother, as so many others did at that time, started making the

Christmas cake at least a month before Christmas. It was a sure sign that Christmas was on its way and excitement would begin to build. The house lent itself to the traditional Christmas of popular imagination. When I think of Christmas at that time, I'm remembering every Christmas rolled into one – except for the Christmas of 1973.

For me there was the anticipation followed by a gradual realisation, as the day drew nearer, that Christmas wasn't going to happen. Despite my having absolutely no idea of what was going on elsewhere, I spent that Christmas feeling odd and lonely. For the first time in my life, Christmas was not a family occasion. Not by design, as I remember, but simply because everyone was in the wrong place, and there was no effort made for us all to meet at Polraen. My mother was in California with friends. My sister was with her husband, Tony, at their flat in Holland Park, in London, and I was left feeling very much alone. Polraen remained sadly deserted and dark that winter.

X

While my father spent his Christmas pacing around Diane's apartment, he reflected that his family was spread around the world but wanted to ensure we would all be together when we heard the news of his death. He was determined that his 'ultimate solution' was the only way out at this stage. He had arranged a few weeks previously for both my sister and me to be in New York at the beginning of January 1974, having decided it wouldn't be right to take his life over Christmas, not least because, for the rest of us, it would forever turn Christmas Eve into the anniversary of his death. The realisation that, at that moment, even death was denied to him, made him angry. There was no escape.

I can only imagine how he must have felt when he woke, alone, in that tiny New York apartment on Christmas morning. I wonder if he thought of Polraen, more than 3,000 miles away, deserted and quiet. Through all his great successes and terrible failures, it had come to this. Fortunately, Diane returned from her parents that evening, so he didn't have to spend Boxing Day alone as well.

He told her there was a major problem with Bronxville, but the Bahamas deal with Hayward was promising. He added that Thorpe had asked Hayward to give an advance on his commission, and he had agreed to do so, but he and Thorpe had to report to Hayward's partners. The two would meet in Miami on the Saturday and hop over to The Bahamas to meet with Hayward and his associates the following day.

Although she didn't say so at the time, Diane didn't entirely buy the story and insisted on going with him, following on a later flight. My father resisted, fearing that once she saw Thorpe and him together, she would realise matters were far more serious than he had let on. But she put her foot down.

'I have spent Christmas without you, and I'm not going to spend New Year's Eve alone,' she told him.

On Saturday, 29 December, my father arrived in Miami and booked into the Miami International Airport Hotel. His arrival in Miami boosted his optimism and, when he met Thorpe in the arrivals hall, Thorpe, too, seemed to be in an ebullient mood. In fact, it was a bizarre mood. After supper, instead of going to bed, Thorpe insisted on walking up and down the long airport concourse doing a series of impressions. His behaviour was so extraordinary that my father was becoming alarmed. As they walked, Thorpe kept muttering, 'We'll get the money out of those fucking millionaires! We'll show them we mean business. Wait till I've talked to them!'

He sounded like a man going out of his mind. Then he added, 'Did I tell you Jack phoned and wanted me to fly direct to Freeport? Well, I told him I had to go to Miami first. You'd arranged for someone to come here from Washington to give me a full briefing. That impressed him!'

My father was staggered. Lie was being piled upon lie. Eventually, it dawned on him that the real reason Thorpe was pacing up and down the concourse was that he was hoping to pick someone up. A young man caught his eye and, telling my father he would see him later, Thorpe followed the man through an exit door. My father waited in case he returned. Sure enough, after a few minutes, he reappeared. He seemed happy.

'He got in his car and drove off, but when he saw me, he put on his headlights.'

'I'm afraid that doesn't mean anything,' my father said. 'It's not the UK where we drive in town at night on our parking lights, in the States it's illegal to do so, even in towns.'

Thorpe refused to believe the explanation and remained happy that, at the ripe old age of 45, he was still capable of pulling younger men. The charade continued for another half an hour before he gave up and went to bed.

Diane arrived shortly before midnight, and she and my father also turned in for the night. The next morning Thorpe knocked on their door and burst in. He was carrying a bottle of whisky from which he was taking regular swigs. My father was growing more anxious by the minute, while Diane was baffled by Thorpe's extremely odd behaviour.

Hayward arranged for a private plane to pick them up. They hadn't told him Diane was with them, so she took a commercial flight. My father described travelling in light planes as something from which only a masochist could derive pleasure, and storm fronts were causing heavy turbulence. My father didn't suffer from travel sickness, but, as the small plane bumped and tossed toward Grand Bahama, Thorpe, with a stomach full of whisky, turned pale.

Hayward was waiting at the airport and explained that two of his colleagues were leaving to spend the weekend on the private island of another partner, Wallace Groves. They had come to the airport and were waiting in an anteroom, so the five of them could discuss the proposal. Thorpe and my father were alarmed by this. They insisted it was not right for such decisions to be made at an ad hoc meeting at the airport, and they wanted time alone with Hayward first. Hayward admitted they could be right, so it was arranged that Hayward, Thorpe and my father would fly to Groves's island the next day. I have no doubt whatsoever that Thorpe and my father had no idea at all what they were getting themselves into, or the kind of people they were dealing with.

Wallace Groves was connected to the Mob and involved in organised crime. One of his silent partners in The Bahamas was Meyer Lansky, the Mob's accountant, and a major mafia figure in his own right. Groves spent two years in prison for fraud earlier in his career, but this hadn't discouraged him. His involvement in the development of Freeport as a haven of casinos, tax avoidance, bribery and corruption, and paying the Mob at least a million dollars a year in return for its co-operation, is well documented.

Thorpe and my father were unaware of Groves's background and that he knew exactly who needed to be bribed in Washington for a deal to go through in The Bahamas. My father and Thorpe were lambs to the slaughter. With the meeting postponed until the following day, they checked in to the Freeport Holiday Inn. Diane arrived from Miami soon after them, but remained in the background, with Hayward and his partners unaware of her presence. That evening, Thorpe, my father, Hayward, his wife and one of his partners, Edward St George, dined without her. By now, my father was completely drained and felt unable to get through the evening, so he pleaded a severe migraine and left early. But when Thorpe returned to the hotel later, he insisted on pacing around in the same way he had done at Miami Airport, evidently on the lookout for a male companion. Eventually, he struck up a conversation with a couple of young men in the bar. My father returned to Diane in their hotel room. An hour or so later, they, and other hotel guests, could hear a noisy party in Thorpe's room. Many of the hotel guests were British and would have known exactly who Thorpe was. His lack of discretion was astounding.

Diane managed to fall asleep, but my father lay awake contemplating the level to which he and Thorpe had sunk. Yes, they were desperate, but that was not an excuse for anyone, least of all a former MP and the leader of a political party. Hayward had always shown them both nothing but kindness. If their plan succeeded, my father would be paying off his debts with money stolen from a friend.

'If we failed and Jack marked us down for what we really were,' he later wrote, 'then the Liberal Party – the ideal and inspiration for our youth – would lose its biggest financial backer, who was so badly needed. I got out of bed and swallowed two Mandrax. Soon I was in a world as delusory and dangerous as Jeremy's.'

That world was far more dangerous than he realised. It also seemed to have escaped Thorpe's attention that the leader of the Liberal Party being sued for fraud by Hayward would have brought down the whole party.

In the morning, Thorpe's hangover left him in no condition to be having meetings of any kind, let alone one as important and risk-filled as that with Hayward and his partners. My father ordered orange juice for him and hoped he would sober up. When Hayward arrived to take them to the airport, he explained Thorpe was not well and went back to his bedroom to try to rouse him. Eventually, Thorpe pulled himself together and joined the others in the hotel lobby. The short flight to Groves's island, however, was turbulent and he vomited throughout. When they landed, by sheer force of willpower, the politician in him took over. Thorpe got off the plane and enthusiastically shook Groves's hand, while surreptitiously dumping his sick-bag in a bin.

The semi-tropical island was beautiful, with immaculately trimmed lawns and banks of flowers. As Groves led them to the main house, Thorpe remarked on the peacocks strutting beside them.

'Yes,' said Groves, 'They're friendly birds and get to know you quickly.' He paused and looked Thorpe straight in the eye. 'They also make good eating.'

When the meeting began, it was Thorpe who put their case to Hayward and his associates, and he did a reasonable job. He strengthened their argument by describing the fictitious meeting he'd had in Miami two days before with the 'official' from Washington. Fortunately, no one asked for details, such as the official's name or what department he worked in. But their story was met with the same polite scepticism my father had faced in New York on Christmas Eve. Thorpe then tried something he had mentioned to my father, but which my father thought he wouldn't go through with.

Thorpe and my father were in a grand house on a private island in The Bahamas, surrounded by opulence – a living room furnished in leather and oak, being waited on by a butler and servants. Still, they had no idea of the kind of people they were dealing with.

Thorpe leaned back in his chair, put his arms behind his head and said, 'Well, gentlemen, it seems to come down to this. Have you got enough money, or haven't you?'

There was stunned silence. After a menacingly long pause, Groves looked directly at Thorpe, holding his gaze and said, flatly, 'Yes. We've got enough money.'

CHAPTER FIFTEEN

THE ESCAPE

IT WAS FORTUNATE the meeting with Hayward and his associates failed. Had my father and Thorpe succeeded, they were embezzling half a million dollars from an alleged mobster, who wouldn't have been over the moon when he eventually found out – and he would have found out.

Despite his misgivings about Thorpe's plan, its failure left my father in a worse position than before the two men concocted their hare-brained scheme.

Some of the events that followed are taken from private notes discovered in my father's archive and were created using pseudonyms.

That evening, he returned to Diane at the Holiday Inn and confessed everything, including that he lied about having completed the Bronxville deal and had attempted to swindle Hayward and his partners. She was deeply shocked to have been made complicit in such a scheme, but not surprised. She had suspected for quite a while something was wrong.

'It's no longer simply a matter of bankruptcy,' my father said, 'or even that I have lied to everyone that Bronxville is completed. I have to protect Jeremy and the Liberal Party. When Jack discovers the truth, and he will realise what happened when my finances collapse, if I'm not around, Jeremy can put the blame fairly and squarely on me.' He paused, almost crying. 'And that means there is only one thing for me to do.'

There was silence while Diane stroked his hand. My father said, 'Darling, I must. I just can't take any more.'

Diane didn't, initially at least, try to talk him out of suicide. She had spoken to my father's psychiatrist friend, Jim Pencheon, some time before and understood the futility of that approach. Pencheon and Diane decided that, despite my father's protestations to the contrary, he probably would be able to stand the ignominy of bankruptcy, hard though it would be. She gently talked him through it.

'Look,' she said, 'I'm not going to dismiss your wishes. That would be cruel, to force you to live against your will. But death is so final. I don't think you should consider it until every other option has been considered. Sure, if you take your life, you won't be aware of the ramifications, but others will. Not least me.'

My father sat silently. He had considered the effect of taking his life on those who loved him many times and, particularly on Christmas Eve, it had stopped him from going ahead with his 'ultimate solution'. But he could only take so much. 'I know you're beyond handling your affairs yourself now,' said Diane, 'but couldn't someone else take over?'

'How could anyone do that if I'm still around?' he said, 'Whoever it was would constantly be in touch with me to ask what to do next. That's not relieving the pressure – it would be exactly the opposite. I still wouldn't be able to sleep at night.'

There was silence again. Then he raised his head and added slowly, 'Unless I disappeared.' Then, with a little more enthusiasm, 'We could live in Florida or somewhere for six months until the fuss has died down.'

'How would Jack react?' asked Diane.

'That's a good point,' said my father, 'It could be even worse when Gerald Whitmarsh discovers Polraen no longer belongs to me. In fact, none of my creditors or friends are going to be happy when they realise they've been lied to.'

'True,' said Diane, 'Some of them are bound to try to find you.'

'Indeed,' said my father, 'If I'm going to disappear, I need to really disappear. It needs to be somewhere from where I can't be extradited. Probably South America.' He thought again for a moment, then said, 'And I can't take cash with me as anything I have belongs to my creditors, including money. If I take anything, I would be guilty of actual fraud.' He had clearly forgotten he was already guilty of actual fraud, having failed to tell Whitmarsh who Polraen belonged to.

At first, this was just fantasy talk, but Diane took it seriously. She saw it as a way of avoiding my father taking his life, particularly if disappearing meant she would be with him all the time. This was a very serious undertaking for Diane. She would be giving up her whole life – her apartment and a very lucrative career with fantastic prospects in New York – but she was prepared to do that to be with my father and help him through, even if it meant living as fugitives in South America. My father started to raise objections, but she cut him short.

'Do you think I'd care about anything if I lost you forever? One day you'll repay me. I've given you more than money. You owe it to me to give me the chance of a life together.'

Diane was, of course, unaware of Sally and that my father had never discussed divorce with my mother. But Diane's words seemed to lift him from despair towards faint hope. Although the meeting with Hayward and his associates resulted only in an incredulous response to Thorpe's final statement, there was one more meeting with Hayward to come – though what he and Thorpe felt it could achieve was anyone's guess. Diane begged him to cancel the meeting, thinking they would just be piling deceit upon deceit, but my father felt he had to – for Thorpe's sake. His rationalisation was that, if he could raise the money from Hayward, it would enable him at least to complete the Bronxville deal, then repay his debt to Hayward. If, from the very beginning, my father and Thorpe had put a genuine proposal to Hayward that he lend my father half a million dollars in return for a share in the Bronxville profits, he might have jumped at the opportunity. But their warped sense of reality led them to think that embezzlement was more likely to succeed.

My father's meeting with Hayward was without Thorpe and was unusually formal. My father felt he put the case much better than he had done before, but, as he talked, he could feel Hayward seeing through the lies, but also weighing carefully whether he should take the gamble.

Perhaps if, right at the beginning, Thorpe and my father had been firmer when they initially put the proposal to Hayward and said, 'If you're in, great. If you're not, let us know now so we can move on,' Hayward may have been prepared to gamble, given the risk of losing out on an $80 million deal. All their travelling around the world to see Hayward and his associates, trying to persuade them to pay them, gave off a distinct whiff of desperation. As soon as Groves came into the picture, with his nose for a con, they stood no chance.

Diane and Thorpe discussed the idea that my father should disappear. Thorpe was alarmingly quick to approve of the plan. It would, after all, allow him to tell Hayward the whole embezzlement plot was my father's and get himself off the hook. For Diane, it was simply a case of wanting any life with my father, rather than none.

It was agreed earlier that Thorpe would meet with my father and Hayward at Hayward's house. Thorpe was there first, and, when my father arrived, he had a thought.

'Would you two like to be alone?' my father asked. Before Hayward could answer, Thorpe jumped in.

'No, of course not.' They sat and chatted for a while about the attitude of Hayward's associates. Then, Thorpe tried a different tack.

'Jack, it's almost as though you don't trust us.'

Hayward pondered this for a moment. 'Alright. Now Peter can leave us.'

This was a shattering moment for my father, though, considering the plan, he may have deserved no better. He realised instantly that Hayward considered the scheme to be his and Thorpe duped into it. But this released my father from any responsibility for Thorpe and his actions.

Whether my father disappeared or took his own life, Thorpe would be off the hook and the Liberal Party's funding safe. He could leave a letter to Hayward accepting responsibility and another to Thorpe offering an apology – problem solved for Thorpe. He said goodbye to Hayward and walked back along the beach to his hotel and Diane. Not long afterwards, Thorpe returned. Incredibly, he had good news to proclaim.

'It's going to be alright. We shall get the money!'

My father was gobsmacked. 'Are you serious?'

'Absolutely!' declared Thorpe. 'All Jack wants is an assurance from the chairman, or someone high up at Mobil, and a similar assurance from Henry Kissinger.'

My father continued to be gobsmacked.

This was, of course, a preposterous suggestion. It would take months to get a commitment from Mobil, and Kissinger almost certainly wasn't even aware of the project. I think Hayward told Thorpe to test whether my father was a man of his word by insisting on confirmation from the very top people. Anything less would expose the fraud. My father was furious.

'Jeremy, you know full well that none of that is possible within the time frame I need the money! It's probably not possible at all!

Why are you coming in here and saying it's going to be alright when, quite patently, it isn't?'

Thorpe sat on the bed like a scolded child. The next day, he had a meeting with the Prime Minister of The Bahamas, Lynden Pindling, to ensure the Bahamian government would approve the sale of the properties, part of the plan to convince Hayward it was all genuine. He went ahead with the meeting and Diane and my father returned to Miami.

With Hayward and his associates apparently onto my father and Thorpe's scheme, and with creditors snapping at my father's heels for substantial sums of money, his 'ultimate solution', or, alternatively, his plan to disappear, needed to be put into effect extremely quickly.

The following evening, Thorpe returned from The Bahamas and joined Diane and my father for dinner at the airport hotel. Unsurprisingly, it was a subdued evening, without the usual jovial banter between the two. Instead, the conversation turned to the details of my father's imminent disappearance.

'Just to put your mind at rest,' my father said, 'I intend to take full responsibility for the Hayward scheme.'

'I appreciate that, Peter. You know I do,' said Thorpe. 'I must say, Beseli, I like the idea of your disappearing much better than suicide,' he said, jovially. My father was not amused, but he did manage to respond.

'I like it better than being eaten like a peacock by Wallace Groves!' he said, 'But there's one thing still bothering me. When Hayward receives my letter, he might feel he has a duty to prosecute me for attempted fraud.'

'I hope I can deal with that,' said Thorpe, slowly and thoughtfully. 'I can put it to him that it would not exactly be helpful to the Liberal Party if he and I had to go down to the Old Bailey to testify against you!'

'That's a fair point. But you'll have to be careful if you are going to prevent him suspecting that we colluded.'

My father thought for a moment. Up to that point, he and Thorpe had only been discussing my father lying low somewhere in America or another friendly country. But, after his earlier discussion with Diane, he thought the risks of doing so were too great.

'Perhaps it would be simpler for me to disappear to a country from where I can't be extradited,' he said.

Thorpe responded immediately. 'I think that would be right, Pedro. Anywhere in mind?' It was a very blasé statement in response to such a serious proposition.

'I presume it will have to be somewhere in South America.' My father looked down and pushed his food aside. Thorpe had echoed his and Diane's plan.

On 2 January, my father and Diane saw Thorpe off from Miami. It was a sad farewell for such close friends and, as he disappeared through the gate, my father wondered if he would ever see him again. He hoped he would. He and Diane returned to New York to plan the disappearance. The favour my father did for Diane's father over his errors was about to pay dividends.

By this time, it appears my father had been working for the US Government for many years. Although he never confirmed this, Diane believed he had been acting as an adviser to the National Security Council, hence his involvement with the Vietnam peace talks. As there were still some small matters to be cleared up with regard to Diane's father, he told his boss about his plan to disappear. His boss was referred to as Mr Robinson in my father's papers, almost certainly a pseudonym.

At first, Robinson received the news without comment, but, a short while later, he took my father aside and said he was very disturbed. They talked privately in a corridor, apparently in one of the government buildings.

'What's gone wrong?' asked Robinson. 'The whole idea of us taking care of Miller was so that he would do the same for you.'

'My problems have worsened and it's impossible for me to ask Miller for more money. Simply because I cannot provide any more security for further loans. I've reached the end,' my father replied.

'Let me reiterate,' said Robinson, 'We only helped Miller because of the help he had already given to you and on the assurance that any further help would be forthcoming when necessary. This was supposed to ensure that we continued to get something in return – namely your services! Now it appears that will not be the case and we've lost your services for nothing. Hardly a satisfactory outcome.'

My father remained calm. 'Honestly, I've received all the help I can reasonably expect. I can't and won't ask for more. I'm sorry. I've served you well and, to a great extent, to the detriment of my business.' Then, in a more desperate tone, 'Everyone wants too much from me. Surely I'm entitled, after all the work I've done for no reward, just to ask that you keep faith with Miller?'

There was a pause while Robinson thought.

'Okay. For the moment. But I'm keeping a close personal eye on this.' With that, he left.

Not long after New Year's Day, my sister, Paula, and I had returned to New York in the expectation of helping my father with the completion of the Bronxville deal, blissfully unaware of everything that had been taking place in The Bahamas. On Friday 4 January, I went into the office on 5th Avenue as normal. My father was at his desk. I said hello and made some tea.

'I have to go to Los Angeles on business on Wednesday,' he said, casually. 'After my meetings there, I have to go to San Francisco and it's possible you may not hear from me until next week.' This was how he usually explained he was undertaking secret work for a few days. I had no reason to doubt what he told me. 'If that's the case and you haven't heard from me by Sunday,' he continued, 'I need you and

Paula to come here on Sunday morning. In the safe, you'll find some documents relating to the Bronxville deal, which should complete automatically next Monday or Tuesday. You'll find the documents contain some straightforward instructions and some of them will need to be mailed that day for the completion to go through.'

Again, I had no reason to doubt what I was being told. I knew the combination to the safe, so I simply acknowledged the request, and we moved on to other things.

My father spent the weekend of 5 and 6 January alone in the office. He wrote letter after letter – to me, my sister, my mother, his creditors and others, explaining everything and that he had to disappear. He said later that they were two agonising days, which I'm sure they must have been. He had to admit to his family he had been lying for a long time and, of course, my dear mother would discover her husband had deserted her.

This proud man had to confess to his family, and everyone else that he was, to use his own words, a 'ruined, discredited failure'. In those letters, he included all the money he could lay his hands on – $700. Split into $200 for me, $200 for my sister and $300 for my mother. Then, on the Monday and Tuesday he pretended to all of us that everything was normal, in the full knowledge of what was about to descend on us. I can't remember the last time he walked out of the office – it wouldn't have registered at the time – but, whenever it was, he would have known he was not going to return. I guess he just said, 'Goodnight,' to me, as he always did.

On Wednesday 9 January, he flew to Los Angeles. He intended to stay at a cheap motel, but thought that might arouse suspicion as he was supposed to have just completed a major deal, so he booked into the Beverly Wilshire. The trip and the hotel were paid for by Diane, who had just received a major promotion at work but was giving it all up to be with my father.

When he arrived in Los Angeles, he received a call from Robinson, which surprised him. Because of the time difference, it would have been late at night in Robinson's home city of Washington.

'Well, this is disappointing,' said Robinson.

'I don't understand,' said my father.

'I'm very surprised you're going through with your plan. I assumed in the end Miller would help you and avoid this solution,' he continued. 'You seem to have forgotten that last summer Diane put a plan to her father which provided that any amount necessary should be provided by him to see Bronxville through, or had you forgotten that?'

'No, I hadn't forgotten.'

'Even to the extent, if necessary, of him selling all the assets he managed to retain as a result of the two of us helping him, so you could all set up a motel business in the Caribbean. What happened to that little plan?' Robinson was getting tetchy.

'Yes, it's true she put that plan to her father. But I made it absolutely clear to Miller it was not to be considered, let alone put into practice, as it would mean depriving him and his wife of their hard-earned security,' said my father.

Robinson could hardly contain his fury.

'I don't think I've ever heard anything so ridiculous. If it wasn't for you, he wouldn't *have* any 'hard-earned security'. He, and possibly his wife too, would be in prison! That's the kind of security they would be experiencing now!' he continued. 'And, anyway, buying a motel in the Caribbean is hardly giving up his security. The whole thing is absurd. No, you are not keeping up your end of the bargain and it looks as though we're going to lose your services. I'll have to reconsider Miller's position.'

My father became desperate. 'Look, please! When I'm away Miller will do all in his power to deal with my debts and creditors. With his help I should be able to return to real life, and you will once again have my services. If he's prosecuted, everyone loses.'

Robinson pondered this for a few moments.

'Okay, here's what we'll do. I'll continue to make sure Miller is taken care of under two conditions: one, that Miller genuinely does do everything in his power to protect you and, two, under no circumstances will you consider your "ultimate solution". If you do, all bets are off. I'll call again on Friday evening to see what's happening.'

With that, Robinson put the phone down.

The first condition was fine because my father knew that Miller would do all in his power to help. The second, however, was almost intolerable because, to be deprived of his 'ultimate solution' – and the insurance payout – meant he had no way of repaying Miller should neither the Bronxville nor the Bahamas deals go through – a fantasy he was still clinging to. He felt stripped of his cocoon of comfort which, in turn, was his protection against his conscience. In hindsight, it might well have been a good thing as it ensured he could no longer fall back on lies and deceit.

True to his word, Robinson called again on Friday 11 January, not long before Diane was due to arrive in Los Angeles.

'Has Miller arrived?' Robinson immediately asked.

My father was surprised. 'No, he's not due to.'

'I'm shocked,' said Robinson, 'I assumed that once Miller realised you were actually going to carry through your plan and disappear with his daughter he would do anything to prevent it. By going away you are breaking faith with me and my department and, if you continue, then Miller is also breaking faith by allowing you to do so. That being the case, my undertakings from last night no longer apply.'

At this, my father lost his temper.

'This is absurd! Diane's father can't go on bailing me out forever. Anyway, it will take at least $100,000 to dispose of the three most dangerous creditors, Chase Manhattan, National Westminster and Whitmarsh.'

'More rubbish,' said Robinson, scornfully, 'If they are paid even a small amount, it will be better for them than taking action against you and getting nothing. If Miller goes to see them with a chequebook in one hand and a pen in the other, he will dispose of them for about a tenth of what's owed. Anyway, $100,000 is peanuts to him.'

My father disagreed. 'Miller is the biggest creditor of all. I cannot ask him to go in still deeper, throwing good money after bad.'

'Let me remind you yet again. Miller won't have "any" money, good or bad, if we don't protect him'.

Nothing had been resolved, but the conversation had to end because my father was due at the airport to pick up Diane. When he met her, he told her the plan for her to stay at the Beverly Wilshire with him had to change as he was expecting phone calls from Robinson and had to be alone. Understandably, this irritated her, but she did as asked, despite the difficulty of finding a hotel which would accept the couple's two dachshunds, which she had brought with her.

Later that night, Robinson called again. He asked if Diane had brought a solution with her other than to disappear together.

'No,' replied my father, 'Nor did I expect her to. She accepted my refusal to allow her to ask her father for anything more and knew it would be useless to do so, if only because I would not accept anything more from him.'

There seems little doubt that Robinson was trying to ensure my father didn't take his own life, or disappear. But the conversation seemed to be going around in circles.

'Let me remind you, again,' said Robinson, 'Over a year ago, I received a call from Diane, and I confirmed to her our intervention with Miller's problems. Why on earth has she not overruled you?'

But, as before, the conversation went nowhere, while my father implored Robinson to honour his commitments made the night before. My father also asked him to reconsider his second condition of the night before, namely that my father wouldn't be able to use his 'ultimate solution'.

'There is absolutely no chance of me reconsidering that,' Robinson said, angrily, 'If you take your own life, we will make sure it does not benefit Miller in the slightest. In fact, quite the contrary – everything will be reopened.' Whether it would have been or not will never be known, but it was a good way of trying to ensure that my father didn't take his own life.

'Very well,' said my father, 'If you will renew your pledge to take care of Miller, I will commit to not resorting to the ultimate solution.'

Then Robinson's attitude changed.

'Well, yes. It's quite possible, although not certain, that the outstanding issue with Miller could be dropped entirely. I can't promise this, but I am able to say at worst it will be only a small amount.'

With this assurance, my father felt able to send a memorandum to Miller saying that it appeared he would be safe once my father had disappeared. He then met Diane for their last dinner in the US. When he returned to his room, Robinson was soon back on the phone yet again.

'Any further news? Is the plan still in effect?'

'No and yes,' responded my father, curtly.

'Will Miller be able to deal with the three most dangerous creditors?'

'I can't be sure, but Whitmarsh is the biggest problem because of the second charge on Polraen.' With a shock, he realised his error. He remembered that he hadn't told Robinson of the fraudulent second charge he had given to Whitmarsh in return for a loan. Robinson questioned him on every aspect of what had happened and was shocked and angry.

'Of all the things you have done, this has to be the most irresponsible,' he said. My father couldn't deny it.

Robinson continued. 'It's quite simple. If necessary, Miller must abandon his interest in the house. That will settle it.' He then went on to outline in some detail all the potential errors Miller had made and the potential consequences.

'I must add a third condition,' he said, 'to the ones I gave you last night. Namely, our co-operation depends on Miller doing absolutely nothing to protect his own position that would in turn endanger yours.' With that, the conversation ended.

My father was dumbstruck.

On Saturday 12 January, Diane and my father checked out of their separate hotels and headed together for Mexico.

CHAPTER SIXTEEN

THE BLACK-LETTER DAY

SUNDAY, 13 JANUARY 1974, is a date indelibly imprinted on my memory. It marked not so much a turning point as a moment when one life abruptly ended, and a new one began. I was just 21.

After another late Saturday night at Fridays bar, I set my alarm for 10am in case I hadn't heard from my father, as instructed. There was nothing from him, so, despite not being in the best shape, I called my sister, who agreed we should meet at the office at 11am. I left my apartment that morning without so much as a backward glance, as always. The next time I saw it, my life had changed beyond all recognition.

It was a typical January morning in New York – bitterly cold with the wind funnelled down the avenues of high-rise buildings. Often, I would take a cab or a bus to the office, but, for some reason, on this occasion, I decided to wrap up warm and walk the seven or eight blocks. As I walked, I became increasingly uneasy. Why was I doing this on a Sunday morning? What was so important in the documents that they had to be picked up today for delivery on Monday? Why couldn't they wait until Monday morning? And why hadn't he simply given me the documents the previous week for me to deal with as and when appropriate. Why were they in the safe and why did I have to be with my sister to collect them? None of this had crossed my mind before, but, on the cold walk to the office, I couldn't make sense of any of it. Paula was waiting for me at the building. I think she may have started to worry as well.

'I wonder what this is about,' she said.

'Well, we'll soon find out,' I replied.

We took the small elevator to the seventh floor, walked down the old building's narrow corridor to the office at the end and unlocked the door. It was a small office, painted pale blue, with just three rooms. The entry door led into a small reception room, with the door to my father's office off it. In his office, the safe was beneath one of the windows, with a lovely view over 5th Avenue. It was a place where I would often sit and 'people watch'. The safe was a combined combination and key lock, which took a while to open. I was becoming apprehensive. Finally, I swung the door open. Inside, there was a large envelope on which was written: 'Take this to your mother's apartment and open it there.' Why on earth take the Bronxville documents to Mum's? Now I was becoming really worried, but we still had no idea of what the envelope contained.

My sister and I walked to my mother's apartment on the corner of 57th Street and 1st Avenue. We didn't say much. We were confused and worried, but we had no idea at all what we should be worried about. The next day the Bronxville deal would be completed, and our family would be significantly wealthier. We arrived at the entrance to the apartment block and pressed the buzzer on the intercom.

'Mum, it's us,' I said, 'I've some documents Dad left at the office for us, and he wants us to read them with you.' She appeared only slightly surprised.

'Oh. Okay. You'd better come up then.' She released the lock, and we made our way to her apartment, where she was waiting in the doorway.

'This is a surprise,' she said. 'What's happened?'

I explained how Dad had left instructions for Paula and me to collect the Bronxville documents from the safe that morning if we hadn't heard from him. 'The envelope said to open it with you.'

My mother remained perfectly chirpy. 'Okay. That's what we'd better do then.'

Curious and anxious, we stood in her living room and opened the envelope. It contained three sealed letters, one to each of us. I passed them out, placed the large envelope on the coffee table and opened mine at the same time as my mother and sister opened theirs. In that moment, our lives fell apart. This is some of what I read:

> *My very, very dear Son,*
>
> *I think you have suspected the truth for a long time and the only reason I have not told you is because I wanted to protect you as much as I could. As things have turned out your ignorance of the true state of things will ensure that no one can accuse you of having done anything wrong.*

Suspected the truth? What truth? My ignorance of what state of things? The awful reality didn't arrive as a sudden lightning bolt; it dawned gradually as I continued to read:

> *Yes, Bronxville is off. Not for the reasons I gave you but because the original deal fell through many months ago... But of course I kept lying to people about the true position – including you. I had little alternative. I owe National Westminster, Chase, Fred Miller (who has been wonderful), Gerald Whitmarsh and others a vast sum of money and only Bronxville or the Grand Bahama deal could have saved me. When it*

was clear on December 14th that Bronxville would take weeks or months to complete, I was pretty desperate. So, I enlisted Thorpe's help to try and get the Bahama deal through quickly and to get an advance on my commission. It almost came off and then complications arose, and I was in just as great a mess as ever.

At this point, I thought I was reading a suicide note. As they read their letters, my mother and sister started crying.

Now this is what I have done. I had two or three choices open to me ... the third choice is the one I have taken and it is to disappear to South America to a country where I cannot be extradited.

I had entered a surreal world. This kind of thing didn't happen to people like us. This was the stuff of Hollywood and gangster movies; it didn't happen to real people.

I hope that when everyone realises this, they will all work together to help the deals go through and for the mess to straighten itself out so that I can come home again either to America or to Britain.

I have written to Thorpe, and I know he will do all in his power to help me. Apart from his real affection for me he will seek to avoid bad publicity for the Liberal Party... I have no money and no assets worth speaking of, and nothing 'hidden away'. (I wish I had, it would go to your mother.) I am enclosing an envelope with this letter with a little money in it to help you when you get to England. I am so sorry it is so little and you are of course entitled to your wages which I cannot pay you. But I have to give Paula a little also and the rest to Mummy.

Attached was $200. My entire worth. He went on to explain what he thought we should do to save the deals and keep the businesses going. It was readily apparent that most of it was the fantasy of a desperate man:

> *The great thing for you to remember Paul is that you have done nothing wrong yourself. All the fault is with me and you have been deceived by me as much as anyone else. You can show this letter to anyone you like… If you are ashamed of me and even hate me Paul it is no more than I deserve but I can only say that while pride, ambition and selfishness have been my worst faults I have tried as best I could to protect you, Mummy and Paula and I have loved you all so much and wanted so badly to pull off one of these deals so that none of you would be hurt. Try to remember something good about me – though off the top of my head, old son, I can't suggest what.*
>
> *Try to learn something from my errors and from the wrongs I have done to so many good people. Remember how I got into this mess – chiefly by going into politics with no money behind me and by getting involved with the damned Plastic Carton project at a time when I was too busy with politics. It is like quicksand you know, you go deeper and deeper and deeper. Whatever you do in the future, Paul, for goodness' sake keep out of debt. It does not matter how humble the job is that you have to do or how much you have to go without. In the end the only real peace of mind is knowing you can face the world without fear. That is something I have not been able to do since 1963 and it was no one's fault but my own. Even if we say Plastic Carton brought about my real downfall, which it did, that does not alter the fact that I was in the House when I could not afford to be and therefore got involved in something*

which did not get my attention otherwise I would have seen all the weaknesses.

Paul, I love you more than I can tell you. I am proud of the granite of which you are made. You are my most wonderful, beloved son. If there is a God anywhere one day I shall see you again.

God bless and keep you safe.

Daddy xxxx

I sat down on the sofa, stunned by what I had just read. My mother and sister were sobbing, both convinced he had either committed suicide or that he was sleeping under a park bench somewhere, thinking he couldn't bear to tell us his true intentions, but I found I couldn't cry. It was just so bizarre and unbelievable I don't think I quite believed it was true. It must be some kind of ruse, I thought, to put people off the track. We were broke and my father had run off to South America to escape the law? No! Surely not!

But as we talked it through and the reality sank in, we had to gather ourselves. The question for all of us was what on earth did we do now? We had just hours to think before Monday morning when the business world and the press would wake up to the reality of what my father had done. We needed to act. My father had added the following note to me on a separate sheet of paper:

Paul dear, because Mummy will want to see the enclosed there are one or two things I did not say. First, Diane's apartment could be available to you if you want it over here. Her father is of course Fred Miller and his telephone number is ... Get in touch with him I beg you. His address Paula has.

If I hadn't been in such a state of distress, this would have infuriated me. I had some knowledge of the existence of Diane, but I had no idea he had disappeared with her. Even then, that thought didn't cross my mind. I imagined him sitting in a one-room shed in somewhere like Bolivia, totally destitute and alone – or dead. And, in his last letter to me, he was asking me to keep secrets from my mother. But I did. She thought that, although he had disappeared for now, there was a possibility he might return – a thought that kept her going until his death. Who was I to tell her there had been someone else?

I ignored his suggestion with regard to the apartment. What on earth did he think I was going to live on if I stayed in the USA? At least in England I had a right to unemployment benefit and, apart from the $200 he had left me, the one other item I had in my possession was an air ticket home.

My mother decided she would talk to her boss at the United Nations and see if she could get a paid job there. She wanted to stay in New York, where she felt she had a future. Whatever my problems were, my mother's were tenfold. On a quiet Sunday morning, out of the blue, she lost her husband and her entire life was turned upside down in the space of a few minutes. She was in her late 40s and had not done paid work since before meeting my father. Now, she had to pick herself up, quickly, and consider how she was going to survive. How she managed to, while still loving my father and missing him for the rest of her life, is a testament to her incredible strength.

We decided that my sister should also stay in New York, for a while at least, to help Miller clear up business matters in the USA. She stayed at Diane's apartment, as my father suggested. It was also decided I should use my ticket and return to the UK immediately as there were many matters that needed to be cleared up there, not least breaking the news to people, some of whom would be devastated.

When we experience disaster in our lives, there's that dreadful moment of waking the following day, then, after a few seconds, the reality of what has happened dawns. Your heart sinks and you become nauseated by adrenaline. This was very much how it was for me.

While the sudden loss of my father, to what exactly I didn't know, was distressing and preoccupied me, I had to focus on getting back to England – and soon. Fortunately, I had the pre-paid open ticket from JFK to Heathrow, but there were more pressing issues.

The first problem was how to get out of the apartment hotel I lived in. I paid a monthly rent, which was where the problem lay.

A few weeks previously, I'd had an argument with the management about cockroaches. I reported seeing one in my room and asked them to lay down powder. They hadn't done so, and we'd had a row, after which I withheld my rent until they did something about it.

I was in arrears and now had no money. I hadn't put my rent money aside, partly because Bronxville was about to make me rich. If the hotel management found out I was on the move, they might well refuse to let me leave and call the police.

My rent was paid in advance, so I owed two months' rent, far more than the $200 I then had. I felt my only option was to do a runner, but making my way nonchalantly through reception loaded with all my worldly possessions was not an option. I would have to pack just a small suitcase of essentials, leaving the rest behind – and leave via the fire escape.

I phoned BOAC – now British Airways – to book a flight. They had one seat available for the overnight flight that evening. I took it.

Previously, I had simply requested a limousine to get to the airport. Now, I didn't even have enough money to take a cab, so it would have to be a bus. But I didn't know where to take the bus from...

By about lunchtime, I had my single suitcase packed, but I wasn't going to leave my guitar behind. Somehow, I had to get these down the fire escape without anyone noticing.

I opened the door, checked the corridor was clear, picked up my meagre belongings and slipped out quietly. I made my way swiftly down the corridor towards the fire exit. Then it dawned on me – fire escapes in New York are on the outside of the building. How was I going to get away with it? I didn't stand a chance.

I thought I should try a lower floor at least, so I got the lift down to the first floor. At the end of the corridor was an exit sign. I scuttled along, opened the door and found a staircase.

I made my way down the stairs as quickly as I could. Finding myself next to the kitchen, I looked for a way out and found a back door leading out to the bins. I slipped out into the back alley and ran to the street. I stopped, collected myself, then walked casually away from the hotel towards the United Nations building.

As I walked, the implications of how my existence had changed overwhelmed me. In less than 24 hours, my life was transformed from one of careless luxury to that of a furtive runaway. I had already become a criminal, ducking out of paying the rent I owed. When I got back to England, I would have to break the news of my father's disappearance to people who would not take it well. And within a day, I would be homeless. Where the hell was Dad?!

Finally on the bus, I sat, staring into space. I looked at the expressionless faces of my fellow passengers and wondered if their reasons for going to the airport were anything like mine. Through the window, the world carried on as if nothing had happened. I worried it might be the last time I saw the city I had come to love. On Saturday night, I partied into the small hours at Fridays, spending freely. Now, I felt like a hobo. How could someone's life change so much in such a short space of time?

When I checked in, there was a single seat left, at the very back of the plane. My seat couldn't recline and, even worse, I was in the middle, unable to stretch my legs. Throughout an overnight flight, I had to sit bolt upright, through heavy turbulence. I spent seven hours staring into dark space, largely how I saw the rest of my life.

I got no sleep at all, arriving in London exhausted. I was simply too tired to take a bus into central London, so I changed the remainder of the $200 and spent some of it on a taxi to the office in Pall Mall. I knew Maureen, my father's secretary, would be waiting there. My first task was to tell her she had no job, and no prospect of being paid any money she might be owed.

When the taxi dropped me off, Maureen was there, waiting for me.

'What do you mean "disappeared"?' she said. The shock on her face was clear to see. She sat down on the chair opposite my desk and faltered for a moment.

'He's gone away,' I said.

'Gone away? Gone away where?'

'I don't know. That's what I mean by disappeared. He left my mother, my sister and me a note on Sunday morning to say the business is broke and he's, well, run away, basically. To be honest, I don't even know if he's alive. Maureen, I have to tell you there's no money. I'm afraid you have no job and there's nothing to pay you with to date.'

I waited for an angry outburst, but it didn't come. Maureen was completely level-headed, which was a relief. Her first thought was for me.

'What are you going to do?' she said.

'I have absolutely no idea. At the moment what I desperately need is sleep and a way to get through the next few days.'

'I'll have to look into what I can do about money,' she said, 'but if there's anything at all I can do to help, you will tell me?'

'Thank you. Of course I will. I'm so sorry.'

'I'll make you a cup of tea and then I'd better go,' she said.

She organised herself, got her bags together, left me a cup of tea and walked out of the door.

'I'll see you soon then,' she said. It would be 40 years before I did.

CHAPTER SEVENTEEN

A SICK, SICK MAN

AFTER LEAVING THEIR separate hotels, on Saturday, 12 January 1974, my father, Diane and their dogs set off down Interstate 5 in a small, rented car to San Diego and the Mexican border. They passed through customs and left the country of Diane's birth, and my father's dreams, at 3pm, driving off into what they hoped would be oblivion.

The contrast between the clean, modern city of San Diego and the squalor of Tijuana was a stark reminder of what they were doing, and it overwhelmed them. They made their way down the coast towards Ensenada, the next town of any size, which was a considerable improvement. They found a run-down motel with some kind of kitchen facility for $9 a night and settled there.

My father's total net worth was $69, in cash. He expected to feel some sense of relief, but, of course, he didn't. He had swapped worrying about debts and the likelihood of going to prison for worrying about those he had left behind, which exacerbated his depression.

The following afternoon, Sunday 13 January, they went to the beach. While Diane played with the dogs, my father looked at his watch and realised we would have opened the envelopes back in New York. There was no turning back now. He later recalled his feelings.

Paula had small, exquisitely beautiful hands, and suddenly I thought of those little fingers tearing open the envelope and finding the letters, including the ones to her and Paul. Both my children were young adults. Paula was almost 25 and had been married for three years. Paul was a few months short of 22, but to me they were still only children. I sensed the appalling shock they must have received and thought of the overwhelming responsibility I had thrust upon them.

The next passage he wrote was curious:

My thoughts turned to Diane's father, Fred. I had asked him to come to my office on Monday January 14th for what he expected would be no more than a routine business meeting with me. Instead, he would be instantly confronted with the problem of whether to accept the power of attorney I had left him; added to that would be the realisation that the money he had lent me was in jeopardy – or totally lost. So was his expectation of future employment, which had been the basis of his loans.

What is noticeably missing is any mention of Miller being shocked that his daughter, Diane, had given up her whole life, including seeing her parents, to run off to South America with this man who might have defrauded her family. Surely that would have hit him harder than any financial loss? Yet, my father didn't mention that at all.

These words taken from my father's memoir are at odds with other documents I found in his papers. I believe Miller knew exactly what was going on, that his daughter's disappearance came as no surprise to him and his feigned 'shock' was to protect him from any perception that he was involved in my father's escape. The other

documents suggest Miller's loans to my father were not related to his potential future employment, which he hardly needed, but to return the favour of my father's help in getting him off the hook.

On the beach back in Mexico, Diane returned from playing with the dogs and sat down next to my father, putting a comforting hand on his knee. He looked at her.

'I can't go through with it. I must just take what's coming,' he said.

Diane paused for a second. 'You know I'll stand by you whatever you decide, but aren't you being a little impetuous? I think your original assessment was right and a cooling off period is vital before you confront your creditors.'

'But their anger might be exasperated by the belief I have been cowardly by disappearing.' He held his head in his hands. 'I just don't know what to do.'

Diane was more practical. 'Look. Leave things for just a few days. Apart from anything else, you must rest. Look at you, you're in no state to be making decisions.' She paused again. 'Tomorrow, I'll drive back to San Diego and phone Paula. I can tell her I know you're alive and safe.'

My father thought for a few moments. 'Maybe I can keep in touch with New York through you.'

They walked back to their motel, ate supper and had an early night.

During the night, my father woke, feeling something enormously heavy pressing on his chest. He nudged Diane awake.

'I can't breathe,' he said.

Although it was a warm night, he was cold, yet sweating. He sunk back into sleep, but the pain from the crushing weight on his chest continued. He later remembered little of what followed.

Diane, of course, called the emergency services. The doctor told her it was a coronary occlusion, and he should be transferred to hospital immediately. But he steadfastly refused to be moved in the belief that, if he was going to die, he wanted to meet death in that tiny cabin with Diane, not in a chaotic Mexican hospital. Diane was far more frightened than him, but did not feel she could force him to do anything, particularly when the doctor agreed that stress could be fatal. He was allowed to sleep, but Diane could not be sure he would wake in the morning, so she sat up all night with him.

The next morning, he did wake up, eventually. He felt weak, but the pain was gone, and his breathing appeared normal. He was desperate to get back to California. He was convinced he was near the end and, if he was going to die, he wanted it to be in the country he loved, and regarded as his home. So, on Monday 14 January, Diane packed the car and drove him back across the border to San Diego, where she tried, again, to persuade him to go to hospital. He refused, insisting instead that she call Paula in New York as soon as possible and report back. Diane made the call.

Diane might have been a little more optimistic than was warranted, but she told my father that, although Paula had not recovered from the shock, she and I had quickly taken control and our chief concern was to know that he was safe. She was right – it was – but at that point we hadn't taken control of anything. My sister confirmed Miller came into the office that day, expecting a meeting with my father, but instead we had shown him the letters. That was only partly true, as at that stage I was already making a beeline for the airport and never saw Miller. It was my sister who gave him the letter.

My father hadn't told Diane his biggest worry was that if Miller failed to placate the creditors and my father ended up unable to return, not only would he be banished forever, but Miller would most likely have problems with his previous errors again.

My sister was working with Miller to try to placate my father's creditors, not knowing that Miller had been given a charge on our family home, Polraen. At the time, both my sister and I believed

Miller was as shocked as we were at my father's disappearance. While my sister heard from Diane quite soon, it was many months before I heard the truth, mainly to protect me from having to lie to creditors about his whereabouts – I genuinely didn't know where he was. Had I lied, prison might have been my reward.

In May and June of that year, a full five to six months after my father disappeared, I received letters from Miller seeking to enlist my help in reaching settlements with my father's creditors and claiming to be the largest creditor, owed over $350,000. There was no mention of his charge on Polraen, so it appears that funds from the sale of the property went to Whitmarsh, as they should have done. I now realise the letters in my father's papers written to me by Miller were, in fact, from my father, who was using Miller as a front. The writing has all his hallmarks and goes into the kind of detail only he would have known. Even more disturbing is that throughout his descriptions of how to deal with the creditors, and their lawyers, my name is put forward as someone who had knowledge of some aspects of the business, when, in reality, I knew nothing.

During their escape to Mexico, my father told Diane nothing of the complications concerning her father. But the pressure of not knowing how Robinson was reacting to the whole debacle became too much for him. After crossing the border back into San Diego and calling my sister, they drove up the coast a little way in the direction of Los Angeles and stopped off for a day or two in the small coastal town of Oceanside. He decided he had to call Robinson. This worried Diane as she thought there was going to be no further contact between the two men. Even worse, she feared he was sinking back into his web of lies again. He always called Robinson in secret, so they arranged for my father to use a phone box, while she went to get some groceries. But Diane doubled back and hid behind the phone box, trying to eavesdrop my father's conversation. My father's question was simple.

'Does the agreement over Miller hold good?' he asked.

'I can assure you it does,' said Robinson.

'So, I understood correctly when you said last week that Miller's affairs would be cleared up completely within six months?'

'That's correct,' said Robinson, 'but it's worth remembering that, if we lost your services completely, we could re-open on the basis of the two years that were not dealt with originally – so don't go getting any ideas about some "ultimate solution".'

'But after that,' said my father, 'he could move on the matter of the house without danger to himself? I mean, if he moves to realise his charge on the house immediately, and as a result, Whitmarsh charges me with fraud in my absence, in your eyes, Miller won't have settled my issues. If that's the case I won't be able to come back, and Miller might have problems again. But if he comes to an agreement with Whitmarsh without declaring his charge, and Whitmarsh settles, then after six months he's also clear with you?'

'Yes, I think that's right,' said Robinson, 'I think after six months have passed, you would be in little danger anyway from your creditors, so it is a matter for Miller to play for time.'

My father stepped out of the phone box – and straight into Diane.

'I've been listening,' she said.

My father was shocked. 'And?'

'I heard enough to know it was about my father. I have a right to know everything and I'm not putting up with any more damn lies!'

On the drive back, he told her the whole story of how the State Department was using the threat against her father to ensure he would continue to fund and support my father. My father was worried that, because he had been spreading a web of lies about his business interests over a number of months, Miller might simply not believe him, refuse to help and put himself in danger as a result.

'I agree,' said Diane, 'Your credibility is so damaged, the facts might be dismissed. But I overheard your conversation, so I can confirm at least part of them. But, Peter, that's not our responsibility. You must put the matter to my father and don't leave anything out. He can then make his own assessment. If he decides to ignore the dangers that will be his decision taken in the light of knowledge. We will have done our duty to him.'

They drove the rest of the way back to their room in Oceanside in silence, but, over the next few days, they talked of nothing else. It was possible that Miller might quite innocently say or do something that would jeopardise himself. They also had to consider Diane's mother and how my father's inaction might impact her. If Miller was to decide to take every action open to him to eradicate entirely the danger from Robinson, then my father needed to explain to him exactly what needed to be done. And so, my father sent Miller a memorandum explaining everything, including the ongoing risk to him..

X

In London, having told Maureen she no longer had a job and that there was no money to pay her what she was owed, I turned to trying to sort out my own life. Shortly after Maureen left, I locked the office, picked up the Buick from the underground car park at the Ritz Hotel, who I could no longer pay, and returned to my apartment in Chelsea. Fortunately, my rent was paid until the end of the month, so I didn't need to move out that same day. But I did need to let my landlady know I wouldn't be able to stay on the following month, thereby breaking the terms of the lease. It was a call I didn't want to make, but I did.

'Hello?' said my landlady.

'Oh, hello. This is Paul Bessell, your tenant in Flat 6 at 32 Draycott Place.'

'Hello, Paul. What can I do for you?'

'I'm afraid I have some bad news.'

'Oh?' Her tone changed slightly.

'Yes. I've just returned from New York where I received the terrible news that my father has disappeared.' I had thought she might show some sympathy, but she didn't.

'Oh,' she said. I wasn't quite sure how to continue.

'Well, the point is, as well as not knowing whether he is dead or alive, I don't have enough money to pay next month's rent, so I shall–'

'What? You're legally obliged to! You have to give me at least two months' notice!' My landlady was shouting down the phone. I was exhausted, both from my journey and the stress of my predicament. I could hardly believe what I was hearing from this very wealthy woman.

'Yes,' I said, 'I understand what's required under the lease. But the plain fact is that I'm now destitute and likely to end up homeless. I simply don't have the money to pay you for next month. But you have two weeks in which to find a new tenant.' Perhaps I wasn't being sufficiently tactful, but I was exhausted, and at my wits' end.

'How dare you!' she shouted, 'Well, let me tell you what's going to happen. I will take the next month's rent out of your deposit and, in lieu of your not being willing to pay the rent for the following month after that, you can get out by the end of this month, and I will sue you for losses.'

'You don't seem to understand,' I replied, as calmly as I could. 'There is nothing to sue me for. I have no money.'

She slammed the phone down. I made a cup of tea and sat down to think what to do. Maria, my girlfriend, was out with friends. She came home later, offering very small comfort. I don't think even she was able to grasp what had happened to me.

I still hadn't rested since fleeing New York. I was so exhausted that I managed to sleep well that night. The next morning, I went to the office with a remarkably misjudged sense of optimism. Maybe, I thought, I could pull something off to keep it open, at least for a while? My hopes were quickly dashed. As soon as I sat at my desk, the phone rang. It was Leonard Ross, my father's solicitor. He was owed next to nothing in fees, but was told by my father that, once the Bronxville deal was completed, he would be appointed the full-time legal adviser to the project.

'Paul, it's Leonard.'

'Oh, hello, Leonard, I–'

'I've received a letter from your father.'

'Yes, I–'

'Get over to this office immediately, do you understand?' he said, and hung up.

I really don't know why I did as he asked. Maybe it was because, at that point, I felt sorry for people affected by my father's disappearance. Now, my response would be to tell him to go to hell. But then, I was little more than a kid, who suddenly had all the responsibility of the world on his shoulders.

I drove for 15 minutes to Ross's office in Dorset Square, where I was greeted by his secretary. Appearing embarrassed, she went into Ross's office to announce my arrival, then came back and sheepishly told me I could go in. Ross was standing behind his desk. I went to shake his hand, but he ignored my gesture and told me to sit down. Then, he came and stood over me, brandishing a piece of paper.

'This is a letter from your father saying he's disappeared to South America. Is it true?' he shouted.

'I'm afraid it is, yes.'

'What did you know about this? I know you knew something. Tell me what you knew!'

I was incredulous. It simply hadn't occurred to me that people would think I was complicit, that the plan had been hatched by both me and my father.

'Nothing, of course,' I said, 'I've just lost my father. I don't know if he's dead or alive.'

'Tell me!' he screamed.

'There's nothing to tell,' I said, 'You know as much as I do.'

'Your father is a sick man! Do you hear me? A sick man! I shall not be letting this go. I shall chase him down wherever he goes! He's a sick, sick man! Do you hear me?'

'Yes. I'm sorry.'

'Don't be sorry. I'll be coming after you for every penny you owe, trust me on that!'

Ross was a man of his word. A few days later, I received an invoice from him for the money I owed – £12. He did chase my father for many years, but to no avail.

Next, came National Westminster Bank, which was owed a lot of money. They asked me to a meeting with them at the Plymouth branch, where the accounts of Peter Bessell Ltd were held. As a director of that company, I was obliged to meet the manager to explain the situation. Plymouth is about 220 miles from London, but quite close to Polraen. Despite barely being able to afford the fuel, I drove down to Polraen for a couple of nights to save what few bits and pieces I could get into the car, which was virtually nothing. The speedboat was there, but I couldn't take it as it was on finance and soon to be repossessed. Then I went to see the bank manager.

I was greeted by a small panel of stern-looking men, obviously senior managers. I quickly realised that, although the meeting was calmer and more business-like – friendly, even – I was being put through exactly the same inquisition as I had been by Ross. Suddenly, I became nervous. *What if these men thought I was complicit in fraud? I could find myself in prison.* My father disappeared to protect himself, and I was left exposed to the whims of people who were going to decide if I was telling the truth. If they decided I wasn't, then I would be in big, big trouble.

Fortunately, I had the letter to me from my father to show them. It was humiliating to have to reveal such a personal document, which they copied for their records, but I really didn't have a choice. They accepted it was a genuine document, not a story made up by my father to cover me, but it was a close shave, I'm sure.

Then came the most difficult discussion. Sally called. She begged me to go to her flat to see her, which I did. She had last seen my father a couple of months previously, when he left to go to New York, having promised he was about to leave my mother, get a divorce and marry Sally. When Sally received her letter from him about his disappearance, she had opened the envelope believing it would be a love letter. Many people are jilted by letter, but to have it happen in that way must have made it doubly hard. There was nobody for Sally to turn to, and, like the rest of us, she couldn't even be sure my father was still alive.

My mother's problems were even worse. She was an incredibly proud woman, who was now having to tell the world that the love of her life had deserted her, completely out of the blue. The man who was so successful and so adored by so many of his constituents had been a fraud for the past few years. Her sister, Anne, called her in fury. Michael, her husband, gave up his architectural practice to work on Bronxville. Now he was broke and in despair, threatening suicide. Anne's life, too, had fallen apart. Like me, my mother was having to bear the brunt of people's fury. Few people seemed to care we were suffering the same problems, only worse. We were rapidly learning who our real friends were. More dreadful for my mother was she lost Polraen, her home. She felt like a nomad, and none of this was her doing. Yet, still she yearned for my father and, in her obsessive love, continued to 'look for him around every corner'.

At this time, I still had no idea Diane phoned my sister from

Oceanside to say my father was alive and okay. For the following six months, I was kept in the dark, presumably to protect me, as I was at least able to say truthfully to the likes of Ross and the National Westminster Bank I had no idea where my father was. It would have been nice to know that he was alive, though.

I now faced the challenge of finding a way to keep the office open, for at least a few weeks or months in the hope of completing a deal to help everyone out, while Miller and my sister dealt with creditors in the USA. I sold the Buick to pay the electricity bill, but I was running out of time to pay the phone bill and the office rent. Despite the help of my closest friend, Paul Mitchell, and coming within a hair's breadth of completing one deal, we simply couldn't keep the office going long enough.

So we closed it and by the end of 1974, I found my dream job working for ATV Music, with the best bosses ever, Eddy Levy and Len Beadle. My sister returned to the UK and found work as an oil trader. My mother, by far the most stoic of all of us, and still deeply in love with my father, had a paid job working for UNICEF in New York, where she was sharing an apartment with a friend.

My father and Diane settled secretly in Oceanside, from where he made regular trips to Los Angeles to continue his secret work. Miller managed to deal with the creditors without telling them where my father was located, in case any got nasty and tried to extricate him back to the UK. Eventually, with the exception of Ross, all creditors were settled and my father began to rebuild a simple, if poor, life. It's a testament to his popularity as a human being that some, notably the senior manager at Chase Manhattan, actually became lifelong friends.

One could be forgiven for thinking we managed to sort ourselves out rather well. But fate had other plans for us.

CHAPTER EIGHTEEN

A PLOT TO KILL

AS MY FATHER disappeared, the Liberal Party under Jeremy Thorpe was experiencing a boom. Thorpe was becoming a national figure. His surge in popularity was phenomenal, with some commentators comparing him with John F. Kennedy and putting him just a couple of points behind the Conservatives and Labour, who were locked in a close, fierce battle.

The February 1974 general election resulted in a hung parliament, with Edward Heath, the incumbent Conservative prime minister, reluctant to relinquish power. The Liberals, even though they had won only 14 seats, held the balance of power. Heath courted Thorpe in the hope of forming a coalition, offering him a Cabinet post. This only served to exaggerate Thorpe's paranoid fear the Scott affair might, at any moment, be exposed. With my father gone, there was no one to control his desire for an extreme solution. Thorpe was just as panic-stricken about Scott as he had been about Hetherington, whom my father claimed he'd wanted killed. In the end, Thorpe refused the Conservative offer, but his political career was now stratospheric, and he had ever more to lose. Scott, meanwhile, was quite happy to tell anyone who would listen about his affair with Thorpe.

It soon came to a head when claims of a plot to kill Scott were made. It was alleged that Thorpe, through various incompetent intermediaries, including David Holmes, conspired to have Scott murdered. The chosen 'hitman' was a bungling amateur, an ex-pilot by the name of Andrew Newton, who was to be paid £10,000 via Holmes and his intermediaries. The money came from Jack Hayward, though he was completely unaware of how it was being used. In October 1975, almost two years after my father's disappearance, Newton approached Scott, pretending to be a bodyguard, who had been hired to protect him. Having gained Scott's trust, on 24 October, Newton met him again. He explained that he had to drive over the deserted Devon moorland to Porlock on business and persuaded Scott to go with him, for Scott's own safety. Scott insisted on taking his large Great Dane, Rinka, with them. Newton, who was frightened of dogs, reluctantly agreed.

Once they were on the deserted moor, Newton pretended to be too tired to drive, and they agreed Scott should take over. When the car stopped, Scott got out, with Rinka, to walk round to the driver's side. When he got there, he found Newton pointing a gun at him. Newton shot Rinka in the head then, pointing the gun at Scott, he said, 'It's your turn now.' But the gun jammed. After several attempts at freeing the mechanism, Newton gave up, and Scott ran away. But he couldn't leave his dog and, bravely, he returned to try to save Rinka's life. Newton jumped in the car and drove off, leaving Scott with his beloved dog, dying in the road.

This attempt on Scott's life has often been ridiculed as 'Rinkagate', but it marked a nadir in British politics that people in high places could even contemplate such things. Despite having had no involvement whatsoever in 'Rinkagate', my father's life was once again about to be turned upside down.

In January 1976, Holmes visited my father in California, ostensibly on Thorpe's behalf. My father picked him up from the airport and, on the drive to his hotel, the conversation turned to Thorpe. After a bit of chat about his leadership of the party, Holmes turned the conversation to Scott, who hadn't crossed my father's mind for the best part of four years.

'The problem at the moment is Scott,' said Holmes, quite casually.

'Who?' said my father, who always tended to think of Scott by his original name, Josiffe. Then he remembered. 'Oh, you mean Josiffe! Don't tell me he's still around!'

'Very much so,' said Holmes, 'He moved into Jeremy's constituency about two years ago and has been happily spreading the tale of their relationship.'

My father thought little of it. 'Well, judging by the size of Jeremy's majority at the last election, it has had little effect.'

Holmes became agitated. 'Voters can change sides on a whim and large majorities can evaporate overnight. Scott has written a book about the relationship. He's hoping to get it published, and has been talking to journalists.'

'The laws of libel will protect Jeremy from that in Britain,' said my father, still unconcerned.

'You're probably right,' said Holmes, 'but there's been a new development and there's now a danger of the whole affair being publicised.' He continued. 'Some time last year, Scott became friendly with a married, but promiscuous, airline pilot and Scott came into possession of a photograph of the man and a girl in the nude.'

My father laughed. Then he realised Holmes was being quite serious. 'What has all that got to do with Jeremy?'

'The pilot's wife was extremely jealous, and Scott has successfully blackmailed the pilot by threatening to show her the picture.'

This aroused my father's curiosity. He had known Scott quite well for a few years in the late 1960s and, whilst the young man had many faults, my father did not have him down as a blackmailer. 'I find that very hard to believe,' he said.

Holmes was a bit put out. 'Well, uh, Scott has deteriorated since you knew him. He definitely blackmailed the pilot.'

With no reason to disbelieve him for the moment, my father accepted Holmes's story, although he was still baffled as to why Holmes travelled all the way to California to tell him about it. Holmes continued: 'By the end of last year, the pilot got tired of submitting to Scott's endless demands and, one night when they were driving across Exmoor, a violent argument developed. The pilot stopped the car and got out. Scott, who had his dog with him, followed. Scott threatened to turn the dog on the pilot who reached into the back of the car, produced a gun and shot the dog, killing it instantly.'

The story sounded somehow rehearsed, but my father was utterly dumbfounded. His love of dogs got the better of him and he saw the tragedy of the whole thing.

'How sad. What breed was the dog?' he asked.

Holmes became impatient at what he saw as an irrelevance. 'I have no idea, but it was a big animal. Anyway, by chance, just as the pilot fired the shot, a police patrol car appeared on the scene. Scott flagged it down and charged the pilot with killing his dog.'

'Serves them both right!' my father responded. 'Are you sure the pilot didn't intend to kill Scott and shot the dog by accident?' He laughed. Holmes hesitated. It was a hesitation my father noted, and remembered many years later.

'Well, anyway, the arrival of the police didn't calm the pilot. He told them he didn't give a damn about Scott's dog and the next time he would shoot Scott, as he was tired of being blackmailed. Then the police arrested the pilot, and he's due to appear in court soon.'

Again, my father couldn't take it seriously. 'That should make a good headline for the *North Devon Journal*!'

But Holmes was in no mood to laugh. 'Exactly,' he responded, soberly, 'and when Scott gets into court, he'll expose the truth about his relationship with Jeremy and, because court testimony is privileged, the newspapers will be able to publish it without risk of a libel action.'

My father was becoming irritated. 'It's all rather silly, David. If that's all Jeremy has to worry about, he's overreacting as usual. Scott wouldn't be allowed to introduce Jeremy's name in court as it's not relevant to the case. But even if he manages to somehow, no responsible newspaper is going to publish it.'

'You're wrong. Scott seems pretty determined.'

'How do you know that?'

'He's been putting it about everywhere that he intends to do so. Do I need to remind you how we always dreaded he would make an outburst that could get reported?' Holmes was getting more and more agitated.

'Fair point,' said my father, 'but moral attitudes have changed enormously over the past few years. I really do think Jeremy is overreacting. The worst thing you can do is encourage him. I speak from experience!'

'Peter, I had expected you to take the matter more seriously.'

'I'm sorry, but even if a newspaper was mischievous enough to print Scott's outburst, no one is going to believe it.'

'That's not Goodman's opinion,' said Holmes.

My father was incredulous. 'Goodman?'

Lord Goodman was one of the country's top lawyers and a member of the House of Lords. There were few, if any, better legal brains. This took matters to a whole new level. My father continued.

'What the hell's Goodman got to do with all this?'

'Jeremy has consulted him. He agreed with his analysis that the situation was dangerous, and Scott must be prevented from mentioning Jeremy's name in court.'

My father's attitude changed completely. If that was Goodman's opinion, he wasn't going to argue the point. He thought he had better start taking the matter more seriously.

'Alright, that's different,' he said, 'Is there some way I can help?'

'Indeed, there is. Goodman suggests you write a confidential letter to Scott's solicitor saying that long ago Scott blackmailed you as well. Goodman will then inform the solicitor that, if Scott refrains from mentioning Jeremy in court, you will take no further action.'

My father turned and stared at Holmes for a second, but quickly returned his eyes to the road. Holmes continued.

'Goodman will tell him that, on the other hand, if Scott brings Jeremy's name into the case you will swear an affidavit and your evidence, taken in conjunction with the pilot's, will result in Scott's arrest, trial and a probable jail sentence for blackmail.'

My father was stunned. There's no doubt he should have rejected such a request out of hand. It was, after all, a pack of lies and, to this day, I cannot understand what made him continue the conversation. Why did he not even question if such a request to lie had truly come from one of the highest lawyers in the land? My father later claimed that Holmes's assertions confused him at the time and, other than one brief meeting with Goodman many years previously, he didn't really know him. Also, as far as he knew, Holmes had never lied to him, and he was not aware that Holmes had any involvement other than that of being a messenger.

'What happens if I write the letter and Scott calls my bluff?' he said at last.

'Peter,' Holmes said, 'Even if Jeremy would let you take a risk, you know I wouldn't.'

My father accepted that. But then something else occurred to him.

'If I write the letter stating Scott has blackmailed me over his relationship with Jeremy, it will provide the solicitor with evidence for Scott's allegations that such a relationship occurred. Surely that's exactly what Jeremy *doesn't* want! This is ridiculous.'

'Yes,' said Holmes, 'Goodman has thought of that. He suggests you should write that Scott had discovered something about your business which he used to blackmail you.'

The whole letter would, of course, have been a lie and, apparently, was being proposed by Goodman himself. This is possible, but unlikely. It probably all came from Thorpe.

'Listen,' he said, 'Scott never had any access to any aspect of my affairs. I didn't have many meetings with him and they were all brief, with my secretary either present or nearby. Okay, yes, I had financial difficulties at the time I was dealing with him, but there was absolutely nothing that could lay me open to blackmail. I'm sorry, but I'm not prepared to manufacture a story along those lines.'

For a while, there was silence. Then Holmes spoke again.

'You could say he blackmailed you over a woman.'

'I could say something about a girl, but, as Scott knew nothing about my life, we would be skating on thin ice.'

'But does it matter?' asked Holmes, 'The letter will be seen only by solicitors. No one else will ever see it.'

They arrived at the hotel and my father waited while Holmes checked in. It gave him a moment to think. His new, peaceful life had been disturbed, suggesting turbulence to come, the very thing he had tried to escape. Despite Goodman's supposed involvement, my father thoroughly disapproved of the proposition. This, no doubt, was the reason Holmes came to see him in person, rather than trying to convince my father over the phone. He'd known my father was going to take some persuading. Once Holmes was checked in, the two men went to his room.

'You've discussed it with Goodman?' my father asked.

'Yes. You know how Jeremy exaggerates. He'll say almost anything if he thinks he's threatened. Before seeing you, I had to be sure there was no risk to you. Goodman said there was none.'

My father was becoming sceptical. He became even more so when Holmes made another startling confession.

'And there's another thing,' said Holmes. 'Scott has been in possession of some letters from you which are damning towards Jeremy. So, on Jeremy's behalf, I paid him £10,000 for their return.'

My father stared at Holmes in disbelief. 'Those letters are worthless,' he said. 'Scott would probably have parted with them for £100. You and Jeremy needed me as your broker.'

The letters he was referring to were brief notes written by my father to Scott in the late sixties accompanying small 'retainers' (as he called them) and discussing Scott's national insurance card. Scott subsequently distributed copies to the newspapers who seemed to consider they indicated some kind of link, but were not incriminating. The press was, for some time, siding with Thorpe as the *Sunday Mirror*'s opinion piece dated May 16th 1976 showed:

'It is true, of course, that the bizarre Mr. Peter Bessell bungled appallingly by paying "retainers" to Mr. Scott. Instead of being grateful, the charming Mr. Scott used these payments as evidence of a special relationship with Mr. Thorpe. Yet what harm has Mr. Thorpe done to Mr. Scott to justify this vendetta?' In other words, the letters did nothing to persuade anyone.

He then produced a letter to my father from Thorpe, which he read while Holmes had a shower.

Thorpe owed my father a great deal, but the debt was reciprocal. Thorpe helped my father many times, not just over the Hayward fraud attempt. He helped my mother after his disappearance and Diane, when she went to London to settle some of the creditors' demands. He even helped me to settle a Pakistani workmate's immigration problem by 'having a word' with the Foreign Office. While the letter to my father was written in a kind of code, it played on their mutual affection and came with the gift of a book, *Life With Lloyd George* by A.J. Sylvester, with the inscription: 'For Peter from Jeremy with affection. From one Liberal to another Liberal about a third Liberal. Vive les trois Mousquetaires! New Year 1976'

The book and letter appealed to my father's sense of vanity. He told Holmes he would write the letter, but not that evening. He needed time to think, and would write it the next morning. But by far the most important thing to him was that the letter would be in confidence.

'David, that's critically important to me and to Diane, her father and my family. I've lost everything, but my reputation has not been damaged – not publicly at least. Now I'm starting again from scratch, and I dare not put my chances in jeopardy.'

His public reputation was not, in fact, as untarnished as he might have believed, but, living 5,000 miles from his home at a time when there was no internet, he wasn't to know that.

'I can assure you unequivocally, Peter, I would never ask you to do something that would put your future at risk,' said Holmes.

'And there's another thing,' my father said, 'Jeremy says in his letter he wants me to say Diane's father had given the £10,000 you gave to Scott for the letters. It's absurd to ask me to bring Miller's name in it.'

'Yes,' said Holmes, 'I knew Jeremy was going to ask that additional favour. But it doesn't matter. It's not important.'

My father drove home and, later that evening, Holmes joined him and Diane for dinner, during which no mention was made of the favour Thorpe requested. My father did record in his memoir, though, that at one point during the meal, after having turned to say something to Diane, when he turned back to look at Holmes, he was staring straight ahead, with a strange, almost hopeless, expression in his eyes.

Soon after Holmes left, my father and Diane went to bed. That night, after some uncomfortable thoughts about what he was being asked to do, my father began finally to fall asleep. But he was soon jolted awake, by a memory of a conversation he had with my mother years ago, in Cornwall.

'That Scott business is going to bring Jeremy down one day,' she had said angrily, 'and, when it does, Jeremy will drag you down with him.'

'Nonsense,' my father had said, 'In any case, how could Jeremy drag me down? It's got nothing to do with me.'

'I don't know how. But you mark my words, he will.'

The next morning, my father took his typewriter to Holmes's hotel and, with the help of a draft which had been sent by Thorpe, together they wrote the letter.

'Who shall I address it to?' my father asked.

'The pilot's solicitor.'

'The pilot's? I thought I was to write to Scott's solicitor. I could have sworn that's what you told me,' said my father.

Holmes appeared confused. 'Oh, I was sure I told you Goodman would tell Scott's solicitor that you had written to the pilot's solicitor.'

My father got up from the desk and looked out of the window, trying to absorb what was happening. He felt sure this wasn't what he was asked to do the previous day.

'I'm sure you said Scott's solicitor yesterday,' he said, 'Oh well, maybe that was a mistake. It probably doesn't make much difference.' He returned to the typewriter.

'What's the solicitor's name?'

'Michael Barnes.'

'Who is he?' asked my father.

'Just some local Devon solicitor.'

'And what is the pilot's name?'

'Andrew Newton.'

Together they concocted a letter which outlined my father's knowledge of Scott and how Scott had tried to blackmail him, most of it a complete fabrication.

When they finished, my father signed it, but still had nagging doubts.

'You know, when I look back on my past, and thinking about my good fortune now, to be at last at peace, I'm not sure I can go through with this,' he said. Holmes sat in silence. My father continued, 'I understand Scott's behaviour in asking for £10,000 from you for the letters and blackmailing Newton, but I'm accusing him of a crime against me which he most certainly never committed.'

'Peter, this has to be done!' said Holmes, sharply, 'Think instead of the injustice of Jeremy's life being ruined when Scott appears in court.'

With that, my father put a copy of the letter in an envelope for Thorpe, along with a brief personal note, kept a copy for himself and gave the original to Holmes. They decided to destroy Thorpe's draft letter and his personal note to my father, so Holmes took them to the bathroom and my father heard the toilet flush. He came back into the room.

'I want to phone Jeremy so he can thank you personally.'

This slightly irritated my father, who had no wish to talk to Thorpe at that moment. 'It's really not necessary,' he said.

'No. I insist,' said Holmes, as he lifted the receiver.

After some difficulty persuading the operator to accept his credit card for payment, he eventually managed to get through to Thorpe's home. Thorpe's wife, Marion, answered.

'Hello, Marion. It's David. Sorry for the bad line. I'm in California. Is Jeremy there?' It was apparent he was not.

'Oh dear,' said Holmes. 'Could you pass on a message to him, please? Simply tell him I called with the message "mission accomplished".'

My father was startled.

He kept repeating those words in his head as he drove Holmes to San Diego airport – 'mission accomplished'. What 'mission'?

As they turned onto the freeway, my father realised this would be his last chance to try to find out if there was something he wasn't being told.

'David, I have to be honest,' he said, 'I don't believe you've told me everything.'

Holmes tensed, staring straight ahead. He mumbled something my father couldn't hear over the traffic.

'Sorry?'

'I said, "alright". The pilot was hired to kill Scott,' said Holmes.

'What? How and where did Jeremy find the pilot?'

Holmes paused for a second, then said, 'Jeremy didn't. I did.'

'Oh Christ, David! We always vowed to prevent anything of that sort! Why? For goodness' sake, why?'

'I knew that would be your attitude, Peter. But everything had changed. Scott had become far more dangerous. When I gave Scott the £10,000, he forced me to promise the same amount annually to persuade him to keep his mouth shut.' He paused, then continued. 'I tried everything to get hold of the letters, but it just made things worse. Jeremy got more depressed and anxious. There was nothing else we could do.'

My father became angry. 'I thought all his ideas of killing Scott had been abandoned years ago. After Florida I was certain he had realised it couldn't be contemplated.'

Holmes didn't respond.

'Thank God it failed,' said my father, 'At least that blasted Scott is alive.'

Holmes replied, convincingly, 'I'm as glad as you are, Peter.'

As they drove, Holmes explained what had happened. He told my father how he found the 'hitman' through friends, a carpet salesman named John Le Mesurier who, in turn, introduced him to a fruit-machine salesman, George Deakin, who might have the right contacts to 'deal' with Scott. He told him how the gun jammed on the moor and Scott escaped. The more my father heard, the more incredulous he became. Then it dawned on him. 'I must have that letter back. I need time to decide whether I should allow myself to be involved.'

'Yes. I understand,' said Holmes, 'It's in my bag in the boot. I'll give it to you at the airport.'

By the time they arrived, there were only 30 minutes until departure and my father could not leave the car at the airport entrance. So, Holmes took his luggage from the back of the car and my father told him he would go and park, then meet him at the check-in desk or gate.

The car park was full, and my father wasted precious minutes finding a parking space. Frantic to get his hands on the letter, he ran through the busy airport. Holmes was not at the check-in desk, so my father hurried to the gate, but he was held up by a security barrier. When, at last, he got through, the plane had boarded, the doors closed, and the steps were being moved away from the side of the plane.

Holmes still had the letter.

Alone on the drive back to Oceanside, my father thought about what had happened. Thorpe and Holmes had relied on three things to get the letter out of him. Firstly, he knew nothing about the murder plot. Secondly, he trusted both of them. Thirdly, their use of a combination of surprise, haste and flattery would be likely to produce an impetuous response. Now he realised just how gullible he had been and, had he written everything Thorpe asked, the letter could be used to shift the blame for the attempted murder of Scott onto him. It still might. But he felt sure Thorpe, being such a close friend, couldn't betray him like that. Still, at least Holmes knew my father no longer wanted the letter to be used and would, presumably, destroy it. Alongside the coast road, the Pacific shimmered under the West Coast sun, he could see surfers out beyond the break, and he began to put the whole thing from his mind. His thoughts returned to his peaceful, Oceanside life, thousands of miles from the world in which he once lived and worked. Holmes's visit, he decided, was nothing but a brief interruption, a reminder of the past.

But his peace was to last only 10 more days.

CHAPTER NINETEEN

LIES PILED UPON LIES

BY EARLY 1976, Diane and my father had settled into a peaceful life on the Pacific shore at Oceanside. With the financial help of Diane's father, my father had restored two small holiday cottages by the beach which were profitably let. But on Sunday 2 February at 3am, the phone rang. Diane woke and answered, then handed the receiver to him. 'Darling, it's Charles.'

'My solicitor? What's he doing calling me at this time of night?' In his dozy state he forgot it was 11am in London, from where Charles Negus Fancey was calling. He sat up and tried to clear his head. 'Hello?'

'Peter, every newspaper in the country has been phoning me. Reporters were here at the office before I got in. What do you want me to do?'

My father was baffled. 'What are you talking about?'

'This Jeremy Thorpe affair, of course,' Negus-Fancey responded, impatiently. 'They all want to see a copy of your affidavit about Norman Scott. I haven't told them, but, of course, I haven't seen it.'

'Charles, I know nothing of an affidavit. Remember, I don't get newspapers here until days later. I just don't know what you mean.'

'Scott had an outburst in court last Thursday, claiming a relationship with Thorpe. Since then, the papers have been carrying a story of an affidavit you are supposed to have written and lodged with me about Scott blackmailing you. Where is it?'

My father's mind raced. What had Thorpe done? He remembered mentioning an affidavit in his letter to Newton's solicitor Michael Barnes. Now it seemed that, not only had Holmes not destroyed the letter, but he also handed it to Thorpe, who was using it to try to clear his name. He found it hard to believe Thorpe could betray him in that way. Was it possible Holmes, afraid of Thorpe's reaction, had failed to tell him my father no longer wanted the letter used? He was now wide awake.

'I'm sorry, Charles. Scott never blackmailed me. His accusations against Thorpe are actually true. For years, I've been trying to protect Thorpe from Scott.'

'Alright,' said Negus-Fancey, 'Then I can issue a statement denying the existence of an affidavit and say that you have no connection with the matter?'

'No. Wait. I must speak to Jeremy first. At all costs, he must be protected.'

Thorpe had just tried to implicate him in a murder plot, yet my father was still trying to protect him. He quickly told Negus-Fancey about Holmes's visit to Oceanside and asked him to get Thorpe to call him. Negus-Fancey was, unsurprisingly, horrified.

'You'll have to write to Barnes immediately and withdraw that letter. The next thing you'll be asked to do is commit perjury.'

'I need time to talk to Jeremy. Meanwhile, I suggest you tell the press I will be issuing a statement tomorrow.'

'I doubt they'll wait that long,' said Negus-Fancey.

'They'll bloody well have to,' said my father and ended the call.

As my father put it, the floodwaters had engulfed him. In truth, he had no one to blame but himself for having been taken in so easily by Thorpe. Incredibly, after the phone call with his lawyer, my father went back to sleep.

At 9am though, the phone started ringing off the hook. The press were onto him. They had found out about his regular payments to Scott but, for the time being, all he could do was stonewall them. The pressure shook him. He needed to speak to Thorpe. Later that morning, Thorpe finally called. My father answered. 'Hello?'

'We've just been watching you on television,' Thorpe began.

My father had given no interviews, so he realised they must have been using old photographs to illustrate the story of his involvement with Thorpe. This, of course, was the very last thing my father had ever wanted to hear.

'Have you?' he grunted.

Thorpe was a little taken aback, so changed the subject, 'How's your health?'

'It's not being improved by all that's going on.'

'Yes, yes. I understand that. I'm sorry, Peter.' Thorpe appeared quite contrite.

'Jeremy, I'm genuinely sorry for all that has happened with Scott's outburst, but the press coverage I'm receiving will do incalculable damage to my prospects of getting back into business. Miller has spent thousands of pounds to give me a new start and if he finds out what's happening, he'll consider it not only ungrateful, but irresponsible, of me to have become involved.'

Thorpe appeared fairly casual and dismissive. 'Oh, don't worry. In a few days it will all have been forgotten.'

My father wasn't in a mood to let go. 'How did my letter to Barnes become public?'

'Cyril broke faith with me and discussed it with the press.'

Cyril Smith became a Liberal MP in the 1970s and was one of the most recognisable political figures of the decade. After his death in 2010, Smith was exposed as a serial paedophile, who preyed on young boys. My father never met him.

Thorpe continued, 'After Scott's outburst in court, I felt forced to show the letter to him, in confidence. I needed to prove there was no truth in Scott's allegations.'

For some inexplicable reason my father resisted the temptation to tell him that showing the letter to anyone was a complete breach of the promises Thorpe and Holmes made to him. Perhaps he was trying to avoid an argument.

'Well, I need to remind you Holmes obtained the letter from me for a completely different purpose.'

Thorpe became defensive. 'But, Peter, I had to prove to the parliamentary party that Scott had something on you, not me.'

That angered my father. 'What the hell are you talking about? Scott never had anything on me!'

For a moment, there was silence. Then Thorpe mumbled, 'Yes, yes, that's right. Yes, that's right.'

In an instant it was obvious to my father that, as happened so many times before, Thorpe had fallen for his own lies. But talking to my father brought him back to some sense of reality. Thorpe continued, 'Okay, I accept you provided the letter on the understanding it would never be published, and I can only repeat my apology. But, honestly, Peter, you have nothing to worry about. It's done no damage.'

'Publishing the bloody letter has done no good either,' my father said, 'Charles told me this morning no one believes it.'

'That's not true,' Thorpe replied sharply, 'The letter is believed. You're relying on the opinion of a young, inexperienced solicitor.'

'Do you not see, Jeremy?' my father said, 'If it *is* believed, it makes it worse for me! Do you have any conception of the effect on people, including my family, of a story that I submitted to blackmail over a woman?'

Thorpe's response angered my father even more.

'Most people will assume the blackmail was over your business affairs.'

'Rubbish,' said my father, 'What would Scott have known about my business? And what was there about it to use for blackmail?'

Thorpe remained silent, so my father continued.

'It will be much better, Jeremy, if we are consistent about what we say, and stick to the truth as far as possible. I'll issue a statement through Charles giving a credible explanation.' He thought for a moment. 'I'll say Scott originally went to you for assistance and you passed him on to me as someone who needed help over a lost National Insurance card. Then, while I was trying to sort out the matter with the Ministry, I gave Scott a little money since he was virtually destitute.' He thought some more. 'Without a National Insurance card, I could not employ him so, for the time being, I put him on a "retainer" of £5 a week, simply as an act of charity. I will also categorically deny Scott ever attempted to blackmail me, or had any knowledge of my private life.'

Thorpe panicked. 'You can't do that! It'll ruin everything! I am begging you, Peter, give me time – time to get this thing under control. I promise afterwards we'll issue a joint statement.'

Did my father seriously believe Thorpe's promises meant anything by now? Was it not clear to him that Thorpe had a habit of conspiring to eliminate those he felt were a threat to his career? But the panic in Thorpe's voice aroused sympathy. They had, after all, been close friends for many years.

'The last thing on earth I want to do is cause you additional problems, Jeremy, but you must understand I have to protect myself too.'

'Alright. Phone Negus-Fancy and give him your statement. Then tell him to speak to me and we'll work out something together.'

'Very well,' said my father, 'By the way, have you spoken to Pauline? She must have been shattered by the press reports.'

'No, I haven't. We got her out of here about a month ago. Christ, it wouldn't have done for her to be around. But I've got her phone number.'

Since my father's disappearance, my mother had been effectively homeless, renting a room off a friend in New York. But that couldn't last forever, so she decided to leave UNICEF and seek employment in the UK. The Thorpes kindly put her up at their Orme Square home while she got herself organised. Unsurprisingly, Thorpe omitted to mention to my father that, during my mother's time with them, he told her my father was a murderer. For many years I was unable to understand why Thorpe told her such a thing, other than deliberately to alienate my mother from my father. Eventually, it dawned on me. Of course! Thorpe always believed my father had murdered Hetherington.

'I have her number, too,' said my father, 'Do you think I should phone her myself?'

'No,' replied Thorpe, perhaps a little too hastily, 'That would distress her more. I'll talk to her.'

I'm not surprised he responded hastily. My mother was not a lady to mess around. If my father had called her, I'm quite sure her first question would have been, 'Who did you murder?' If he'd learned Thorpe had told my mother he'd murdered someone, his loyalty to Thorpe would have evaporated instantly.

My father replied, 'You can tell her anything you like, you know. She knows all about the Scott affair.'

Thorpe was astonished. 'Does she?'

'Of course. She knew about it years ago. But will you phone her?'

'Scout's honour!'

The call ended, and my father went to his typewriter to draft a statement. Five minutes later, the phone rang. It was Thorpe again.

'Peter, I've got it!'

'Go on.'

'All you have to do is issue a statement saying you understand you may be required to give evidence in a criminal matter and therefore you can say nothing. If you do that, no paper will dare to publish another word about you.'

From Thorpe's point of view, this was a good solution. But for my father it would only make matters worse. It would still leave everyone thinking he had been blackmailed by Scott. He also thought that Negus-Fancey was right: this was all the first step in a plan to persuade him to commit perjury. That made him angry.

'Jeremy, there's no question of my giving evidence. I told David that. I'm not going to lie under oath. What are you talking about?'

'Calm down,' Thorpe replied, 'You can't be compelled to give evidence unless you want to. You needn't take my word for that. Ask Negus-Fancey or any lawyer. You can't be forced to be a witness.'

My father didn't understand this at the time, but Thorpe meant he couldn't be compelled to testify in a British Court because he lived outside its jurisdiction. This was obviously well thought through, probably while plans were put in place to hoodwink him into writing the Barnes letter.

'Alright,' he said, cautiously, 'If you can persuade Charles your suggestion is safe, perhaps the statement I've drafted can be altered.' With that he started to read it to him, but when he reached the point where he emphasised Scott had not blackmailed him, Thorpe interrupted.

'Well, that contradicts your letter.'

'No, it doesn't. I only said he tried to blackmail me.'

'No,' said Thorpe, harshly, 'You wrote that he blackmailed you once. That's enough.' He was talking as if what was contained in the letter was true and it was my father's memory of events that was at fault.

'It doesn't matter what I wrote,' my father said, 'There was no truth in it. You know bloody well Scott never blackmailed me. But never mind that, there's something more important than that. Did David pay £10,000 for my letters? I don't believe it.'

My father later wrote in his memoir that Thorpe's reply sounded as if he'd been rehearsing it for weeks.

'Not to my knowledge,' he said, crisply.

'What?' shouted my father, 'Then that story was a trick to persuade me to write that bloody letter.'

'Wait,' replied Thorpe quickly, 'Do you think this phone is safe?'

'I suppose it is. I don't know. But in any case, I've got to know the truth.'

'Let me give you an "Isaac Foot" answer.' He paused, then spoke slowly and deliberately. 'If David crossed the ferry, it was essential those letters should not be found. We had to get them first.'

Thorpe was referring to the Bodmin constituency and an earlier plan for Holmes to take Scott across the river to Cornwall on a ferry and murder him. He was saying, as plainly as he could, the purpose in buying the letters from Scott was to ensure the police did not find them after Scott was killed because they would provide a link to him.

'I think I understand,' replied my father, 'But I want it in plain language. You mean David did hire the pilot?'

'Yes.' Thorpe's voice was sombre. 'That's the worst danger of all.'

'Oh Christ! What a mess! Well, one thing is certain. That can never be considered or tried again.'

'That's right, my God, that's right …'

There was a pause. My father changed the subject.

'Did you know Scott was going to have his outburst?'

'No. We were taken completely by surprise.'

'I see. Tell me. If David bought my letters, how the hell did the newspapers get hold of them?'

'Scott had photocopies and sent them to every bloody newspaper in the country,' said Thorpe.

Another amateurish mistake. Thorpe and my father then agreed on a statement which was released via Negus-Fancey. In it, he outlined the reason he had been paying Scott a 'retainer', only partly true in that they denied a connection to Thorpe. My father was careful to record all phone calls, and this one was no exception. I heard the recording.

It's clear to me from these calls and events that Thorpe was trying to shift the blame for the murder attempt onto my father. But, because of their friendship and shared experiences, my father simply couldn't see it – or didn't want to. For the next few days, the press hounded him relentlessly for more information, even to the point of staking out his house 24 hours a day. The pressure was intolerable. He and Diane were trying to live a normal life, but it was becoming impossible. Somehow, he needed to bring the matter to a close and move on. In an attempt to do so, he made his most ridiculous decision yet. Realising that Thorpe's career was on the verge of being destroyed, and genuinely believing it might result in his suicide, my father decided to take full responsibility for Scott. As soon as he had a moment alone with Diane, he told her of his decision.

'I've been thinking. This has to stop. If it doesn't, Jeremy is going down. I'm going to do a 180-degree turn and take responsibility. My reputation is already in the mud. What difference does it make? But if Jeremy is forced to quit as a result of such a scandal, the Liberal Party will be torn asunder. I can't allow that.'

'It's not that. It's really Jeremy you care about, isn't it?' said Diane.

'Yes. Yes, I suppose it is. If his ship's going down then, by God, my little guns will be firing for him.' My father never lost sight of the fact that, to a large extent, Thorpe's problems stemmed from the fact that homosexuality was illegal in the UK in the 1960s.

He called Thorpe in London. Marion answered. She was strangely cool. My father asked if Thorpe was there.

'I'm afraid he's not available,' she said.

'Then could you please ask him to call me as soon as possible?'

'I could.' That was the end of the conversation.

A short while later, Thorpe did call. He appeared as cool as Marion.

My father asked, 'What on earth is the matter with Marion? Her tone was so cold. What have I done?'

'It's just the strain, Pedro. I'm sure she didn't mean it. We're going through hell here, you know.'

'Fair enough. Well, I thought you should know I've decided to take the blame for Scott completely on my shoulders. You'll be able to face the press and your colleagues with a full confession from me.'

My father wouldn't have been expecting Thorpe to fall to his knees in a show of gratitude, but he was expecting at least some indication of relief – and gratitude. There was nothing.

Thorpe's tone was resigned. 'That's good of you, Peter. Thank you.'

There was a slightly embarrassed silence. Then my father continued. 'Jeremy, I know what you must be going through.'

'Yes,' said Thorpe, dully, 'Every morning I wake up with that terrible sick feeling.'

'Oh, I'm very familiar with that.' Another pause. 'Jeremy, I'll do my best. I'll be thinking of you all the time. Remember you can phone me any time of the day or night. Keep your chin up. We won't be beaten.'

Later that evening, my father allowed the press, who had been waiting outside for days, to return and, to a packed room, he confessed that the payments to Scott had been to keep him quiet about his personal life. Further, he admitted the letter to Barnes was written to clear Thorpe. There were lots of awkward questions, such as to name Holmes, which my father refused to do. He managed to keep the focus of blame on himself. The press now felt scorn for him as he kept changing his story, and appeared unreliable.

Diane had so far been kept out of the headlines. She was still largely unknown. Certainly, my mother knew nothing about her. Then, one morning, a press photographer took a picture of Diane as she was leaving to go shopping for groceries. She immediately went back and told my father, who was furious, but they decided it would now be impossible to keep their relationship out of the newspapers, so it was better to introduce Diane on their own terms.

Together, they spoke to the press about their relationship and allowed photographs to be taken. They should have known the type of headline it would produce: 'The Girl in the Life of Runaway Bessell', which was followed by: 'Her father paid my debts – I hope to marry her one day'.

This was how my mother, even after having been out to California to see him after his disappearance, found out about the existence of Diane. She was shattered. Neither my sister nor I were ever able to tell her that we already knew. Her public humiliation was so great she left the country to work in Libya for several years, in an effort to get away.

My father's reputation in the UK was shot. He was seen as an adulterous liar, who ran away from his debts and whose devious behaviour threatened to ruin Thorpe's career. But Thorpe was in trouble, too. The tenacity of the media soon got the police involved. The shooting of a dog on Exmoor was becoming a pressing matter; the newspapers were not about to let it go. Scott told the police and the *Sunday Express* he was driven onto the moor by someone claiming to be a private detective, who shot his dog then tried to shoot him, but the gun jammed.

Gradually, things were being pieced together. The case was taken over by a very senior police officer, Detective Chief Superintendent

Michael Challes who, when asked why such a senior officer had been assigned to the case, responded, 'I am in charge because of the ramifications of this affair.'

Over the following few months, coverage intensified. Whilst some factions of the press defended Thorpe to the hilt, claiming he was being hounded by an unbalanced individual in Scott, others were tenacious in not wanting to allow an attempted murder and the killing of a dog to go unpunished. Very soon, all the mistakes and misdemeanours in my father's life were going to come crashing down on him in an enormous avalanche.

CHAPTER TWENTY

THE ONLY THING WORSE THAN A MURDERER

ON 14 MARCH 1976, the British establishment closed ranks to protect Thorpe. *The Sunday Times*, edited by Harold Evans, who was convinced Thorpe was no more than the victim of a vicious whispering campaign, published a lengthy article on the affair. The banner front-page headline read 'The Lies of Norman Scott – by Jeremy Thorpe'.

This was accompanied by a lengthy statement from Thorpe along with an in-depth article on page 17, written by their 'Insight' investigative team, titled 'Thorpe's Ordeal', in which my father was ripped to shreds.

Thorpe's statement included the following:

Mr Scott has made the following allegations against me:

The existence of a homosexual relationship with me.

That I stole his National Insurance card.

That the Liberal Party, Lord Byers and others have made him from time to time subventions to keep him quiet.

That, in the incident of the shot dog, my wife or I hired a gunman at a five-figure sum to kill the dog, or Scott, or both, towards the cost of which the Government had contributed.

That the identity of the gunman was, variously, my helicopter pilot, or a Liberal worker in the Devon and Cornwall region.

In addition, it is alleged that I was acquainted with or involved in a correspondence between Scott and Bessell and that I knew about, or was involved in, the purchase of the Bessell letters from Scott for a sum of 2,500 pounds. All these allegations are false.

Apart from one or two trivialities, he was denying virtually everything my father knew to be true. But the 'Thorpe's Ordeal' 'Insight' article was far worse. There was no doubt the intention of the article was to shift the blame from Thorpe onto my father. It described my father paying money to Scott as blackmail to keep his financial affairs quiet. It claimed Scott knew about my father's financial problems because he used to 'hang around' his office. The collapse of my father's business in 1973-74 was described as being the basis for the blackmail. They described his business as that of a 'runner', a junior role delivering trades to a broker for execution. The article claimed my father was interested in the case of the Czar and his family's 'escape' only because he might be able to extract a secret hoard of Czarist gold from Barclays Bank, also that his investigation into the Czar case was proof of his propensity to believe wild fantasies.

My father's payments to Scott were nothing to do with his financial affairs and the article's dates weren't right. His business collapsed in the early 1970s whilst the payments to Scott were made in the 1960s. My father was a broker, not a runner. There was never any chance of getting money for the Czar investigation; it was simply a hobby.

But all this was just the tip of the iceberg. The closer other factions of the press got to the truth, the more intense the pressure became.

While he was being constantly hounded by reporters, I visited my father, in October 1977. It was the first time I had seen him since his disappearance. It was an emotional meeting.

I took Freddy Laker's Skytrain, the first budget airline to the US, from London to LA – never an easy journey. Rather than an 11-hour direct flight to California, my Skytrain flight stopped off in Manchester then Bangor, in Maine, to go through US immigration. The flight took the best part of 16 hours, arriving in LA at 6am. The flight was so arduous that, as we started to descend towards LAX, the passengers spontaneously started to sing 'California, Here I Come!' out of sheer relief. I wasn't in the best condition to see my father again for the first time in four years.

He seemed smaller and much more fragile than I remembered. Could that have been a psychological thing? When someone is your hero, they appear larger than life and you picture them as strong. Now my father had ceased to be my hero, he was just a normal human being, who made mistakes. That's the person I saw at the airport. It was quite a shock to me. But I wasn't angry with him any more. I had begun a new and successful life of my own in the music industry, working as the Creative Manager at April Music, a division of CBS Records.

My father and I hugged, awkwardly, as English men do, and our family had never been tactile.

On the drive to Oceanside, we stopped for a snack and were served by a pretty, young waitress. My father couldn't take his eyes off her. I was quite shocked, and a bit disgusted. He wasn't overtly looking at her; he was giving her sidelong glances, like a dirty old man. For a moment, that's how I saw him. It was a small thing, but it stuck in my mind.

The following two weeks were supposed to be relaxing, for both of us, but we were to be disappointed. Throughout my whole stay, he was hounded by reporters, who constantly hung around the front door. What's more, the father I found in California was a very different man from the one I remembered from home as a child.

My father had been an important man. He dealt with issues and people of national and international significance. He dressed impeccably, always in the most expensive suits, and he travelled the world. Any humdrum tasks were taken care of by employees.

The father I met in Oceanside was a different person. Trivial issues had become significant. If he or Diane went shopping for groceries, there would be a half-hour discussion, and sometimes an argument, about what was needed, followed by talk of who was going to go and what time they would get back. On the day I arrived, I sat while they talked about a bag of nails my father had to buy from the hardware store. It was the kind of in-depth discussion that might once have been reserved for parliamentary debates. I realised he had lost everything and was a shadow of his former self. No longer a big man, he had become small, the complete antithesis of everything he dreamed of and worked towards. Despite all that, he couldn't resist becoming involved in local politics, and was soon well known locally as that English politician who was always prepared to lead some well-meaning cause, such as combating beach erosion.

Their home in Oceanside was a beautiful place to live, no more than 10 metres from a beach lined with palm trees, with dolphins and surfers out to sea. The living and dining rooms were on the second floor, giving an uninterrupted view. The soothing sound of breaking waves was constant.

Yet, in this paradise, reporters were constantly banging on the door, wanting to hear my father's side of an ever-evolving scandal which was hitting the headlines daily in England. My father felt important again; the world wanted to know him. But if he told the truth, he would betray his best friend.

We spent most of my two weeks there discussing this dilemma.

While we also tried to patch up our relationship, it was obvious the Thorpe affair was occupying his mind. A decision would have to be made.

To my mind, the moral course of action was easy. Thorpe had quite blatantly tried to place all responsibility for Scott on my father, so he owed Thorpe no loyalty. But there was a major issue, as I told my father over dinner one evening. He was obviously worried and depressed. It was a while since he had to make such momentous decisions, in a world he thought he had escaped.

'There's a big problem, Dad.'

'What?'

I hesitated for a second, because I was worried that what I had to say might hurt him. But it needed to be said.

'You're forgetting something about the English psyche. It's not so much about the establishment defending Thorpe, although they'll obviously do everything in their power to protect him. No. If you decide to tell the truth, there is something else you need to be prepared for.'

He waited for me to continue.

'Never forget that, in the eyes of the English, the only thing worse than a murderer is a grass. You will be hated.'

This confused Diane. 'What's wrong with exposing someone who tried to have another human being murdered?'

'You're right,' I replied, 'But in England it doesn't work like that. There is a kind of code. It's not right, I know, but that's the way it is. The plain fact is the public may well hate Dad for exposing his best friend. Friends stick together no matter what.'

'Yes,' she said, angrily, 'But Thorpe tried to sell your father down the river.'

'I know that,' I said, 'But people don't follow these things that closely. Depending on how the press reports it, they may well just see one friend betraying another. The fact that it involves an attempted murder will be immaterial. Even though Dad will be doing the morally correct thing, he could well end up being reviled and hated.'

There was silence for some time. I worried about what all of it would mean for us, his family, who had already been more than hurt by his actions. If he turned on Thorpe, we'd have to live through another hell. My father moved to the window and looked at the horde of reporters standing there, eating sandwiches, smoking cigarettes. They were evidently not going to give up until they heard something from him. He spoke quietly. 'Ask them in.'

The small living room was quickly jammed with journalists, eagerly expecting him to comment on all that Thorpe said in the article in *The Times*.

'Gentlemen, I thought I should call you all in to save you a lot of boredom waiting outside.'

There was an expectant silence in the room. Was there about to be a world-shattering new story?

'I have yet to see a full transcript of Thorpe's statements. I cannot comment until I have seen them and have enough information to form an opinion. As you know, my son is here on vacation, a vacation that has already suffered far too many interruptions. I won't be available until after he has returned to London in ten days' time.'

With much mumbling and grumbling, the reporters left, disappointed. My father gambled that over the following 10 days they would probably lose interest. He was right. We got to go to Disneyland, San Diego Zoo, the desert and many other places in California.

But over the next year, the police, as well as the press, put intolerable pressure on him. The British police had no jurisdiction over my father because he was now living in the US but, after much soul-searching, he agreed to be interviewed, in Los Angeles, by

Detective Chief Superintendent Michael Challes, deputy head of the CID, and Detective Superintendent Davey Greenough. My father had not been involved in the attempt to murder Scott on Exmoor, but Holmes admitted it to him, and Thorpe persuaded Holmes to organise it. All the previous attempts by Thorpe to persuade my father to murder Scott were in themselves, of course, a crime. The police were aware they had no case against Thorpe for attempted murder, but they thought they had a very strong case against him for conspiracy and incitement to murder, provided my father would agree to travel to the UK and testify against his old friend at the Old Bailey. The fact the police were prepared to go to the expense of sending one of their most senior officers and a colleague to Los Angeles to interview my father was an indication of how seriously they were taking the investigation.

The decision to testify or not was not an easy one. Quite apart from how he would be likely to be vilified for being a grass, there was the expense of the trip, the potential risk of being prosecuted himself, simply for having listened to the original conspiracy, as well as for the attempt to defraud Hayward. My father was also by then not a well man, having contracted emphysema through his years of chain-smoking. The thought of testifying in front of the world's press and having to face his old friend in open court was not an attractive proposition. By simply saying no, he could remain in peaceful obscurity on the coast of California. Agreeing to travel to the UK would thrust him headlong into the frantic world of politics, corruption and the press once more. Did he really want or need to do that?

The moral aspect lay heavy on him. While he had been able to restrain Thorpe, all the talk of murder had been just fantasy talk – or so he had thought. But, as soon as my father disappeared, it seems Thorpe put his fantasies into action and conspired to murder a young man who wanted nothing more than to get his

National Insurance card back. Politicians are like actors in that one of their motivations is the limelight; it makes them feel special and important. Despite the pleasure and peace of his new life, the lure of the limelight could have been irresistible to my father. He would once again be the centre of attention. He might even be able to make some money from writing a book about the whole affair. The meeting with Challes in Los Angeles took place at the office of my father's lawyer. My father liked him immediately. Both were born and raised in Somerset, and found they had a great deal in common, including Challes's first beat as a policeman being in my father's home city of Bath. Challes was a gentle West Country man who couldn't have been more different from my father's brash LA lawyer. The start of the meeting highlighted the cultural gulf. Challes was warm and friendly; my father's lawyer, Allen Susman, was businesslike, in the style of a typical Beverly Hills lawyer.

Brief pleasantries over, Susman got down to business.

'So, Chief Challes, may I ask the purpose of your visit here? Is it to obtain information?'

'Indeed it is,' responded Challes, dryly.

'And more importantly to my client,' continued Susman, 'are you seeking an undertaking that he will testify in criminal proceedings? Will he be asked to make depositions?'

'That depends on the outcome of these meetings,' said Challes.

'I see,' said Susman. 'If my client co-operates with you, what guarantee of immunity will he be given?'

'I have no power to grant immunity,' Challes responded firmly.

My father quickly interjected, 'I'm quite satisfied I've committed no offence in any matter relating to this police enquiry. I have no interest in asking for immunity.' Susman gave him a look which said, 'Shut up or leave the room!'

'Perhaps it's worth me pointing out,' said Challes, 'that there is no way I can force Mr Bessell to come back to England as a witness.'

After a few more points of clarification, it was agreed that Challes and Greenough, his assistant, would travel to Oceanside the next day to interview my father at length, with my father's chosen witnesses present. Four days of intense interviews followed, resulting eventually in my father providing the police with a lengthy statement. Challes and my father also issued a brief statement to the press, in which he stated: 'The question arose whether I would return to Britain to give evidence in the event of a trial. While I have not ruled this out, I was not asked, nor did I give any undertaking to do so.'

But the die had been cast. Challes would give the results of his investigations to the Crown Prosecution Service, which would make a decision as to whether or not to charge Thorpe, and his accomplices, with conspiracy to murder. It was quite evident that, without my father's testimony, the case would not be strong enough to charge Thorpe. It all rested heavily on his shoulders. Eventually, he caved in.

X

At 9pm on 6 May 1979, I was met at the drop-off zone at London Heathrow Airport by a Special Branch officer. After establishing my car would be looked after and taken to another exit, he swished me along private corridors, through security with a wave of a card and guided me to the arrivals gate of Pan Am Flight 100 from New York. There, I met my father's solicitor, Lionel Phillips, who was already waiting, along with a barrage of reporters and photographers. The arrival of my father in the UK to testify against Jeremy Thorpe in what was billed as 'The Trial of the Century' was headline news. The flight arrival time meant it could be covered live on the evening news bulletins.

I was allowed to go to the end of the airbridge so I could stand next to the aircraft door and greet my father relatively privately before facing the throng. He got off the plane, looking as immaculate as ever, despite his now terminal emphysema and having just endured a long flight. Our greeting was brief, with no chance of a hug, before we walked up the airbridge and straight into what could only be described as chaos. Reporters were shouting, pushing and shoving. Security men were doing their best to clear a path.

My overriding memory, apart from the mêlée of photographers keen to get a clear shot of my father, was the blinding lights of the TV cameras shining straight into our eyes, making it incredibly difficult to see where we were going. The Special Branch officer, who was evidently used to this kind of thing, did a magnificent job of steering us in the right direction.

The shouted questions, which my father's political instincts forced him to appear to ignore, were mostly hostile. Through it all, he kept smiling, as if he were arriving on holiday.

'Mr Bessell, did *you* conspire to murder?'

'Mr Bessell, how does it feel to grass on your best friend?'

'Mr Bessell, are you a bankrupt?'

'Tell us about your women, Mr Bessell!'

It was as if all my father's sins came back to haunt him in one terrible minute. My warnings a year or so earlier were to prove prophetic. Yet he was back, the centre of attention, and we walked through, giving the impression the world was a happy place for us.

Just a few miles away in my sister's tiny flat in Kensington, my mother lay curled up in the dark on the floor in a corner of the room, sobbing and alone. Reporters banged on the door, shouting, 'Mrs Bessell! The world wants to know your story!' The world was anything but a happy place for her right then.

It had become a pattern of our lives that my sister would take care of my mother, and I would take care of my father. This was ironic given my sister was my father's favourite, and I was my mother's.

After I'd helped my father through the scrum at the airport, once we were in the car, we finally had some peace together as I drove him to his hotel. We spoke about anything but the trial. It was a reminder to me that, behind the chaos of cameras and excited journalists, the life of any celebrity is as normal as anyone else's. When we arrived at the hotel, despite the large throng of reporters, none of them recognised my father. I'd had to park the car in a nearby car park, from where we walked back to the hotel entrance. As we waited to cross the road and enter the hotel, one of the reporters, with his camera round his neck and notebook in hand, sidled up to me, looked around furtively and almost whispered, so the others couldn't hear, 'Are you staying at this hotel?'

'Yes,' I said.

'Have you heard of Peter Bessell?'

'Yes,' I said again.

'Have you seen him here? Do you know what he looks like?'

'I've absolutely no idea,' I said, as my father stood right next to me. And with that, we strode anonymously and confidently into the hotel.

It might have been the same incompetent reporter who did much the same thing at my sister's block of flats. Having gained access to the building, a typically grubby-looking reporter was wandering around looking for anyone who might be connected to the Bessell family, or even just someone who knew what they looked like. As he waited for the lift on my sister's floor, she, her husband, my mother and I came out of her flat and stood right next to him. It was obvious to us that he was a reporter. The lift doors opened, and we all got in together.

As we descended, he said, 'I'm looking for Paula Bessell. Do you have any idea which flat she's in?'

We all shook our heads and said we had no idea who he was talking about. We got out of the lift on the ground floor and left him to what would be, presumably, a long and fruitless evening searching for people who were no longer there, whom he'd already spoken to.

The next day, my secretary Heather put a call through to me at my office at CBS.

'It's the Nigel Dempster column from the *Daily Mail*,' she said.

'Put them through,' I said to Heather.

The voice was friendly and female. The Nigel Dempster column was a well-known gossip column.

'Mr Bessell?'

'Ah, yes,' I replied, 'What can I do for you?'

'I understand you have recently divorced?'

I was taken aback. It was true that my wife, Joan, and I recently separated and divorced, very amicably. I was now in a new relationship, with Jill; Joan was also in a new relationship, with a pop star called Dave Dee, of Dave Dee, Dozy, Beaky, Mick & Tich fame. But we were still on very friendly terms. However, the combination of anything connected with my father and a pop star was too much for the press to ignore. My caller established that Joan, Dave, Jill and I were all very happy with our personal relationships, and then the following morning's headline read: 'Bessell's Son Has Problems of His Own'.

This was nothing, though, compared with what my father was about to go through. His days in court, facing a hostile judge, and in front of the world's press were to prove traumatic in the extreme. The atmosphere of the courtroom alone had been enough on occasion to overwhelm many famous witnesses.

CHAPTER TWENTY-ONE

ONE MORE WHOPPER

THE CENTRAL CRIMINAL Court in London was – and remains – the most intimidating of courts. Commonly known as the Old Bailey, after the street on which it stands, it has many courtrooms. But Court Number One, where the Jeremy Thorpe trial was held, is steeped in gruesome history and hangs heavy with the drama of many famous trials, including those of Oscar Wilde, Dr Crippen, John Christie, the Krays and Peter Sutcliffe, otherwise known as the Yorkshire Ripper.

For barristers and judges, a case in Number One Court at the Old Bailey was the ultimate accolade in their profession. The judge sat on a high dais, which is the full width of the court. The witness box was awkwardly placed to the right of the judge, a little below him or her and slightly in front of the jury box so the jurors got an excellent view of the witness's right ear and the back of their neck but may never look them in the eye.

The witness box itself is extremely uncomfortable for the witness – it is just too wide to enable the occupant to support themselves by resting their hands on the side rails, while the ledge in front is just too low for them to lean on. At that time, judges liked witnesses to stand upright, and not fidget, as a sign of respect to the court.

For someone in poor health, like my father, simply standing in the witness box was a very unpleasant experience. But the most intimidating place in the courtroom is the dock.

The dock faces the judge on the same level as the dais, enclosed on three sides by a plate-glass and wooden barrier, about six feet high. The front is about half that height so that the judge, clerk, lawyers, the jury, distinguished visitors, the press and the public all get a fine, uninterrupted view of the defendant who, although innocent until proven guilty, was very much exposed, seated on an upright wooden chair. At the rear of the dock, an opening in the floor and a staircase lead to the cells. A man or woman can face few experiences more intimidating and humiliating than being in the dock at the Old Bailey.

It was into all this that my father was thrust on Tuesday, 8 May 1979. First to arrive on the first day of the hearing was Thorpe himself, along with his wife, mother and uncle, Sir Peter Norton-Griffiths. They were greeted at the main entrance by Jack Gamble, the Keeper of the Central Criminal Court, who then personally escorted them via a lift to one of the rooms adjacent to Court Number One, normally reserved for consultations between clients and barristers. This was an unusual way for a prisoner to surrender his bail.

My father arrived about 10 minutes later, with his solicitor Lionel Phillips. Immediately on entry they were searched for concealed weapons and then escorted, by one of Challes's assistants, to the main public lobby and then into a small room to wait. The Old Bailey policeman who unlocked the door turned the three small chairs and table upside down.

'Just checking for bugging devices,' he said.

Although the court session started with the preliminaries, at which my father was not allowed to be present, it wasn't long before Challes himself came in and said he wouldn't be needed that day. He didn't realise it at the time, but George Carman, Thorpe's barrister, was arguing fiercely my father should not be allowed to testify at all.

The next morning, Wednesday 9 May, Phillips was delayed picking my father up from the hotel, so he went to the court alone. As soon as he arrived, a policeman came through the swing doors and indicated he should follow him into the courtroom, where the judge, Mr Justice Cantley, was waiting, looking sternly down at him from his high dais.

Cantley was the epitome of the staid judicial figures of the time. Being the judge of such a high-profile case would assure him of his place in legal history. He was, no doubt, determined to make the most of it. Sixty-eight at the time of the trial, he remained a bachelor until the age of 55 and understood remarkably little of 'real life', having been cocooned within a very closed community. Auberon Waugh, who wrote *The Last Word: An Eyewitness Account of the Thorpe Trial*, and whom my father respected enormously, noted Cantley's undoubted conservative views on sex by quoting a press report of Cantley's remarks when trying a case involving a 23-year-old man injured in a bulldozer accident. When told the accident had affected the man's sex life, Cantley enquired if he was married. 'No,' replied counsel.

'Well, I can't see how it affects his sex life,' said Cantley.

This was the attitude towards sex and marriage my father was about to face. But, on that morning, he knew nothing of Cantley's background, as he looked up at him glaring down from beneath his wig.

'Is your name Peter Joseph Simons Bessell?'

Cantley had pronounced my father's third name 'Simmons', but my father thought better of correcting him.

'Yes, my Lord.'

'Are you aware you may be a witness in this case?' he asked sternly.

'Yes, my Lord.'

'It appears you held something of a press conference here yesterday.'

As my father couldn't for the life of him think what the judge was referring to, he didn't know how to answer. Cantley continued.

'There was a report in an evening paper. Have you seen it?'

'No, my Lord.'

'Then look at it.'

A clerk handed him a crumpled newspaper cutting. The article outlined how he was hoping to drink plenty of cups of tea. Cantley glowered at him.

'Well? What have you to say?'

My father explained as best he could. 'Yesterday, before the proceedings began, a reporter asked me about my tea-drinking habits. As far as I recall that was all that was said, my Lord.'

'Before proceedings began?' For a moment Cantley softened. But then he became stern again. 'Now, remember this. You are not to discuss the case with anyone. If a reporter approaches you, take his name and come and tell me about it. Otherwise, you too will be in danger.'

My father had been duly humiliated in public and in front of the press. But that was just the tip of the iceberg.

Back in Oceanside, two years previously, when I advised him that he might be perceived as a grass if he testified against his best friend, not even I had the faintest notion it would be the judge who harboured the strongest grudge.

My father was finally called into court to testify on Friday 11 May. As he walked into the court to be sworn in, he was haunted by the shrunken figure in the monstrous dock of Thorpe, the friend he had not seen since bidding him farewell at Miami Airport a few years ago.

He took the oath. The judge looked down, smiled and told

him he could sit if he wished and did not need to ask permission. Then, his manner changed abruptly as he warned my father that an immunity from prosecution, which had been granted to protect him from overzealous previous business acquaintances, and encourage him to appear as a witness, did not extend to perjury. Clearly the warning would have caused the jury to regard him with suspicion from the outset. They were not informed that he had offered to waive that immunity in the firm belief there was nothing he could be prosecuted for. But the offer was turned down because, according to the Director of Public Prosecutions, there were so many aspects of my father's life the defence could attack that one more wouldn't make any difference!

The first couple of days' testimony involved the 'examination in chief' in which the barrister for the prosecution, for whom my father was a witness, Peter Taylor QC, questioned him on the events surrounding the aspects of the affair in which he was involved, including Thorpe discussing murder with my father in the House of Commons. Then, it was the turn of the defendants' barristers to cross-examine him. In the dock with Thorpe were David Holmes, John Le Mesurier and George Deakin, all of whom were allegedly involved in the conspiracy to kill Scott on Exmoor. When Taylor finished guiding my father through his testimony, Holmes's counsel, John Matthew QC, began the cross-examination. Matthew homed in on my father's immunity, suggesting it was a licence to embellish his story to secure a conviction. But, more importantly, he turned to the contract my father had signed with the *Sunday Telegraph*.

Unknown to the court, the Crown Prosecution Service refused to cover my father's legal expenses. These fees were large and the only way he could cover them was to enter into an agreement with the *Sunday Telegraph* to co-operate on pieces to be published after the trial. The fee to be paid was £50,000 (£235,000 today) but in the event Thorpe was acquitted, the amount would be halved to £25,000. Evidently, in the eyes of the defence, this agreement amounted to yet another inducement to my father to embellish his testimony to secure the conviction of Thorpe and the other defendants. Holmes's barrister also said they were aware he was writing a book and suggested such a book would be unpublishable without a conviction, again intimating my father had reason to embellish his testimony.

'No, sir,' said my father, 'The book will be published anyway. There are many things about the lives of your client and Mr Thorpe that need to be said and are not at all libellous.'

Nevertheless, the fact the jury was not aware of the reason behind my father's contract with the *Sunday Telegraph*, and he had no way of making them aware of it, gave the impression his motivation was greed. It was an incalculable blow, but worse was yet to come. Next was George Carman QC, Thorpe's counsel. Despite his small stature, he was a brilliant and tenacious advocate. Carman began with a four-part question on why my father had returned to the United Kingdom to testify.

'First, a sense of justice?' Carman asked.

My father tried to answer without sounding pompous. 'That affected my decision.'

'Loyalty to the Liberal Party?'

'That was also a consideration.'

'Revenge?' he asked, smoothly.

'No, sir. I have no occasion for it.'

'Money?'

'No, sir.'

Carman had the *Sunday Telegraph* contract in front of him, which suggested otherwise. He then asked if my father had been a lay preacher. When he was told yes, Carman asked why, as a man who preached the Gospel, he took no action when Thorpe proposed murdering Scott. Should he not have told someone in the Liberal Party? It's unlikely, of course, that anyone would have believed my father if he *had* told them.

'I accept it was wrong of me not to do so, but I believed that Mr Holmes and I could always prevent your client from putting his intentions into practice,' was the only answer he could give.

Then Carman went for the jugular. He turned to the Florida charade with my father and Holmes. He referred to the episode as incredible, then added, 'And there is something more incredible. Before Mr Thorpe, on your account of the matter, was sending Scott to his death in 1971 in the United States, you have asserted that he proposed to you the murder of another person in 1970?'

For a moment, my father thought Carman had taken leave of his senses in mentioning the matter. He was, presumably, referring to Hetherington.

'Yes, sir.'

Carman then named Hetherington and asked if it was correct that Thorpe appointed him, and not Holmes, as the executioner on that occasion. The court was stunned into silence.

'Yes, sir,' said my father.

At that point, Carman might have shown his hand. But he didn't. Instead, he asked whether my father had told a number of lies about the whole case.

Referring to the years he had protected Thorpe, my father replied, 'Yes, sir, for the protection of your client.'

'Have you told any whoppers since 1976?'

'Not to my knowledge, sir.'

At this point, Carman turned to the judge and asked if it might be a suitable moment to adjourn until the next day. Quite evidently the judge was enjoying this particular exchange far too much. Seemingly forgetting himself, he said, 'Oh, I think we have time for one more whopper!'

Judge Cantley's comment displayed a lack of neutrality, which stunned the court just as much as the exchange between Carman and my father. Carman continued, bringing up the attempt to defraud Jack Hayward of half a million dollars. My father pointed out he and Thorpe were both involved, and that the plan had been Thorpe's. He added, 'I very much regret having to say that Mr Thorpe's only motive was to help me. Disgraceful though the entire episode was, Mr Thorpe's intention was unselfish.'

Carman returned to the topic of Hetherington.

'You have now told us there were two people Mr Thorpe wanted murdered. Is that all? Or will you have some others to tell us about tomorrow morning?'

In his memoir, my father wrote: 'My inclination was to treat it as a joke, which indeed may have been Carman's intention, but even in the second or two before I answered, I remembered that Jeremy had not been joking in either case.'

'No, sir,' he answered, quietly.

The court then adjourned. The press were astounded at the Hetherington affair and that it should have been introduced by the defence. What could be the reason? The anticipation of the following morning's testimony reached fever pitch. Carman didn't disappoint. He returned directly to the topic at the start of the next day in court. He took my father through an outline of what had occurred. Then, remarkably, and in the same tone of voice that one might use to ask the time, the judge asked my father, 'Did you kill Mr Hetherington, Mr Bessell?'

My father was stunned. The words that started to come from his mouth were 'Good God, no!', but he managed to say, 'Goo … ~No, my Lord!'

'I suggest,' said Carman, 'that you told Mr Thorpe you had killed Hetherington,' and he laughed and replied, 'You should have spent more time canvassing for your successor instead of murdering people – then we might have held your seat!'

'That, sir, is a complete fabrication.'

Carman paused and glanced uneasily at Thorpe. Then he continued.

'You must have thought, Mr Bessell, that you had a homicidal maniac on your hands as Liberal leader?'

'Yes. There were times when I thought Mr Thorpe had a sick, crazy obsession about murder, sir.'

In the hours that followed, Carman homed in on my father's questionable past – the lies he had told on behalf of Thorpe, his sex life, his business problems, his addiction to Mandrax. It was as if his whole life caught up with him in one day. The headline the next day was blunt and damaging: 'BESSELL – DRUG ADDICT'.

But Carman's reason for bringing up the Hetherington affair was still unclear. Everyone was already well aware of my father's failings. What advantage could there be for the defence in bringing up Hetherington? The following day, Carman returned to the subject. After questioning my father about the night of his meeting with Hetherington, Carman produced a book of newspaper clippings. It showed that on the Monday morning, 15 June, Thorpe and my father spoke at an election meeting with Liberal candidate, Paul Tyler, at Liskeard – the morning my father said he phoned Thorpe in North Devon. He realised at once he had mixed up his dates.

'You see, Mr Bessell, it takes a long time, does it not, to nail you down in your lies?' Carman was triumphant.

'No, sir. I have not lied. I have made an error in day or date for which I cannot immediately account. That is all.'

Carmen continued. 'There would have been no need for you to telephone Mr Thorpe at his home in North Devon when you were seeing him that morning in Liskeard?'

'That has to be right, sir.' My father's mind was racing, but the knock-out blow was simple.

'It has to be right,' said Carman, 'not only because you saw Mr

Thorpe in Liskeard on the Monday morning, but because he and Mrs Thorpe spent the night before at your house at Looe.'

'I have no recollection of that.' Something was wrong, but he was hopelessly unsure of himself.

Carman wasn't about to let go. 'Mr Thorpe has. And at last, Mr Bessell, we have pinned you down to a lie on oath.' Perjury is a serious accusation.

'No,' my father replied sharply, 'I accept there is an error in days or dates. That is all and, given time, I can provide the correct answers.'

'Yes, Mr Bessell, it takes time to explain lies. The error is in your distorted and tainted mind.'

'Sir. No one would be so stupid as to concoct a story which could so obviously be shown to be wrong. I repeat. It is an error in dates.'

Carman continued to press my father on many issues, nearly all of which my father was able to deal with. But the Hetherington issue stung, and Carman's performance was generally accepted as a turning point for Thorpe.

After a whole day of battering my father, Carman eventually said, 'I suggest, Mr Bessell, that you are right when you say you have a credibility problem. I suggest, too, that you are a person who is incapable of being believed?'

At last, the judge intervened. 'Mr Carman, that is a question for the jury. You don't expect him to agree with you, do you?'

'Well, he might,' Carmen replied.

The judge sighed. 'Very well,' he said.

Carman put the question again.

'If I thought I was no longer capable of being believed,' said my father, 'I would not be here at the Old Bailey. I would be in Oceanside, California.'

And, on that note, Carman sat down. To my father's relief, the cross-examination by Carman was done. So was the court – for the day.

CHAPTER TWENTY-TWO

A HUMBUG

BACK AT HIS hotel, after his first day's testimony, my father frantically went through his records regarding the dates of the Hetherington issue. He quickly established the problem was due to an incorrect diary entry he had made previously. It was important he get the information to the prosecuting counsel as quickly as possible, so the matter could be cleared up, and it could be proved that Carman had made a monumental error in raising the Hetherington matter. After all, it revealed a second occasion on which Thorpe incited a person to commit murder. He had expected Detective Chief Superintendent Challes to call him at his hotel the following morning, when he would pass on the information, but Challes didn't call. When his solicitor, Phillips, picked him up to return to court just after 9.30am, my father realised he had left his notes behind.

On arrival at court, they went straight to their small room next to Court Number One.

'I've forgotten a note I wrote last night for Taylor about Hetherington,' my father said to Phillips. 'It's vital he gets it.'

'Alright,' said Phillips, pulling a notebook from his pocket. 'Tell me what you want to say, and I'll get it to him.'

My father dictated it to him, and he hurried off to find Challes to pass the note on to Taylor before the court began the morning sitting. When the time came, my father resumed his place in the witness box, expecting the Hetherington mix-up to be resolved and Carman made to look silly. The rows of lawyers were in position, but he noticed they were busily talking amongst themselves. Suddenly, they got up and streamed out of the court.

When they returned, the judge made his entry and Taylor immediately asked that the jury and my father be sent out. About 10 minutes passed before the policeman signalled to my father that he was to return. The jury was back; Carman jumped to his feet. With simulated rage, he accused my father of contempt of court, an accusation which had him completely mystified. But he looked at Lionel Phillips and saw that his face looked ashen.

'Have you discussed this case with your solicitor?' Carman raged.

'Yes.'

'Is this a note you dictated to him this morning?' He handed over two small pages from Phillips's notebook.

'His Lordship told you, you are not to discuss the case with anyone and now you admit to having flagrantly and deliberately disobeyed His Lordship's orders …'

The judge backed him up. 'Do you remember I gave that order?'

'Yes, my Lord. But I did not think that it extended to talking to my solicitor–'

The judge interrupted angrily. 'When I said anyone, that meant *everyone*, Mr Bessell. What have you to say for yourself?'

'All that happened was that at the end of each day I share a taxi with Mr Phillips who drops me off at my hotel. As I could not say anything to him in the presence of the driver, he got out with me, and we stood for a moment on the pavement exchanging opinions on how the day had gone.'

Carmen interjected, 'And discussed with him how you should deal with the following day's evidence?'

'Did you discuss the following day's evidence?' the judge asked.

My father described in his memoir his feelings at this point:

'Had I not been so shaken, I might well have exploded with laughter. Clearly, I would have needed to be gifted with clairvoyance to discuss questions that might be put to me before I heard them.'

'No, my Lord. I meant no disrespect, nor did Mr Phillips. It did not occur to me that I was barred from talking to my lawyer.'

'But I said you were to talk to no one,' the judge thundered.

'Yes. I accept that, my Lord.'

'You may have to accept a lot more than that, Mr Bessell. I will deal with this matter later. Let us proceed.'

My father continued his testimony in a state of shock and worry about what was to befall him.

Taylor commenced his re-examination.

'Mr Bessell, when you require legal advice, to whom do you go?'

'My solicitor, sir.'

'Exactly.' Taylor was exasperated and shot a glance at the judge.

My father awaited the clarification on the Hetherington issue. Taylor asked a few more questions, clarifying what had happened with Jack Hayward and the matter of my father's immunity from prosecution.

'Mr Bessell, have you immunity in the United States, where you live?' Evidently this was intended to show that his immunity in the UK was meaningless.

'No, sir.'

The judge interjected. 'But there is no suggestion, is there, that any part of the attempted fraud on Mr Hayward took place in the United States?' Meaning my father couldn't be prosecuted there in any case.

'I put the same proposal Mr Thorpe had put to Mr Hayward to one of Mr Hayward's partners in New York.'

The judge jumped at the opportunity to give him another unnecessary warning.

'I believe you saw Mr Hayward with Mr Thorpe in The Bahamas, and from my notes you also saw Mr Wallace Groves?'

'Yes, my lord.'

'Then you'd better keep away from The Bahamas.'

My father was becoming more and more exasperated with the way in which he was being treated. But he said nothing and waited for the next question from Taylor.

Taylor smiled at him. 'Thank you. That's all, Mr Bessell.'

That's all? *That's all? What about Hetherington?*

My father thought he must have misheard Taylor. Surely he was not simply going to allow the judge's final admonishment to be the last thing the jury heard from his appearance in the witness box? He stood in the box, staring at Taylor.

'You can go, Mr Bessell,' said Taylor.

He walked slowly through the well of the court, glancing up at Thorpe as he did so. Thorpe was sitting upright in his chair, looking considerably better than he had done on the first day.

That evening, I picked my father up from his hotel in Russell Square to take him to dinner with my then partner, Jill. To describe him as furious doesn't begin to do justice to his mood. He was incandescent. I'd never seen him in such a state. It was beyond him how a person who was not in the dock, but merely there as a witness, could be treated with such contempt.

Over dinner in a packed restaurant, my father discussed his feelings with us. Unfortunately, he had quite a loud voice and, half-way through dinner, a man at an adjacent table suddenly stood up and thundered, 'I cannot bear to listen to this any more. It's disgusting!'

The whole restaurant went quiet, as the man left with his partner. The three of us were very embarrassed. It was another, stark reminder to all of us my prophesy that my father would be resented as a grass was coming horribly true. My father decided he'd had enough. As he had now been discharged as a witness, he decided there was no point in remaining in the UK simply to be hounded by the press, so he returned to Oceanside to await the outcome of the trial and to work on his book.

On Thursday 7 June, the court was packed for the opening of the much-anticipated defence. The world was desperate to hear what Thorpe had to say once he was under oath in the witness box. As David Holmes was first on the indictment, he was to be called first. His barrister, John Matthew, stood and uttered one sentence.

'My Lord, on behalf of Mr Holmes, I call no evidence.'

Gareth Williams QC, counsel for George Deakin, put Deakin in the witness box, who explained he had introduced the alleged hitman, Andrew Newton, to David Holmes, but he had believed this was to help deal with a blackmailer and didn't know anything about a plot to murder. When he had stepped down, Denis Cowley QC, on behalf of John Le Mesurier, called no evidence. Then it was Carman's turn. Everyone leaned forward eagerly in anticipation. Journalists had their notebooks at the ready. Now was the moment. Carman stood.

'My Lord, on behalf of Mr Jeremy Thorpe, I call no evidence.'

The court was stunned. And disappointed. The press were going to be denied their moment. Was this a tacit admission of guilt? Innocent people usually can't wait to get onto the stand and defend their innocence. Why was he not prepared to 'vigorously defend' himself as he had claimed he would? Surely this would be a disaster for him.

But it was a masterstroke on the part of Carman. Thorpe would not have to stand there for hours, under oath, explaining away all my father did to protect him from Scott. He wouldn't have to explain Hetherington, nor would he have to explain his involvement with the Hayward fraud and the fake telephone call, during which he pretended Diane was a Washington official, nor would he have to explain a myriad other difficult situations. Instead, he could rely on Carman having simply discredited the prosecution's witnesses and pleading that there was no case to answer. As it turned out, Carman wasn't the only one Thorpe could rely on; he could also rely on the establishment to look after him, in the form of the judge himself, Justice Cantley. What followed has often been described as one of the most prejudicial events in British legal history, the judge's summing up for the jury.

On Friday 15 June, the court adjourned for the weekend. On Saturday my father flew to New York to await the jury's verdict before continuing his journey to London to discuss a publishing deal for his memoir. On Monday, the judge began his summing up.

'The four accused are men of hitherto unblemished reputation,' the judge began, reminding the jury that Thorpe was a Privy Councillor, the former leader of the Liberal Party and 'a national figure with a distinguished public record'. This ignored the discussion, in court, of Thorpe's involvement in an attempt to obtain £20,000 from Hayward by deception in addition to the fraud attempt with my father.

He discussed the 'tainting' of witnesses: 'The pursuit, not of justice, but of profit, has tampered with the quality of important evidence.' He added that, if there had been an enterprising media in Biblical times, Judas Iscariot 'might have thought the 30 pieces of silver the least of his rewards'. In this way, he linked my father's name to the ultimate grass, Judas, ignoring his need to fund his legal expenses.

'Mr Bessell is plainly a very intelligent, very articulate man,' he continued. 'He must have impressed the voters of Cornwall very much. He has told us he was a lay preacher, at the same time, as he put it, being sexually promiscuous. And therefore, a humbug.'

He went on to say evidence that might be affected by financial considerations should be looked at with distrust and treated as 'dangerous', unless corroborated. This was, of course, a reference to the *Sunday Telegraph* agreement. Then came his most remarkable comment in referring to the Hetherington episode as one my father had invented: 'The fact that a man tells a lie in a case does not mean he is lying all the time. You cannot say a witness is disqualified if he is caught in one lie.'

If Cantley really believed my father lied about Hetherington, it was no trivial matter. He had said, under oath, that Thorpe had incited him to murder Hetherington. In the case of such a significant lie, the judge would have had no option but to refer the issue to the Director of Public Prosecutions, who should have charged my father with perjury. The judge did not.

In the words of Auberon Waugh, from his book about the trial, *The Last Word:* 'It had been as deliberate and prolonged destruction of one witness as anyone was likely to hear. Whether it was justified, or whether it was an abuse of judicial power is something which would have to be decided between Joseph Cantley and his Maker.'

The summing up ended on 20 June, and the jury retired to consider their verdict. They had a lot to consider; it took them two days. My father's testimony was only part of the proceedings – Scott himself had played a significant role – but that testimony was central to confirming everything Scott claimed over the years.

On Thursday 21 June, my father sat alone in a small hotel room in New York, waiting for news that did not come. The more he waited, the more he doubted his decision to testify. Whatever the result, it was a disaster for him – and his friend. If Thorpe were found not guilty, the damage would still be so great he would probably never be able to rebuild what had been an outstanding career. A 'not guilty' judgement also meant that my father's hands would be forever tied with regard to what he could say about the affair. Publishers would be unwilling to print his book. It would effectively end any hope he had of telling his side of the story and clearing his name, a disaster for him.

But a guilty verdict might be even worse. He was absolutely convinced such a verdict would cause Thorpe to take his own life – and he felt he would be unable to live with such a burden, and might have to do likewise.

On Friday 22 June, I had a business lunch at an Italian restaurant in Soho. As we were eating our desserts, Jill came running into the restaurant.

'The jury's out.'

'And?'

'He's innocent,' she said.

The shock reverberated through my body, but I like to think I hid it reasonably well. My father had been made to look a complete fool, and a liar, in the eyes of the world. It was a terrible moment, the first of many such moments I would have to endure for the rest of my life. I paid and left the restaurant to call my father at his hotel, but I could not get through.

In New York, it was early morning. The phone rang in my father's hotel room, waking him. It was Diane.

'He's innocent,' said Diane.

'Thank you,' he said, quietly, and gently put down the phone.

At that moment, every part of my father's life caught up with him – his childhood, his parents' break-up, his war years, his first wife's death, his marriage to my mother, his deceitful affairs, his money problems, his parliamentary career, his jet-set life, his children, keeping his three lives separate, his suicidal feelings, the Mandrax, the attempts to prevent murders from being committed … All of it had returned to haunt him over the two weeks of the trial. Yet, despite everything, he was pleased Thorpe would not go to prison.

Alone in his hotel room, my father sat on the edge of the bed… and fell apart.

CHAPTER TWENTY-THREE

ESPIONAGE?

SO THERE WE have it, in my search for my father I have gone from his days as a humble tailor in Bath, to an international business tycoon and the disaster of the Thorpe trial. Yet still, remembering the picture my mother found in my father's briefcase and his words 'it's someone we have to get rid of', there is the overriding question of his secret work. Did it exist at all? Did they 'get rid' of people? Diane mentioned to me on more than one occasion she thought they did.

In the 1960s, how easy it would have been for a man who wished to live three separate lives to pretend he was involved in some kind of espionage. At a stroke, he gave himself a simple excuse to disappear, sometimes for weeks on end, with no contact other than that which he allowed. There was no internet and there were no mobile phones to help track him down. And of course he wouldn't have to remember which lies he'd told to whom; he could tell the same lie to everyone. It would take some nerve, though, to live with the perpetual fear of being found out.

But what if that person *was* involved in some kind of espionage or secret government work? For obvious reasons, he could never prove it if challenged.

If my father was indeed involved in some form of secret work, it would validate many of his actions and his overall trustworthiness.

If he wasn't, he is guilty of the most awful act of betrayal to all who loved him.

A spy is someone 'employed by one nation to secretly convey classified information of strategic importance to another nation', so not necessarily an enemy nation. A spy may, for example, act as a secret adviser to a friendly country, not passing on specific sensitive information, but secretly informing the other country of likely attitudes and reactions at home to events and policies in the foreign country.

If a UK MP was working for the United States government advising the US how the UK might respond to certain US policies, would that make the MP a spy? What if that MP was giving public support to US actions without the UK government knowing he was being encouraged and briefed by the US, even if not being paid to do so. Would that make him a spy?

My family's life changed dramatically over the course of just 12 years. In 1952 I was born into a poor family. By 1964, my father was an MP. His beautiful wife, who didn't need to work and was always there to support him, wore fur coats, dressed in Gucci and other designer brands and looked very much the part on his arm. His London laundry business was so successful that he sold his interest and opened an investment brokerage. All this came at a cost, though. He had an office in Mayfair, the most expensive part of the West End of London; a large house in Cornwall, with cleaning and gardening staff; two children at expensive private boarding schools; a non-working wife; several very expensive cars; stratospheric travel expenses, mostly between London and New York; a West End apartment for his mistress, Sally; and a few secretaries and research assistants. His general standard of living added to the expense – weekends away with girlfriends in Paris and The Bahamas; gentlemen's club memberships; and fine dining. His monthly outgoings could not have been met by his meagre

MP's salary – £3,250 a year in 1964 (roughly £54,000 in today's money). His total outgoings, in today's money, must have been about £120,000 a month, so he would have had to be earning an additional £70,000 a month from his business, to which he was able to give very little time.

Having established his reputation for living the high life, to lose that status would have been an unbearable loss of face to a man whose public image was his very existence. Unfortunately, his dedication to his constituents left him little time to spend on his business, which began to suffer. By 1965, his income was falling behind his expenses.

In addition to his stressful financial problems, he had his campaign to run for the 1966 general election. And there was also his secret work. On that day in Cambridge, when my father told me about his secret work for the government, he hadn't told me exactly what it was that he did, as it was 'covered by the Official Secrets Act'. Of course, it's possible he simply made up some cock-and-bull, glamorous story to keep his son in awe of him. But my sister, Paula, has very similar recollections, and there are other things which point to his claim not having been made up simply to impress.

If my father was telling the truth, what was this secret work, and who was it for? If he wasn't, what did he stand to gain by fabricating such a story? The obvious answer is that it would have been a very convenient cover for his numerous extra-marital affairs. While there's no doubt he used secret work as cover when it suited him, it's unlikely that was its main purpose. There were too many people outside the family who also suspected he was doing secret work of some kind. No government agency would come forward to say, 'Yes, your father worked for us', but it might be possible to have it confirmed that he did *not* work for any secret government agency.

In April 2019, I contacted MI5 – Military Intelligence, Section 5, the UK's domestic security agency – to ask if they had any files on my father. They let me know that they will only release information more than 50 years old, and only if they consider it to be non-sensitive. MI5 is not subject to the Freedom of Information Act. Four months after my initial enquiry, I received a response informing me they did indeed hold information on my father, but that only a small part of it fell outside the 50-year rule. They let me know they would study the file and, if suitable for release, they would include it in the next batch of files due to be released to the National Archives, scheduled for 2020/21.

Then Covid struck and all schedules went out of the window, but, in January 2020, I followed up. Eight months later, in August, they let me know that they had reconstituted the file, which had been microfiched some years ago. They were reviewing the file to see if it was suitable for release and if any redaction would be required. As this was a slow and painstaking process, they anticipated the file would not be released before mid-2021.

I realised they might never release the information, and they were under no obligation to give me a reason. The closer I got to finishing the book, though, the more I realised the importance of knowing at least something. In a last bid, I contacted MI5 again on 6 September 2023. They responded in detail, including the following information:

> *We have looked again in detail at the information we have on your father and considered whether we might now be able to release material from it to The National Archives. We have, however, concluded that the file is not suitable for release. This is because much of the information on the file ... comes from sources that we have to continue to protect. And any information on that file that was received after 1973 – even though much of it is from open sources – remains subject to our policy of releasing nothing that is less than 50 years old.*

The letter went on to outline one small aspect where they had investigated contacts he made with the Romanian Embassy whilst an MP and had found nothing untoward.

Private Eye magazine claimed, in an article titled 'A Duff Inquiry', published on 15 May 1987, that he was an F-Division agent for MI5: '… Peter Bessell, former Liberal MP for Bodmin, for instance, was an F Division agent for all the time he was in Parliament, and afterwards.' MI5's F Division was specifically tasked with hunting down 'internal subversives'. *Private Eye*, however, was notoriously unreliable.

In the 1960s, the implication was that he was working for the UK, but he may have been working for the US, as he certainly said he was in later years. Henry Kissinger claimed not to know him and said that he was a fraud, yet I have correspondence between them showing them to be on first-name terms.

I also have correspondence, dated 17 March 1967, between my father and Mr William Brubeck, Political Councillor at the US Embassy in London, regarding my father making a visit to Vietnam in support of the US position there. My father's letter outlines how, although he would publicly be making the trip as a fact-finding mission for the UK Liberal Party, it would actually be used as an opportunity to promote US interests. My father's letter ends: 'Perhaps we should have a word before Easter, you know where to reach me. Peter'.

The letter shows that the men's relationship was obviously close, and my father was confirming that he was prepared to promote the interests of the US Government with regard to Vietnam and not be the independent observer his public persona would suggest in the UK. It's no wonder the US put some value on his contribution to their diplomatic efforts surrounding the Vietnam War, as Britain was a big player on the international stage at the time and there was a great deal of resistance in the UK to any support for the war.

His Vietnam trip would have resulted in him being regarded as a friendly alien on whom the US could depend upon for support and advice on the UK Government position in many areas.

My father was also, apparently, on friendly terms with both US President Richard Nixon and President Lyndon B Johnson. On 19 March 1976, he wrote to his solicitor as follows:

> *I may have told you that I knew Richard Nixon slightly. I saw him twice during the early days of Watergate. He persuaded himself he was a sort of embattled hero being persecuted by his friends and enemies alike. He concluded that in those circumstances he was justified in taking any action to cover up the scandal. Nixon is a patriot (yes, really) and by his own lights tried hard and conscientiously to serve his country. But he lost that motivation when the net began to close in around him.*

I found in my father's papers a document written by him, explaining that he was able to use his contacts to get Diane's father, Fred Miller, help with his business errors. It's hard to imagine you could achieve that without some very influential friends who had not only the power, but also the motivation to help.

Gordon Winter, a South African secret agent and the author of *Inside BOSS*, about South Africa's apartheid-era Bureau of State Security, claimed that my father was an agent for the CIA. My father always angrily denied this, and I believe him that it was either a fabrication or a mistake.

Diane kept a file in later years labelled 'Unadmitted Person' in which she kept detailed reasons for her belief that my father was engaged in secret work and that he worked as an 'unadmitted' adviser to the US National Security Council. There are several letters from my father to my mother in which he refers to his work in coded form.

There are many documents in the 'unadmitted person' file, which Diane left me, but the most interesting are:

- A note from Diane outlining her reasons for believing he worked as an unadmitted adviser to the US National Security Council.
- A detailed description, by my father, of his contact at the White House who revealed the Chivers Papers to him, Dr Robert Miller (not related to Diane's father). I have established there was a Miller on the White House staff at the time. I have no doubt some papers existed and that my father saw them. My father's affidavit goes into enormous detail about his meetings with Dr Miller and in describing the documents. These descriptions were verified by Sally.
- Various memoranda from my father outlining details of his meetings with his 'bosses', in which he names Lloyd Hughes, Charles Martin and Everett Simmons as his contacts in Los Angeles. I have not been able to track them down.
- A nine page memorandum, using coded names, outlining the business error with Diane's father.
- A sealed envelope left by my father to be opened in emergencies only. Diane opened it after his death. There was a note in his handwriting with the words: 'USE MY PHONE ONLY (the number will not work with yours). DIAL 757-7635. Ask for Peter Bessell and say who you are.'
- A piece of lined notepaper with the words: 'Note Kissinger and White House #'s in old Diaries in desk'. I have checked his diaries and can confirm the numbers are there.

- A note outlining how a typewriter repairman, who came to service my father's typewriter at Oceanside, recognised him from President Nixon's West Coast home at San Clemente.

- A handwritten note by my father, not addressed to anyone and not dated, outlining the terms of a contract for the position of 'Consultant on S.E. Asia' for 12 months. It names Everett Simmons and Martin as his contacts.

- The memorandum from my father to Fred Miller, his wife Doris, and Diane, dated 29 March 1980, outlining a meeting he'd had in Washington regarding his pay and contract. The memorandum was written with coded names, but he attached the real names on a separate sheet, along with the suggestion that the sheet should be destroyed. The attached names included Charles Martin (Justice Department), Lloyd Hughes, Mr Zbigniew Brzezinski (President Carter's National Security Advisor), Mr Friendly (a co-ordinator between the National Security Council and the Department of State), Mr Lowenstein, and Secretary of State Vance. There is a handwritten note by Diane at the top of the first page saying 'Remove'.

- A note from Diane pointing out that soon after my father's death his office was broken into and *only* the files relating to his secret work were stolen, nothing else. As she wrote, 'The bastards!'

My father's affidavit on the Romanovs and the Chivers Papers mentions his contact at the State Department. It's a sworn statement in which he states his willingness to repeat the contents in a court of law. The contact is not named.

Further to all this, Diane stated in a letter to my father's solicitor, that he continued his secret work for many years as payment for the favour done to her father.

But the item about the meeting with Brzezinski in 1980 is the most critical of all. If I could just prove that meeting took place, or could have taken place, it would go a long way towards verifying my father did undertake some kind of secret advisory work for the National Security Council, or the State Department. Apart from Brzezinski and Secretary of State Cyrus Vance, none of the other names are generally recognised as being involved with the National Security Council. It would have been very difficult for my father to know these people had he not been an insider or done a great deal of research, for which he didn't have the time. The names he attached to the memorandum weren't simply written as a list – there were misspellings and suggestions he might have misheard names, the most obvious being he wasn't sure if one of them was Lowenstein or Lobestein. If he was trying to fool people with this list, I think it unlikely he would have gone to the length of misspelling names – he would have wanted the reader to believe he knew them personally.

The meeting took place at the State Department in Washington during the presidency of Jimmy Carter. An online search at the Jimmy Carter Library in Atlanta revealed nothing. But most of Brzezinski's files relating to that period remain heavily redacted and classified, as do the personnel files. It's impossible to prove the meeting happened, but did any of those people exist? And did they have any connection to Brzezinski? This is where I focused my research.

The only hope I had of finding anything of use was to visit the Carter Library in Atlanta in person which, in March 2025, I did. I was aware it would be an incredibly long shot. I spent countless hours leafing through folder after folder, until – finally – two names popped up.

The first was Al Friendly, mentioned in a short memorandum from David Aaron to Brzezinski – 'The attached is self-explanatory. Al Friendly called me and is willing to arrange this.' Finally, I knew that a Mr Friendly had been connected to Brzezinski. Two days later, I found another memorandum from Friendly, this time addressed directly to Brzezinski.

Finding one name lent credibility to my father's story, but I really needed another. As I sat in the library, I thought if my father had been advising the National Security Council on something, what might it have been? There are millions of files in the library. What were the chances that I'd stumble across the right one? Then I remembered my father became deeply involved in work on Rhodesia's bid for independence in the 1960s. Might he have been advising the Americans on southern Africa? I asked for a folder on Rhodesia (now Zimbabwe). It was all but empty except for a list of items which had been removed and remain classified. Bingo! On that list was a memo of a meeting between US democrat politician Allard Lowenstein and Under Secretary Newsom, dated 27 February 1979. If this Lowenstein was present at the meeting my father claimed to have attended, it was very shortly before his death, as Lowenstein was shot in his Manhattan apartment on 14 March 1980, in suspicious circumstances.

Above all, there was no reason for the contents of the memorandum to be fabricated. If my father had wanted to do that, it would have been much easier, and less expensive, to have gone to Los Angeles and pretended there had been a conference call. He didn't need to travel all the way to Washington, particularly when he was becoming increasingly unwell, unless it was absolutely necessary.

I believe my father *was* involved in advisory work for the US National Security Council, either directly or indirectly through a go-between, and seemingly not always willingly. My father was, I believe, and will remain, an 'unadmitted person'.

Obviously, none of this confirms that my father was a spy, or an adviser, to any government. It does show, however, that he was involved in secret activities of some kind.

I spent a week at the Nixon Presidential Library, in Yorba Linda, California, where I ploughed through seemingly endless files which might have revealed some connection between my father and the US Government, particularly concerning Vietnam. Other than the connection to Kissinger, I found nothing of significance, though that's not to say there is nothing hidden within the millions of documents in the library.

My father always publicly denied he was a spy, particularly when some UK newspapers claimed he had been one. He was adamant he would not have been a spy while he was an MP, as he always maintained that 'being an agent for a foreign country while being a Member of Parliament would be the most despicable act of treachery'. In another letter to his solicitor, dated 8 February 1978, he refers to a conversation he had with Barry Penrose and Roger Courtier, the authors of *The Pencourt File*, a book on the Thorpe affair, in which they claim that he told them he was involved in espionage:

> *For my part, the only serious error is over my alleged association with the US secret services. Needless to say, I have never at any time been the agent of the US or any other government. I have resisted denying this to press only because I do not want to discredit* The Pencourt File.

Despite the spy denial, my father never denied working for the National Security Council; in fact, he suggested on a number of occasions that he did.

There are many indications that he may have been a spy, or an 'adviser', but many denials, and no concrete proof either way. If he was *not* involved in secret work of some kind, why would he have invented such a story and kept it going right up until he died? And why would so many seemingly well-informed people agree that there is at least the suspicion that he was some kind of secret agent? My father might not have been a spy in the traditional sense, certainly not for the CIA, which he detested, but the fact that he appears personally to have known two US presidents is suggestive.

There are contradictions in his letters to his solicitor – a claim that he was not involved in espionage for the US, while revealing his relationship with Nixon. The story he told Thorpe about his experience in a Vienna nightclub leads one to wonder what he was doing in a nightclub in Vienna. The city was a centre for espionage for many years, particularly for the Russians during the Cold War, not least because of Austria's neutrality and the city's location in eastern Europe. My father had a deep love for Vienna, particularly its musical culture, and often spoke wistfully of his time there as a young man. But exactly when, or why, he spent time there is a complete mystery. His activity during the war for the Ministry of Information was most peculiar when you consider that he was a conscientious objector, so would have been regarded with suspicion by the UK authorities. He was hardly the kind of person to have been placed in a sensitive role.

Everybody likes to believe they know something that no one else does. It makes them feel special and helps their social standing, whether with regard to high-level government business or village gossip. What easier way to achieve this than to suggest that one is some kind of secret agent? My father was often accused of being like Walter Mitty – the fictional character who lives a life of fantasies, imagining himself to be a wartime pilot, a surgeon and a devil-may-care killer. My father was plagued by feelings of inadequacy, brought about by what he saw as his lack of education compared to his university-educated peers, like Thorpe. Despite his great intellect, he was always looking for ways to compensate for that perception. This may explain his exaggeration of the achievements of his father, for one thing.

The core of my research has been focused on my father's secret work. Above all else I have to know if what he had been telling his family was, at least, partly true. If none of it was true, and his life had only been deceptions and lies, it would be an unbearable burden for me, my sister, and our children.

But the nearest I have come to proof was the extensive document I found in his archive in which he tells, almost as an outline for a movie, the entire story using pseudonyms. This document is the glue in which all the disparate events come together in one place and suddenly make sense. This is the place where he discusses his dealings with 'Robinson' from his secret work, and all the episodes that led to his disappearance. I know much of it to be true because I was there for part of the time.

Would it stand up in a court of law? Probably not. But I'm sure he intended it to be found and confirms, to me at least, he indeed had secret masters and he was an 'unadmitted person' of some kind. But – a spy? No.

CHAPTER TWENTY-FOUR

THE AWFUL TRUTH

AS WITH ALL biography and autobiography, the reader's overriding questions are always: How much of this is actually true? Which of these events happened as described? Is the witness dependable? In this case, I, as the author, am asking the same questions.

'Whatever you do, do not be perceived as trying to defend your father,' was the professional advice I received when I started writing this book. But I'm my father's son. Am I to blindly accept he was a pathological liar because it makes good copy? Or do I assess reasons for his behaviour, which is very different from defending him? And what would anyone else have done differently in his situation? Many readers may be feeling, 'Stop doing this to yourself! Can you not see him for what he was? It jumps off every page that he lied and deceived everyone throughout his life!' Yes, I can see why people might feel that way. But now that I've completed my research and found out as much as I reasonably can about his life, I'm forced to come to a conclusion, for good or bad.

Let's begin by considering the worst-case scenario.

My father stole petrol coupons during the war. He had an affair during his first marriage and continued to have affairs and flings throughout his marriage to my mother. It's possible he set fire to his business in the early 1950s to get out of financial trouble. He led at least three personal lives: his family life with my mother and his children; another with Sally; and a third with Diane. Each of these lives was kept secret from the other, though both Sally and Diane knew about my mother, my sister and me. In this worst-case scenario, he also created a secret world where he claimed he worked covertly for both the UK and US governments at a high level, which gave him a convenient excuse to disappear from one personal life in order to spend time in another. He was obsessed with sex. In his business life, he lied many times, once committing fraud by promising Whitmarsh there were no other charges on Polraen, and attempting it on another occasion with Hayward. Was he a complete charlatan? After all, these are indisputable facts.

But for all that, he wasn't a wicked man. He was a wonderful father during my childhood and spent a great deal of time helping those less fortunate than himself. He was adored by most of those who knew him. Perhaps he was driven by ambition? Or a need to conquer? Many politicians are. One of Diane's most endearing characteristics was her ability to judge a person not by their actions, but by what had *caused* those actions. It's easy to think of a thief as a bad person, until you consider the desperation that drove them to commit their crime. We are often too ready to judge and condemn, without knowing anything about someone and their life. That's not to say there aren't people who are simply bad, but my father was not one of them.

There is one terrible fact I can't escape: my father's actions all but destroyed my mother. Yet she didn't stop loving him for one second; and I don't believe he stopped loving her either.

Cruelly, he wrote in his farewell letter to my mother that he would be back in six months. That was a fantasy, but perhaps he actually believed that fantasy and clung to the dream that those he left behind would save his business and he would return to my mother. Perhaps he was, quite simply, a fantasist. But he was a religious man, who wrote to her many years before, stating that, 'before God', *she* was the woman for him. Is it possible that he remained with Diane because her father had money and, in the end, he had little choice? I know that thought crossed Diane's mind more than once, despite which, she stayed with him until he died in 1985. Another example of someone knowing him to be a rogue, yet loving him without question.

I've discovered in my mother's papers that she went to see my father in California, twice, about a year after he disappeared. At the time, I didn't know about these visits, during the course of which my mother remained completely unaware of the existence of Diane. She thought my father was living as a pauper in a shack he was too ashamed to let her see. She travelled to Los Angeles and stayed in a motel, where my father called her.

'Hello, Mama,' he said calmly. She started to cry.

'Where are you?' she said, sobbing.

'I can't say,' he replied, 'All I can tell you is I'm near San Diego.'

'Can I see you?'

'I'd love to see you. But you will need to travel closer to me. I can't get to LA.'

'Peter, how could you do this? Why didn't you tell me?' she said.

'Let's talk about it when we meet. Take a bus to San Diego and I'll see you at the bus station.'

As she wistfully gazed at the ocean on the coastal bus ride, despite all the heartache and betrayal my father had caused, she prayed that their meeting would be the beginning of a reconciliation. She could love no other man. She couldn't wait to see him again.

The bus pulled into the station and the casually dressed and suddenly slightly frail figure of my father came into view. My mother's overriding impression on first seeing him and talking to him was similar to mine a few years later – 'He was a shadow of the man he used to be.' Gone was the overwhelmingly self-confident politician and businessman who only dealt in issues of significance; in his place was what she referred to as a 'small man', lacking self-belief and obsessed with trivial matters. But it made no difference to her feelings for him.

First, they had tea at the bus station, then they went for a drive along the Pacific coast, parked and reminisced. Did they touch or kiss? I don't know. But my mother did leave some notes on their conversation. Apparently, he brought sandwiches, which she noted had been immaculately prepared, but, as she watched him eat them, the bottom fell out of her world yet again.

'I'm not sure what I want to do in the future,' he said. My mother was speechless. She had hoped, assumed, prayed the meeting was to pave the way for their eventual reconciliation and to allow him back into society. She was destined to cling to that hope for the rest of her life. Her notes of their meeting are succinct: 'He left me at hotel – drove away – to where?' And then an odd entry: 'I didn't sleep – he did, well.' This suggests to me that they might have spent the night together. My mother returned to New York and collapsed. A short time later she received a small package from California, heavily marked 'personal'. It contained a recording by Richard Tauber, the renowned tenor they both loved, of 'The Dearest Maiden' – a song about first love being the best love. It tortured her, and she was unaware the whole time of Diane's existence, which she only learned about years later, through a newspaper headline. Yet, even then, she retained her hope that she and my father might be together again.

When my mother went to California again, she stayed in a small apartment in Santa Monica, where my father stayed under the pseudonym of Dr Hoffman. My mother asked him why he needed a pseudonym. He said he needed it for his secret work. When it was time for my mother to go, he offered to run her to the airport. She said she'd rather he didn't, but he took her anyway. Their parting then was the last time she ever saw him. I don't know if they hugged. I also don't know if Diane was aware of these meetings. I didn't dare ask her for fear of the distress it might cause her.

As for the secret work, the person whose opinion on this matter I trust most is Diane, who died in 2020. She lived with my father from the late 1960s until his death in 1985. Like everyone else, she wondered if such work existed. Even after their 'disappearance', when they were living in California, my father's secret work continued. He used to make regular solo trips to Los Angeles for meetings. Both before and after his death, Diane worked hard to find out what she could.

It's quite possible my father was continuing to use his secret work as a ruse to get away to Los Angeles from time to time to do whatever it was he wanted to do – meet women presumably. But the whole story was so complex it seems implausible that he would have needed to go to such lengths simply to spend time with another woman, particularly when he and Diane had an agreement that they could have affairs, as long as they were discreet. Diane's parents, Fred and Doris, moved to Oceanside to live with them. Miller paid for a substantial property by the beach with two large houses for the two couples to live in and two small cottages to rent out as vacation lets. My father renovated the cottages, which were in a poor state, entirely on his own. This gave Miller a return on his investment, and I believe my father was paid a small sum from that income as payment for the upkeep of the property.

Whenever my father needed money, however little – to go to Los Angeles on secret business, for example – he had to write begging letters to Miller. The reason Miller paid up was because he believed that, at some point, the Government would pay my father, or my father's memoir on the Thorpe affair would earn enough money for him to pay Miller back.

I used to be grateful to Miller for supporting my father, but I later believed it was the very least he could have done, given how my father arranged for Miller's business errors to be buried and left him able to continue living as a wealthy man. My father may have pretended to continue his secret work after his move to Oceanside simply to ensure Miller continued to support him.

The contradictions in my father's life are practically irreconcilable. He went from being almost a pauper to a man with significant wealth, and back again. He was a pacifist who was accused by Thorpe of being a murderer. There were unresolved questions about his parents. He preached to the most puritanical of congregations while living a fairly debauched life. He suffered from depression at a time when there was not much help to be had. But his real problem was that he was completely unable to say no to anyone. He gave, both financially and as a friend, when he was in absolutely no position to do so. He gave his time and effort to his constituents when he should have been focusing on his businesses. He was unable to tell my mother he couldn't afford the house, or me that I couldn't have a speed-boat. The growing burden of his debt brought out the worst in him.

Was he a fantasist? Yes, almost certainly. Undoubtedly, he got himself tangled up in a web of his own making.

Did he tell the truth at the Thorpe trial? Yes, he did tell the truth. I know he did because I was party to some of the discussions and events concerning Thorpe at the time. There's also little doubt that if he was going to be dragged halfway around the world to give evidence, he intended to try to use the trial to his advantage in some way. Unfortunately, the deal with the *Sunday Telegraph* proved to be disastrous, although it did set the legal precedent that witnesses would no longer be allowed to enter into that kind of arrangement with the media before a trial.

When it was all over, he had no independent income on which to survive. He had no pension, and no social security, as he was not a US taxpayer. He could not return to the UK because of his health. Diane saw everything he ever wrote, including his private letters, so he would always write bearing her in mind. He was financially dependent on Diane's father, who was probably entirely unaware my father was compelled to continue working for the US Government under the threat that they would re-open the case of Miller's errors if he didn't. In his final years, he had no independence and wrote a lengthy explanation of this in the form of an outline for a play or movie. He went from being an international politician and businessman, to having no life of his own whatsoever. Many may say he deserved his fate and, sadly, that is certainly how he felt.

There's no getting away from the fact that he was a charlatan in his personal life. He admitted it, and offered no excuses. As his child, it was a shock to grow up and find out he had been deceiving us all, in so many ways. Incredibly, all the women he loved forgave him, even when they found out the truth. All my mother wanted, more than anything in the world, was to know that my father loved her.

While researching this book, I visited my sister to compare memories of various events and confirm my own were accurate. We discussed the idyllic life my father and Diane led once they had settled in Oceanside. They had a beachfront property on the Pacific Ocean. They would wake daily to the sound of waves, in which they could watch dolphins play, and beyond the break, they could see migrating whales pass by. My father and Diane undoubtedly loved each other. He had to make just the occasional trip to LA to continue his part-time secret work, it was a world away from the days of poverty and business disasters when he first married my mother. Then Thorpe interrupted this blissful routine.

'Of course he was having an affair with a woman in Los Angeles,' my sister said.

'What? *What?*'

She looked at me, surprised that I hadn't known.

'How do you know?' I asked.

'He told me,' she said, matter-of-factly.

Over the years, I had reached the point where there were so many accusations and revelations about my father I thought I could no longer be surprised or shocked. But I was both surprised *and* shocked by what my sister told me. I thought he and Diane were living a life devoted to each other, but it appeared this was not the case. I also doubted, for a moment, that he had been travelling to LA for 'secret meetings'. It felt like a final blow which I did not want to face. So, I went back to the archive and searched some more. Had every trip from Oceanside to LA been for nothing more than a grubby affair?

Diane suspected as much, but concluded my father's illness had rendered him incapable of sex. She felt that, at worst, it was a friendship, which she would not deny him. His lover was the receptionist at the motel where he stayed on his trips to LA. Diane discovered that the relationship was a result of his staying there, rather than the reason for his visits.

During the 11 years they lived together in Oceanside, Diane carefully monitored whatever my father did. It seems likely to me that he was indeed an 'unadmitted person', working under some kind of duress. His affairs followed on from that.

In the early 1980s, my father's emphysema worsened to the point he no longer had the breath to walk and was eventually bed ridden. On 26 November, 1985, he suddenly sat up, held his hands to the air and called "Please, God, take me now." On 27 November, he died in his sleep. It was a true blessing that, after the trauma, crippling depression and unending tension of his life, his God allowed him to pass peacefully.

X

Not long after my lunch with my mother in Felixstowe, she started to develop difficulty in walking. Then, one day, she fell while going upstairs. Following that, she started having hallucinations, getting up in the middle of the night and standing alone at the top of the stairs, terrified, because she could hear someone knocking on the door. As these hallucinations became worse, it was clear that she was no longer capable of taking care of herself. Following another incident, she was taken to a hospital in Ipswich.

At this point, my mother was in her late 80s and her dementia was worsening. Her night-time hallucinations became worse. She would see thousands of spiders crawling over her and try, frantically, to clamber out of bed, but she was incapable of doing so without injuring herself. The nurses became impatient with her. When it was time for my sister and me to leave her in the evenings, she would beg us to stay because she was so frightened of being alone. We would stay and hold her hand like a child until she was asleep. The hospital had failed to diagnose that my mother had Dementia with Lewy Bodies, a type of progressive dementia characterised by visual hallucinations, among other symptoms. It was only going to get worse. Eventually, she was moved into a home. Her deterioration once she entered the home was rapid, her mobility quickly all but disappearing. We knew that when she could no longer swallow it would be the end.

A few days before she died, my sister and I visited her. The nurses had placed her in an armchair in the communal room. As we entered, we saw her, unable to move, slouched in the chair, with her head down. We thought she was probably asleep, but she wasn't; it was simply that she no longer had the ability to keep her head up. But when she heard our voices, she strained and raised her head slightly. She could still talk, though only very quietly.

'Hello, Mum,' we said, as cheerily as we could.

'Oh, hello,' she said. Then she paused thoughtfully.

'Where's Daddy? I thought he was coming with you.'

My sister and I looked at each other for a moment.

'Mummy, I told you Daddy died a very long time ago. He's not here,' my sister said gently.

Her response was as if she had heard of his death for the first time, the kind of shock we all feel when we suddenly lose a loved one. She raised her head again.

'NO! NO! NO!' she cried. She stopped and thought for a moment. Then she asked, 'Did he love me?'

X

One morning, three days later, as I drove the two hours to the home again, I thought of everything that had happened over the past 40 or so years and what our lives had become since my father's disappearance, particularly my mother's life. Through all the heartbreak, the financial difficulties, his reappearance, her learning of Diane, the Thorpe case, the need to earn an independent living, her one, overriding concern was knowing if he had loved her.

My sister had been with our mother all night. In my heart, I knew I was probably going to be with her as she died in just a few hours, perhaps sooner. I had determined to tell her that my father *had* loved her, so that she could die in peace.

When I entered the room, she was lying on her side, completely paralysed. She could not talk; she could not even blink, but her eyelids were very slightly open. The nurses had placed her in the foetal position and came in occasionally to put drops in her parched eyes.

Paula sat in an armchair by the side of the bed, with my mother facing away from her. I stood on the other side, between the bed and the window, watching her expressionless face and listening to her laboured breathing. It was obvious the time was getting close. For a couple of minutes my sister left the room to talk to the nurses. When she did, I said to my mother, 'Don't worry, everything is fine.' I don't why I said that or what it could possibly mean. In the end it simply didn't feel right to say to her, 'Daddy loved you,' because, at the time, I couldn't pretend to honestly know. And I felt it wasn't a moment for pretence. But maybe it was.

My sister came back in and sat down. I could hear what I knew to be the death rattle in my mother's breathing. Incredibly, I saw a tear force its way from her dry eyes. I had no way of knowing if it was from sadness, fear or the absolute desperation of not knowing about my father's love, but she was going. Then, she stopped breathing.

The awful truth is that I completely failed to allow her to die in peace. My father had taken his secrets to his grave.

ACKNOWLEDGEMENTS

'FINDING DAD' has certainly not been a lone project, and I am indebted to many people, in particular:

Special thanks to my agent, Andrew Lownie, for his support and belief. Also to my reader and editor, Mischelle Priebe, without whose faith, guidance and encouragement this book would not have been possible.

Thank you to Tim Tate, author and documentary maker, who persuaded me my father's story was worth telling, giving valuable time, advice and contacts in the process.

Thank you to Sharon, Daisy, Oliver and Adam for understanding the importance of this book to me, and putting up with various moods over the past six years!

And finally, thank you to my sister, Paula, who gave her blessing for me to open up and investigate the deepest of old wounds, when lesser people would have preferred them to remain closed.

PHOTOS

My father, in his mid-teens, with the mother he adored, but who abandoned him as a child.

My father as the young man whose good looks and charm attracted many young women.

Left to right: My father, me, my sister Paula and my mother in 1952. I see my mother looking at her husband, whom she adored. At this point, she already knew of at least two of his affairs. What is she thinking?

My father's first campaign, Torquay, 1955. In later years this homespun style on a budget would be replaced with American-style razzmatazz.

On board the Queen Elizabeth bound for New York, circa 1959. My mother's first trip to the US – the country that would become her home.

My father was forever making us laugh, despite his inner despair.

Campaign publicity shot in the gardens of Polraen, 1963. *Credit: From the collections at Kresen Kernow - GE2H3727.*

My father *(below)* on his way to winning Bodmin at the 1964 general election. Large cars and loudspeakers had replaced the humble campaign bicycle.

Polraen and his first American car. For a while, my father fulfilled his dreams.

The crowd hear the election result and my father's 'victory' speech at the 1964 general election. This was the only time I saw my father cry - in this case with happiness. Just eight years earlier he had been destitute and on the verge of suicide.

An esteemed Liberal MP. Addressing the Liberal Party conference and celebrating Thorpe's election as party leader with the Parliamentary party *(my father is third from the left)*, little knowing the horrors that awaited.

Before the fall. Supported by my father's apparent wealth, I lived a life of flashy American cars and my beloved speed-boat, with apartments in Manhattan's East Side and in Chelsea, London.

DAILY Mirror

THORPE

NINE chilling words summed up Jeremy Thorpe's attitude to the man he had come to fear, a court heard yesterday.

What he told me about Norman Scott, by ex-MP Peter Bessell

'It is no worse than shooting a sick dog'

By SYDNEY YOUNG, GEOFF LAKEMAN and SIDNEY WILLIAMS

Bizarre

Spurred

Full court story: Turn to Pages 15, 16 and 17

The Thorpe affair explodes.